Forward Poetry Regionals 2011

Edited By Jenni Bannister

First published in Great Britain in 2011 by:
Forward Poetry
Remus House
Coltsfoot Drive
Peterborough
PE2 9BF
Telephone: 01733 890099
Website: www.forwardpoetry.co.uk

All Rights Reserved
Book Design by Neil Daniels
© Copyright Contributors 2011
SB ISBN 978-1-84418-585-6

Foreword

We at Forward Poetry have now spent an impressive 23 years in the publishing industry and retain our enviable position of being the largest publisher of new poetry in the world. Our founding belief is that creativity is something that should be accessible and enjoyable to all, and with more than two decades worth of experience, we remain just as committed to breaking down the barriers of elitism.

For this anthology we have selected verse from our talented writers that, while varying in style and content, each express and communicate thoughts, feelings and ideas to the reader. As a result this imaginative collection is one bound to inspire just as much as it entertains.

Contents

Chris Mary Creedon, Fulwood	1
John Dillon, Pendlebury	2
Ray Lennard, Macclesfield	2
Julie Spackman, Leeds	3
Lilian Kujawiak, Widnes	4
Gladys Brunt, Beighton	5
William Reilly, Liverpool	6
Anne-Marie Pratt, Howden-le-Wear	6
Thomas Speight, Halifax	7
Michael Spencer, Hessle	7
Jeannette Facchini, Hartlepool	8
Molly Timpson, Leeds	8
Carole Bloor, Cadishead	9
Lillian Fitzgerald, Moston	9
Sarah Harrop, Priest Hutton	10
Frania Vickers, Leeds	10
Samantha Taylor, Oldham	11
Barbara Bentley, Appletree Village	12
Mary Parker, Maltby	13
Joyce Adams, Lakeside	14
Terence Powell, Dresden	15
Margaret Mathers, Barrow-in-Furness	16
Rachel Sutcliffe, Golcar	16
J Malcolm Robinson, Bentley	17
Manal Ahmed, Leeds	18
Eric Hyland, Aspull	19
Ann Ashworth, Swinton	20
Barry Bradshaigh, Blackpool	21
Rae Alderson, Flixton	21
Stephen Wooley, Croxteth	22
Taranom Movahedi, Leeds	23
Beryl Mapperley, Bridlington	24
Julie Merdassi, Castlefields	24
Lorena Valerie Owens, Durham	25
Betty Allison, Gilesgate Moor	25
Trevor Huntington, Emley	26
Asraa Hafeez, Cheadle	28
Michael McNulty, Runcorn	29
Heather Pickering, Horsforth	30
Letty Linton, Sunniside	33
Ruth Margaret Rhodes, Knaresborough	33
David Sim, Normanby	34
Valerie Lancaster, Southport	35
Arthur Aston, Townville	36
P Brewer, Cleveleys	37
Jacqueline Burns, Salford	38
Geoff Kendall, Chorley	39
Jessie Horsley, Bolton	39
Gay Horton, Bollington	40
Suzanne Beevers, Earlsheaton	41
Vera Seddon, Gatley	42
Gary Thompson, Whitefield	44
Henry C Culpan, Halifax	45
Margie Fox, Cheadle	45
L Growney, Crosby	46
Emma Simister, Morecambe	47
Ann Warren, Grange-Over-Sands	48
Denise Clitheroe, Preston	49
Margaret Robertson, Gt Lumley	50
Lesley Elaine Greenwood, Bradford	51
Elizabeth A Wilkinson, Runcorn	52
Helen Smith, Darlington	53
Joan O'Toole, Blackrod	53
Qesma Mohammed, Manchester	54
Dean Beardsley, Old Denaby	55
Joy M Humphreys, Preston	56
Barbara Turner, Sale	56
Edna Sarsfield, Southport	57
Caroline Connelly, Faifley	57
Alan Ernest, Sheffield	58
Angela Butler, Allithwaite	59
Brenda Hughes, Holland Moor	60
E S Arries, Houghton-le-Spring	61
Terence Smith, Sheffield	63

Christine Pudsey, Cleethorpes	63
Ramandeep Kaur, Bradford	64
Ivy Bates, Lymm	64
Harry Patrick, Carlisle	65
James Hazell, Rochdale	66
Carolie Cole Pemberton, Manchester	67
Jonathan Curry, Killingworth	68
Shirley Temple Beckett, Widnes	69
Peter Corbett, Liverpool	70
Audrey Watson, Wakefield	71
Eric R Sephton, Stretford	72
Elizabeth Mason, Knutsford	73
Mary Braithwaite, Southport	74
Marie Greenhalgh, Burnley	75
Jean Paisley, Hebburn	76
Angela McLaughlin-Bolton, York	77
Gary Austin, Southport	78
Colin McCombe, Moreton	79
Stuart Elsom Wright, Halifax	80
Snowman, Lymm	80
Barbara Ward, Pickering	81
Arya Mati, Manchester	81
Denise Jarrett, Leeds	82
Lee Smith, Woodhouse	83
Doreen Goodway, Airedale	84
Joyce M Chaffer, Yeadon	84
L E Marchment, Hathershaw	85
Olivia Barton, Balderstone	85
Mary Hoy, Bootle	86
Norah C Darbyshire, Daisy Hill	87
John O'Connor, Little Hulton	88
Joan May Wills, Kendal	89
Joseph Knott, Whitworth	90
Christine Naylor, Airmyn	90
Dorinda MacDowell	91
Cynthia Gibson, Ripon	91
John Flanagan, Leeds	92
Luke Greggain, Whitehaven	92
Kenneth H Wood, Ormskirk	93
John Fudge Jnr, Sunnyside	93
Clare Marie Zeidrah Keirrissia Marshall, Langley	94
David Charles, Lytham	96
Adrian McRobb, Cramlington	97
Karen Collins, Wrightington	98
Sue Hardy-Dawson, Harrogate	99
Robert Lockett, Bootle	100
Leslie Hogarth, Carlisle	100
Philip Moore, Walton Village	101
Marjorie M Armstrong, Carlisle	102
Jenifer Ellen Austin, Sproxton	103
Maureen C Bell, Gateshead	104
Elaine J Seagrave, Woodseats	105
Wayne Pugh, Brasside	106
Terence Leslie Iceton, Leeds	107
Ed Collins, Southport	108
Beryl Eastwood, Hull	108
Bianka Hannam, Ellesmere Port	109
Howard Peach, Cottingham	109
Bernard Shaw, Barwick-in-Elmet	110
Paul Kelly, Walton-le-Dale	111
Alex Branthwaite, Sunderland	112
Andrew Gill, Chester	113
Yvonne Valerie Stewart, South Shields	114
Alma Taylor, Manchester	115
Jennifer D Wootton, Bradway	116
Jacqueline Zacharias, Naburn	116
Robert H Quin, Knutsford	117
Janet Rocher, Wirral	118
E Joan Knight, Great Houghton	119
Anthony Gibson, Hartlepool	120
D Ritchie, Roseworth	121
Michael Riley, Farringdon	121
Ann Warner, Prestwick	122
June Knight-Boulton, Newton-le-Willows	122
Erin Fitzgerald, Liverpool	123
S D Sharp, Stockport	123
Frank Oldfield, Hackenthorpe	124
Peter Branson, Rode Heath	124
Christina Batley, Rochdale	125
Rachel Wilson, Silksworth	125
Dorothy Jessup, Keighley	126
Rachel Van Den Bergen, Levenshulme	126
Carol Taylor, Wakefield	127
John Sears, Congleton	128
Allen Beit, Birkenhead	129

Joan Evans, Upholland	130
Michael Harrison, Aintree	131
Dot Young, Durham	132
Kathy Denton, Horwich	133
P Mitchell, Morecambe	134
Nick Pearson, Gipton	134
Carole Revell, Hull	135
Linda Gray, Ashington	136
Peter Cardwell, Keighley	137
Ian Lowery, Upper Denby	138
Joyce Hudspith, South Stanley	140
Norman Mark, Carlisle	140
N G Charnley, Blackpool	141
Margaret Whitaker, Brighouse	141
Betty Graham, Whitefield	142
Leila McLeish, Carnforth	143
Jim Spence, Dufton	144
Ernie Graham, Millom	145
Edna Mills, Riding Mill	146
Jenny Bosworth, Louth	147
Maureen Dearden, Keighley	148
Ed Gardner, Boston Spa	149
M Noad, Thornaby	150
Kathleen McGowan, Newcastle Upon Tyne	150
Margery Rayson, Daltongate	151
Lyn Crossley, Burnley	151
John Masters, Marske-by-the-Sea	152
Maria Jenkinson, Blackpool	152
Margaret Bate, West View	153
William Nicklin, Widnes	153
Ian Bosker, Leigh	154
Hilary Jean Clark	155
Wendy Anne Flanagan, Rishton	156
Andrew Gruberski, Dewsbury	157
Robert Hogg, Guisborough	158
Donald John Tye, Wallsend	158
Paul Judges, Leavening	159
Sandra Meadows, Lymm	159
Christopher Robin Slater, Newcastle Upon Tyne	160
Ann Eddleston, Worsthorne	160
Kiran Ali	161
Eric Prescott, Southport	161
Rodger Moir, Allerton	162
Pauline Walsh, Blackburn	162
K Chesney-Woods, Sacriston	163
Vivienne Fitzpatrick, Bradford	164
Arthur Pickles, Waterfoot	164
Paul Hough, Barnsley	165
Joan Lister, High Pittington	165
Marlene Jackson, Wath-upon-Dearne	166
Irene Patricia Kelly, Bolton-on-Dearne	166
Lynette Coote, Harrogate	167
Linda Hardy, Southport	168
Jackie Richardson, Underbarrow	169
Philip Corbishly, Rossendale	169
Christopher Hayes, Bolton	170
Wayne Barrow	171
George Gutherless, Withernsea	172
Denise Evans, Thornaby	173
Jacqueline Bulman, Great Harwood	174
Bryan J Holmes, Wheatley	175
Florence Broomfield, Ashton-in-Makerfield	176
Elaine Sands, Standish	177
Jillian Minion, Millom	178
Dawn Williams-Sanderson, Newbiggin by the Sea	179
Heather Aspinall, Heaton	180
Kathleen June Jinks, Eston	180
Austin Baines-Brook, Gomersal	181
Alison Scott, Heaton	182
Geatana Trippetti, Heaton Mersey	182
Nigel Miller, Sandbach	183
Shirley Gray, Sheffield	183
Peter Roebuck, Prestwich	184
Nicola Karunaratne, St Helens	185
Anita Cooling, Boston Spa	186
Ian Lennox-Martin, Carlisle	187
Elizabeth Mary Dowler, Bulwark	188
T McFarlane, Wavertree	188
Elaine Briscoe-Taylor, Shipley	189
Marian Williams, Davyhulme	189
Sheila Donetta, Swansea	190
Sylvia Joan Higginson, Timperley	190

Barbara Sherlow, Preston	191
William Jebb, Endon	192
Gwendoline Douglas, Hull	193
Sue Gerrard, St Helens	194
Betty Lightfoot, Swinton	195
Doreen Tattersall, Cowpen Blyth	196
Frances Gibson, Beragh	197
Claire Gordon, Mottram	198
Ian McNamara, Belfast	199
Sheila Storr, Gargrave	200
Jacqueline Bartlett, St Martins	201
Lorna Hawthorne, Armagh	202
Robert Bannan, Townhead	202
J Williams, Swansea	203
Ann Voaden, Nantymoel	204
Sylvie Alexandre-Nelson, Swansea	205
William Waring, Belfast	206
Annie McKimmie, Portsoy	206
Barbara Rodgers, Belfast	207
John Harrold, Bettws	207
Maureen Cole, Felin Foel	208
Margaret Non Williams, Saundersfoot	209
Samuel McAlister, Carrickfergus	210
Brenda Liddy, Belfast	211
Michael McGuigan, Carrive	212
Mary Leadbeter, Beaufort	212
G Aldsmoor, Broughty Ferry	213
David John Hewett, Dyfed	213
Paul Kurt Lockwood, Welshpool	214
Violet Burggy, Kilmuir	214
Roger Paul Fuge, Llwynhendy	215
Angela Cole, Llangunnor	215
Gaynor Evans, Bridgend	216
Doreen E Todd, Portglenone	217
Graham Thomas, Llanelli	218
Philip J Mee, Kinmel Bay	219
Joshua Peters (12), Redbrook	220
Shirley Johnson, Falkirk	221
Elizabeth Phillips Scott, High Valleyfield	221
Hugh Campbell, Lurgan	222
Pauline Uprichard, Lurgan	223
Samantha Forde, Magherafelt	223
Ian L Fyfe, East Kilbride	224
Hilda Marjorie Wheeler, Llanon	226
Glenys Allen, Pendine	227
Alan R Coughlin, Limavady	228
Bill Hayles, Prestatyn	229
Norman Bissett, Edinburgh	230
Kathy McLemore, Dundee	231
James Roland Sterritt, Markethill	232
Padraig Donnelly, Keady	232
Anne Taggart, Armagh	233
Gwyneth E Scott, Colwyn Bay	233
Glenys B Moses, Sennybridge	234
Haidee Williams, Gorseinon	235
Peggy Howe, St Asaph	236
Jacqui Fogwill, Ganarew	237
Rose Innes, South Carbrain	238
Gordon Forbes, Dumfries	239
John Greeves, Magor	240
Julian Ronay, Aviemore	241
Patricia Donaghy, Dungannon	242
Suzanne Swift, Betws-y-Rhos	242
Peter Spurgin, Edinburgh	243
Isla Demuth, Raglan	243
Clifford Jones, Bontnewydd	244
Perry McDaid, Derry	244
June Mary Davies, Cardiff	245
Ann Thomas, Maesteg	245
Hannah R Hall	246
Anne Aitchison, Larbert	247
Oira Newman, Erskine	247
Frances Meenan, Brigade	248
Malachy Trainor, Armagh	249
Malcolm Coles, Rumney	250
Eileen-Margaret Kidd, Peebles	251
Anthony G L Kent, Haverfordwest	252
Patricia Bannister, Denbigh	254
Joyce Hockley, Stirling	255
Audrey Poole, Penarth	256
Colin Burnell, Cardiff	257
James Peace, Glenrothes	258
Patricia McKenna, Pontypridd	259
Celia G Thomas, Aberdare	260
Susan Kelly, Nairn	261
Mark Tough, Castle Douglas	262

John McKibbin, Baillieston 263	David McDonald, Kirkcaldy 295
Rebecca Isted, Cardiff 264	Jean MacKenzie..296
Stephen Maslen, Newport...................................264	Pat MacKenzie, East Kilbride 297
Fred McIlmoyle, Bangor 265	Vivienne Vale, Tonyrefail 298
Isobel Buchanan, Ayr 265	Terry Mullan, Cookstown..................................299
James O'Sullivan, Cork..266	Janet Middleton, Westquarter...........................300
Joan Catherine Igesund, Auchnagatt.................267	Sheena Blackhall, Garthdee...............................301
Jane Bessant, Wainfelin 268	Alexander Winter, Aberdeen.............................302
David Rosser, Ammanford..................................269	Maureen Margaret Thornton, Aberaman........302
James McIntosh Martin, Cowdenbeath 270	Wendy Prance, Cardiff 303
Peter Paterson, Bellshill.......................................272	Kathy Miles, Ffos-y-ffin......................................304
Claudette Evans, Hollybush 272	William F Park, Clydebank 305
Elizabeth Blacklaw, Dundee 273	Liam Ó Comáin, Derry......................................306
Jessica Stephanie Powell, Pontlottyn.................273	Susan Clarke, Llantwit Major 307
Janet Bowen, Milford Haven.............................274	Norma Anne MacArthur, Edinburgh.............308
Robert Black, Annan 274	Robert Wynn-Davies, Whitland......................308
Joan McCradie, Cardiff 275	Betty McIlroy, Bangor 309
Caroline Anne Carson, Thornhill.....................275	Joy Wilson, Clogher 310
Enid Thomas Rees, Mountain Ash 276	Fleming Carswell, Argyll....................................311
Margarte Gleeson Spanos, Llandysul...............277	Katriona Goode, Earlston.................................312
Dorcas Wilson, Linlithgow................................278	Mukeshkumar Raval, India 313
Norman Royal, Grangetown 279	Arthur May, Newport..314
Windsor Hopkins, Tondu 280	Yvonne Clark 314
Alan Pow, Hawick 280	Helga Dharmpaul, Tain.....................................315
Barbro Pattie, Rothesay.......................................281	Joan Kelly McChrystal, Derry City..................315
Mike Monaghan, Bishopbriggs..........................281	Janette Campbell, Cumbernauld......................316
Ian Archibald, Edinburgh...................................282	Gavin Knox, Ballinamallard 318
Aileen A Kelly, Aberdeen....................................283	Laraine Smith, Indiana 319
Bill Torrie Douglas, Fairlie..................................284	M G Sherlock, Colwyn Bay 319
Pam Russell, Yarrow 284	Wendy A Nottingham, Ogmore-by-Sea 320
Mavis Downey, Talgarth 285	Shiksha Dheda..321
George Campbell, Perth 285	Sara Burr, Inverurie 322
Marion McKenzie, Irvine 286	James Quinn, Dumfries.....................................323
M L Damsell, Plwmp..287	Pamela Gibson, Duns..324
Gwyn Thomas, Merthyr Tydfil 288	Anne Black McIsaac, Motherwell....................325
Jeanette Davis, Alva 289	Owain Symonds, Pontllanfraith.......................325
John Bain, Oban..290	Linda Jennings, Glais 326
Caroline Champion, Mathern 291	Anne Williams, Llanelli.....................................327
Miki Byrne, Walton Cardiff 292	Jim Emery, Ballymacoss....................................328
Karl Jakobsen, Dumfries.....................................292	Grace Minnis, Holywood 328
Marie Coyles, Dervock 293	Ruth Lydia Daly, St Dials 329
Margaret Davis, Chepstow 293	Ruth Edgar, Dromore 330
Norah Nelson, Newry...294	Kathleen Wendy Jones, Rhyl 331

Grant Cameron, Aberdeen	332
Veronica Davison, Misterton	332
Teresa Bell, Moneymore	333
Ronnie Simpson, Blairdardie	333
Betty Westcott, Newport	334
Nick Purchase, Grangetown	334
Zoha Khalid, Islamabad	335
Julian Bishop, Fasnakyle	336
Pam Ismail, Llanishen	337
Barbara Fowler, Merthyr Tydfil	338
Alison Drever, Edinburgh	338
Bill Barker, East Wemyss	339
Cameron McIntyre, Newtownards	340
Mary Morton, Keady	341
Robert Simpson, Ballymoney	342
Melanie M Burgess, Aberystwyth	342
Joan Littlehales, Rhostyllen	343
Catherine Keohane-Johnson, Penydarren	343
John Monaghan, Ballygawley	344
Cyril G Payne, New Inn	345
E Hawkins, Denbigh	346
Chelsey-Leigh Clatworthy (16), Blaengarw	347
Fred McIlmoyle, Bangor	348
Frederick Osborne, Bangor	349
George Du Plessis, Boksburg	350
J Pressly-Allen, Knutsford	351
Anthony Dunne/O'Regan, Kilkenny	352
Nancy Tamagno, Ladywell	353
Marjorie Leyshon, Swansea	354
Marjorie Langhorn, Darrington	354
Rachel E Joyce, Cardiff	355
Patricia Todd, St Helier	355
Margaret Kent, Beauly	356
Lesley Downie, Findhorn	357
Nikita Biswal, Delhi	358
Dilys Jones, Hull	359
Beryl Shepard Leece, Wallasey	360
Deborah Wilson, Norton	360
Terry Ramanouski, Widnes	361
Irene Gunnion, Perth	361
Robbie Hillhouse, Ayr	362
Diane Thomson Miller, Uddingston	363
Aubrey Malone	364
Kalie Eaton, McDonough	366
Lee Connor, Norton	367
Christine B Dobbie, Rothesay	367
Susie Crozier, South Hylton	368
Valerie Smallwood, St Helens	369
Graham Connor, Norton	370
Ali Gina Shotton, Ovingham	370
Bob Gleeson, Glasgow	371
Patricia Angus, Glasgow	372
Michael A Johnston, Ballycarry	372
Jean Mitchell, Aberdour	373
John Mangan, Liverpool	373
Oliver Waterer, Accrington	374
Kenneth Cox, Brigg	375
Malcolm Wilson Bucknall, Hornsea	376
Peter Madden, Mytholmroyd	377
Phillip M Rowland, Padgate	378
Shona-Lee Gallagher, Birkenhead	378
Kauser Parveen, Halifax	379
Janice Jackson, Oldham	379
Doris Thomson, Middleton	380
Joyce Hemsley, Sunderland	380
Gwen McNamara, Bagby	381
Dorothy Kenny, Burnley	381
Caroline Corley, Huddersfield	382
Rachel Sutcliffe, Golcar	382
Connie Walsh, Bramhall	383
Ted Brookes, Dunscroft	384
Zena Bain, Kincorth	385
Jean Percival Ford, Almondbury	386
Elizabeth Doroszkiewicz, Northenden	386

The Poems

Almost Supernatural

Born of the memory
of the ages of ice,
struggle through history
as the pure sacrifice -
Snowdrops with leaves green as grass
- firstborn of Earth - but first to pass . . .

Petals questing and bright -
purple, yellow or white
even while chilly winds blow
Crocus still will shine or glow
as Spring tiptoes forth - or back
as though unsure of the track.

A sea of mystic blue
spreads the wild wood through
just before a fresh greening
becomes an overweening
pride of summer foliage -
- passing brief the bluebell age.

Almost supernatural
each flower plucked growing -
- the poignant coming - going -
- iris in water flowing -
each Earth-and-Heaven knowing . . .

The realisation comes as a shock
that our Earth was once a flowerless rock.

Chris Mary Creedon, Fulwood

Perranporth Beach

It was one of those August nights
the moon was shining intensely
with a hole in the top
of my head for a flower
I lay down to count the stars
A silent calm rested on the Earth
the sky was breathing softly
the sea was lapping softly as if to
suggest I was part of a cosmic conclave
and I knew this couldn't last
as my brain finally poured into the sand
with all eternity arranged before me.

John Dillon, Pendlebury

Holidays

Golden days by the silver sea
When the days were happy and bright
Finding shells, hearing Sunday bells
Holidays after tea
When the moon was still o'er a Blackpool Hill
We walked along the sands
On barefoot feet, soft and neat
Gently holding hands
Holidays must end too soon we fear
Hoping for another year.

Ray Lennard, Macclesfield

Unimportant

Life of a dream.
At the expense of a man.
Sorry,
That as precious time,
Turns to years,
His dreams are still but pieces,
Of a jigsaw,
Whose picture is unclear,
Or proves the importance of his existence.

Land of a being.
Clasping hold of little.
Wasting.
Material things he cannot take.
For dust of man,
Will scatter in the breeze,
The cobweb maze of strings.
The ties of his relationships,
Are shredded by his fear.

Thoughts of this world,
Can linger in the mind.
Muttering.
Feeding upon the strength of Man.
Taking from him,
Only that which he has got.
Because unlike the rat-race,
He was a loner escaping,
From a world of hate and greed.

Julie Spackman, Leeds

Bygone Days

(Dedicated to my mum and dad)

Whatever happened to Lalio
And the games I used to play
Whatever happened to Sunday school
I was sent on the Sabbath day
Whatever happened to blind man's buff
And spin the bottle
Going home real mucky and Mother going to throttle
Whatever happened to conker woods
And borrowing a baby
Whatever happened to jam butties
Long walks and the bottle of water maybe
Ration books for the corner shop
Long bike rides where my chain came off
Whatever happened to the nit nurse
That used to come to school
And whatever happened to the cane
That was used freely as a rule
And getting the holes of my father's belt
Across my backside
Running away from home but coming back
at half-past five.
Whatever happened
To skipping in the street
And two red marks on my legs
From the wellies on my feet
Tossing up against the wall
And next-door's dog would pinch the ball
Tying door knockers together
And playing out in all kinds of weather
Brushing the street up, from one end to the other
Until confronted by my mother
Whatever happened to bob a job
Jam on toast and a buttered cob
Whatever happened to Derbac soap
Willy Woodbine and camel hair coat
Whatever happened to scrubbing the step
Like the old folks used to do
Whatever happened to sharabang trips
And days out to the zoo
Whatever happened to the scrubbing board
Old tin tub and mangle
Whatever happened to Dolly Blue
And white peep toe sandal
Whatever happened

To the Christmases I used to know
When Dad would get the shovel out
To move away the snow
Whatever happened
To all my yesterdays
My childhood days of leisure
I have them locked within my heart
For I myself to treasure.

Lilian Kujawiak, Widnes

I dreamt we were together again
Lovers, running and splashing in the rain
Our hearts joyful, our arms entwine
Longing for the day I'd make you mine

I dreamt you were beside me
Collecting shells by the sea
Walking barefoot along the shore
Wishing the pain would be no more

I dreamt there were children, four
Three boys, a girl, you said you wanted more
You know I'll always love you
In my heart I'll forever be true

I dreamt of the future, that could have been
But, our fate and destiny were unforeseen
Death came into our lives, I'll forever cry
As your life ebbed away, I wonder why

I dreamt there was no more sorrow
Forever wishing there'll be tomorrow
Upon waking, reality brings so much grief
But, I know your demise, gives you relief.

Gladys Brunt, Beighton

Cost More

Whenever you look in your local store,
What the price is today, tomorrow it will soar,
The food prices have risen for sure,
Not a penny less, but a few pence more,
Inflation they say has put up the cost,
Shopkeepers make sure profits are not lost,
They imagine our pockets are bulging with money,
If they call that a joke it's not very funny,
The amount of food I once bought, now I only buy half,
And to save on the electric I sit in the dark,
The price of beer in my pub is now beyond me,
So I stay at home with a large mug of tea,
A pipe full of baccy is good as a meal for me,
I cannot pack it in so I let it be,
And I enjoy a chat with my pet tabby cat,
Who sits at my feet and never answers me back,
My life's a struggle has been hard and long,
Now it's like a bell without a gong.

William Reilly, Liverpool

You are my muse.
The reasons why the words flow.
I could say I love you a thousand times
yet it would never be enough.
It is as if I am waking from a long sleep
and there you stand in real life.
You who sets my soul alight
but is only mine in dreams.
Written words can reveal with ease
the longing in my heart.
Yet around you these words dry up.
To say them aloud would break the spell
and reality would raise the curtain of truth.
Could you ever say the words I yearn to hear?
Those of I love you as you pull me near.

Anne-Marie Pratt, Howden-le-Wear

Dreamer

Sat here with a silent whisper in my head
Conscience I hear?
Tick-tock time flies by
Life flashes I'm somewhere else
Who am I?
In a world so huge
Destined to be somebody I don't want to be
In a city so large
So many stories untold
The soft touch of the eccentric figure I see
My head speaks words undeclared before
My individuality found a companion
Anomalous feelings exceeding my body
As she leaves
She vanished like a leaf fluttering away
Back to normality
I thought I had found salvation
My alarm clock ear piercingly wakes me
Just another day . . .

Thomas Speight, Halifax

A Summer Smile

Days are mild, and now seem long,
Breeze not so cold, nor as strong.
Birds are loud, and very active,
Must be finding each other attractive.

In gardens children play, it's music to my ears,
While pollen often fills my eyes with tears.
Flowers now seek some of your affection,
With water and feed, they'll stand to attention.

People seem happy, ready with a smile,
Making the best of this so short while.
The land is beauty, and oh so green,
But I just saw a leaf fall
Whatever can *that* mean.

Michael Spencer, Hessle

In Coxwold's Fields

I want to hear the church bells chime,
In Coxwold's fields
I heard the chimes at close of day
As travellers wound their homeward way
In sunsets soft, and rising heat
When backs were strong
And love was sweet.
In dreams alone do these repeat,
In Coxwold's fields.

I now return when snow lies deep,
And with the countryside asleep
Again those chimes ring true and deep,
In Coxwold's fields

I lift the curtain on the past,
When summer came and went too fast
Through winter's icy grip I'll long
For Coxwold's fields.

Jeannette Facchini, Hartlepool

My Long Wait

I've waited so long for you to mature
Cared for, coddled, who could ask for more?
Did I lose patience? Did I heck,
I thought I'd keep giving you a check.
Time passed by, nothing to show,
I kept thinking, you'll have to go.
Have I wasted my time? I've more to do,
Other things need looking after too.

But wait what's this I see?
After four long years it just can't be.
But yes, at last, a flower to behold,
My 'magnolia' plant can hold its own,
In my garden, pride of place
My beautiful 'magnolia' full of grace.

Molly Timpson, Leeds

Moonglow

I looked up at the moon one night,
it was shining, oh so bright.
There I saw but such a sight,
many angels flying round,
making not a mortal sound.

Wings, they shimmered in the glow,
as they flew on down below.
I stood there quiet as a mouse,
as they flew towards my house.

They danced and twirled, round and round,
with wings they barely touched the ground.
Once they saw me standing there,
up they soared into the air.

I swear I heard a tinkling laugh,
as they flew into the path,
of moonbeams yellow, shining bright,
they disappeared into the night.

That's the last that I would ever see
of angels dancing just for me.

Carole Bloor, Cadishead

The Tree Of Knowledge

My wild imagination
drifts amongst the words,
gathering inspirations
of literate and absurd.
Gifts of information, from
one whose love is shared,
A will 'o' the wisps confirmation,
in Eden's garden fair.
The tree of knowledge revelation,
he who wins first dares!

Lillian Fitzgerald, Moston

If I Were A Bird

If I were a bird, I'd fly to you
I'd fly for miles to be with you
I'd fly over oceans, rivers and seas
Soar over mountains, pastures and trees
If I were a bird

If I were a bird, I'd fly to you
I'd fly over cities in search of you
I'd scan towns and streets, every part
Flying, dying to get to your heart
If I were a bird

If I were a bird I'd fly to you
Safe in the knowledge that I'll be with you
When it is over, my journey is done
Only then will I know, my life had begun
If I were a bird, if I were a bird,
I'd fly to you.

Sarah Harrop, Priest Hutton

Fun-tech

Driving along in our usual car
People stop and stare, as our car passes by.
When we stop people ask all sorts of questions.
What is it?
Where did you get it from?
Answers given with a smile.
Then on we go through the Yorkshire countryside.
Up and down dale, to the next village.
Bringing smiles to people's faces.
Some cheer and wave to see the Fun-Tech on the road.

Frania Vickers, Leeds

Hi Mum,
Each day that I am here I think of you more and more,
The way that you sound, your voice, your call.
You not being well and I not being near,
Helps me keep my promise, never again will I be in here.

I miss your cooking and your cheeky smile,
Missing you so much makes it all worthwhile.
As I appreciate you now and when I see you, will do so much more,
We'll have a great Sunday dinner and a really good talk.

Of the good times and the bad,
Solutions and ideas,
Me and Auntie and you and Grandma,
We'll both get better and have many years.

I realise my responsibility now,
All the things I am capable of and will do,
Someway, somehow,
I will change and do it for you.

I will make you proud,
The daughter you deserve,
The one you had,
I know I can be her.

I love you Mum and always will,
You took care of me growing up and still do,
It is my time now to show you what you're worth,
My complete and utter love and,
For me to be your 'good' little girl!

I love you Mum.

Samantha Taylor, Oldham

I Have A Man Coming Home

I have a man coming home
I am blessed by my man coming home
When I hear his key in the door
And the tread of his feet on the floor
My heart says I want nothing more
Than my man coming home

I have no man coming home
I have no man coming home
I vowed to love 'till death us do part'
And this I did with all of my heart
Now my lot to the end of my life
Is as his widow and not as his wife
I have no man coming home

Oh young ones be happy and say
'I have a man coming home'
When the children have all gone away
When life tells them they need not stay
Let them go with a smile and a wave
Realise a future you have
You have a man coming home.

Barbara Bentley, Appletree Village

The Magic Of A Garden

Weeks of snow and ice, will it never end?
Many birds are hungry and thirsty, trying to fend.

As the snow melts, the eager shoots of daffodils show,
At the first rays of sunshine the snowdrops bow.

The ladybirds are busy; they know spring is on the way,
As we leaf through the bright catalogues and plan for May.

I love Livingston daisies and plant them every year,
I diligently set them around the garden, but I fear.

Come the late spring showers, most are washed away,
But I do not let it deter me: It is a small price to pay.

The smell of new mown grass and the borders full of colour,
I sit on my garden swing for many a heavenly hour.

When retirement comes and you are left all alone and low,
You have time to appreciate what a garden can bestow.

Healthy exercise, fresh air and interest beyond compare,
It more than rewards me for my love and care.

As summer leaves us and the garden turns to gold,
The last fruits are eaten, and we turn the leaves to mould.

My pet blackbird is around, as he is most of the year,
Eating grapes he sits on the step without any fear.

So the magic of the garden fills a great big void,
That comes with retirement and old age, we cannot avoid.

Mary Parker, Maltby

Life Of A Seven-Year-Old Minding His Brother

Me brother's on the prowl again,
I wonder what he's at.
Me mam was just real cross with him,
He's just dressed up the cat.
I wonder just where he has gone,
He may be in the coal.
And that has just reminded me,
Me sister's at the dole.
Isn't life real funny,
She thinks she's got a job.
So sign her name,
Her life's a strain,
But doesn't care a lot.
Me dad well he's just gone to bed,
He has a cold inside his head.
He told me not to make a noise,
He still thinks I'm his baby boy.
After all I am turned seven,
I'll just have to speak to God in Heaven.
Perhaps he'll tell me what to do,
He may give me a little clue,
And tell me where me brother's gone,
I don't want him to get me wrong,
So please dear Lord just tell me?
I must get off to school,
I hope he hasn't wandered
Down beside the pool.
Ah, here he comes, the little pest
I'm sorry God, but he tore his vest.
And thank you God for finding him
I don't know what we all would do,
If you didn't watch the things we do.
Me little brother's safely in,
Thank you God, I'll trot off to school.

Joyce Adams, Lakeside

Please

Please let me see the sunrise
For just one moment more,
And let me hear the plaintive gulls
Amid wild oceans roar,
Please let me feel the salty spray
From off the white-tipped waves,
And let me listen to the tales
Of gold in smugglers' caves,
Please let me see the summertime
With smells of new mown hay
And let me watch the fishing boats
Meander cross the bay,
Please let me wander down the lanes
To hear the chaffinch song
And let me see the white-washed home
Where once my heart belonged,
Please let me see the sunset
Go down upon the sea,
Don't cry my loves I have not gone
For you are part of me,
Please let me see the evening star
As I stand on the brow
Now let me gently pass away
My time is here and now
Please hold me for a moment
Unto the breeze so warm
Then scatter me upon the wind
'Twas there my spirit born.

Terence Powell, Dresden

Christmas Magic

Close your eyes and go to sleep, close your eyes and try real hard.
You've left his glass of sherry and wrote his Christmas card!
There's a carrot waiting for Rudolph and a mince pie on the plate,
So close your eyes and go to sleep, it's getting very late!
You've hung your stocking by the bed, with a letter saying you've been good.
So close your eyes and try to sleep (I really wish you would!)
You know he won't come till you're fast asleep (and I've such a lot to do!)
So please, please, please you need to sleep (and believe me I do too!)

It's quarter to one and I think he's asleep, we try moving presents from where they are hid,
When a voice from above shouts, 'I think he's been! I heard him, I'm sure I did!'
'Not yet dear,' I answer, 'go back to sleep, he won't come while you're awake!'
We're frazzled and tired (please go to sleep) and a drink of the sherry I take.

It's two o'clock and quiet, we lay snowy footsteps from the door,
Sprinkle magic dust, fill stockings, pile presents on the floor.
The snow 'settles' on the Christmas tree at last the scene is set,
We smile and munch the carrot as into bed we get!

It's six o'clock, I'm up and dressed, making all the noises I can make.
'Come on it's Christmas morning, Santa's been why won't you wake!'

Margaret Mathers, Barrow-in-Furness

Morning Walk

Sun shines down through tall trees,
Leaving marbled patterns along the street,
Footsteps pound with regular beat,
As foolhardy runners brave the heat,
Engines roar raising clouds of dust,
Top down becomes a must.
Buttercups soak up the golden rays,
Life gets lazy in the hot heady days.

Rachel Sutcliffe, Golcar

The wall's a disaster
In need of plastering
The room needs papering too
The roses need pruning
The piano needs tuning
But they're not the first in the queue.

No matter how hard
In the garden I try
To keep the pathway weed free
I've tried every day
With SBK
But where I've been is still hard to see

My blue-pink hydrangea
Is in mortal danger
Of dying due to the heat
And just my luck
My old Polo got stuck
As the tarmac melts in the street

The lock on my garden gate
Is in such a state
Needs replacing or oiling at least
The T hinges too
Are rusted right through
Their inclination to work finally ceased

And did I mention
'Twas my intention
To paint all the windows? Maybe not
But sitting out here in the sun
Is so much more fun
So I'll give em a good coat of thought.

J Malcolm Robinson, Bentley

Good Old Days

Good old days,
When smiles were pure,
When cries were innocent,
When 'broken' described toys, not hearts.

Good old days,
Where pain was only physical,
Where hearts were unbreakable,
Where time was so magical.

Good old days,
When happiness was internal,
When friends were truthful,
When thoughts were simple.

Good old days,
Where everyone seemed kind,
Where cuddles were wide,
Where kisses were white.

Good old days,
Full of cheers,
Away from fears,
With innocent tears.

Good old days,
Simple, yet beautiful.

Manal Ahmed, Leeds

Tale Of The Lovespoon

A young man in Wales once carved a spoon,
This he carved for the love of his life.
He gave it to her by the light of the moon,
For he wanted this girl as his wife.

On this spoon that he carved he did put a heart,
This was to tell her he loves her so well.
They'll be together forever and never will part,
And in Wales they always will dwell.

He next carved a horseshoe so that luck it would bring,
And then carved two bells on it too.
Then he carved on some flowers inside a ring,
And these flowers denote 'I Love You'.

So to his girl he presented his lovespoon,
She received it with rapture and joy.
As they walked together by the light of the moon,
Oh her lover was a very happy boy.

So this is the tale of the lovespoon,
These spoons young men give to their lover.
Walking together by the light of the moon,
Their arms entwined with each other.

Eric Hyland, Aspull

The Four Seasons

Winter has gathered her cloak around her and gone,
Taking with her her icy blasts, her slippery pavements,
Her glistening icicles and her carpet of snow.
But, in her favour, she brought with her the holly tree.
The shiny-leaved holly with its bright red berries,
The much-loved ivory mistletoe and the
Delicate but strong-willed snowdrops.

Spring, waiting in the wings, comes dancing onto the stage
to take her place.
Spring, ready to display herself which she does to perfection.
She shows off her trees dressed overall in delicate and
pastel shaded blossoms.
After which the multicoloured pretty primroses appear.
And soon the bright yellow daffodils nodding and swaying
In the breeze.
Soon to be kept company by the multitudes of gorgeous bluebells.

Very soon Summer arrives to take centre stage.
Summer, bold, brash with her optimism.
She came, in turn, bringing deluges and heat waves.
But her sunshine brings out myriads of flowers.
The sweetly perfumed rose, the tall larkspur,
The campanula and the bright red poppy.
It's time to give way to Autumn, but her
Lingering sunshine shows her sadness at leaving.

Autumn, surrounded by the sun's falling rays
Is eager to play her part.
Bounteous Autumn has her own show up her sleeve.
From her we reap the rich harvest of fruit,
Berries, nuts and the ripened yellow corn.
Long shadows foretell the fate of Autumn.
Winter is standing on the horizon, heaving her frozen baggage,
Ready to elbow mild-mannered Autumn aside.

Ann Ashworth, Swinton

Wild rose of Alba sweetest white of bloom,
Whose fragrant lease perfumes its heady flock,
Where field rose musk leaps purple Briar's swoon,
And Egland joy ciders in Woodbine hock,
Pome's common fame that Tyne's its wild convey,
To flower buzz time's Honeysuckle's roam,
In brill'ant Thrush-ing's sway like night-gales play,
As roses scent's blood, makes ruddy petals tome,
A duke crossed Gallic rose in rings betroth,
Which court's agin fleur wore fair's crown consort,
In hybrid Henna, re rich ardent's doth,
To composite a crest of Royal sort.
So is this Albus rose et sprig of broom,
In crimson's bed an English Lys' groom!

Barry Bradshaigh, Blackpool

I see you standing there across the water
A silhouette against the evening light
My farewell cries bounce back to me unanswered
And very soon you'll all be out of sight.
My little boat moves silently and slowly
Propelled by unseen hands on unseen oars
Across the lake the purple jagged mountains
Rise up above me from familiar shores
I drift along in peaceful, calm surroundings
Not knowing yet just where my journey ends
Or who, if anyone, will come to greet me
My parents, long departed, and old friends?
No sound except the ripple of the water
No light except the pale rays of the moon
No sense of time, only a sense of waiting
A feeling that I'll be there very soon.

Rae Alderson, Flixton

Hand-Me-Down Days

Sometimes they seem so far away,
At other times it's just like yesterday.
Money was tight, and few and far between.
If you wore certain clothes,
everyone knew where your mother had been.
Poor families stood out like a sore thumb.
The whole world knew your clothes were second hand.
Now to kit out your kid can cost a grand.

I can't believe how some things have changed.
They're a long way off from hand-me-down days.

Don't get me wrong, I'm not having a go at our parents back then.
I really admire how they coped, living from day to day.
No time to waste a meal, hunger was always a day or two away.

I can't believe how our parents survived with us,
They must have been deranged.
But they got us here from the hand-me-down days.

So we should never forget, how they kept mind,
body and soul together.
We should always remember, how they got us
through that stormy weather.

Stephen Wooley, Croxteth

Even with,
A broken smile
Remains of tears
On her fetching face
Are perceptible.

Undeniably undaunted.
She endures,
The hardship, the calamity
Not a single sign
Just tender smiles.

The glow in her eyes,
It's flickering to non existence
No warmth, no tranquillity.
She distinctly desires
Water, a warm shelter.

She makes no sound
As quiet as a whisper
She awaits your helping hands
God, reach out for her.

Taranom Movahedi, Leeds

Clarification

Here on holiday - mother and son -
Made lots of plans for the days to come . . .
On Bridlington beach they would find a 'spot'
And forget all about 'dot com dot'
See crowd at funfairs - the arcade too
Sample ice creams of every hue
Book seats at the spa for a 'big' name
'Try out your skill' at an open-air game . . .

To the guest house now they made their way
- Watched waves breaking across the bay -
This is such a splendid place
Come and go at your own pace.
They smiled: reminded of a time
A cottage - seeming so sublime
But oh! A bedstead - three feet - no more -
And 'sonny' - grown up - now six feet four!

Beryl Mapperley, Bridlington

Baby

A baby is a blessing
an angel in disguise,
A bundle of beauty
joy and delight
with bright and beautiful eyes.
A baby is a gift from God
to cherish comfort and care.
A baby brings you happiness
with lots and lots of love
and shiny curls of hair.

Julie Merdassi, Castlefields

Reality's Rainbow

We walk hand in hand, my love and I - so close,
Whilst in my heart, I feel only sad and morose.
I mourn for the precious love we threw away -
I wish that it would return again to stay!

We had a dream, the two of us, which now is gone,
A dream of togetherness, of hope, of joy that shone.
Like the pot of gold at the rainbow's end,
So broken now, I fear it will never mend.

Perhaps it was too fragile ever to last,
Reality intrudes on make-believe cruelly fast,
Bringing the realisation life holds less joy than sorrow -
Yet keeping us yearning for that bright tomorrow!

Lorena Valerie Owens, Durham

Make Me Happy

'What is the matter with you today?'
I heard a little girl's mother say.
'I hate school,' were the words said in despair,
As Suzie pulled her long black hair.

'I don't know how to read and write,
Somebody said I was such a sight.
In trousers like a little lad
Which makes me feel so sad and bad.

I get out of bed wondering what to wear
You buy me clothes which make them stare.
The teachers look at me with great sadness
There's never a day filled with gladness.

Take me to another school
Where they will not treat me like a fool.
I'm tired of crying and feeling sick
Move me away! It had better be quick.'

Betty Allison, Gilesgate Moor

Highway To Heaven

Relax;
Marvel at Man's ingenuity;
At God's creation;
The rugged beauty of the countryside.
Horton-in-Ribblesdale.
Ribblehead.
The viaduct.
Obstinate enterprise;
Cheap labour;
Skill and sheer determinism.
Arch after arch.
Pier on pier.
Carboniferous limestone,
Yorkshire grit!
The sun shining on the stark dale;
Lynchet-like terraces on the hillsides.
Bridges and tunnels all numbered.
Squat trees, flattened bushes,
Meadowsweet and wild garlic.
Echoing cries from the tunnel sides
Of long-gone navvies who built for their tomorrow -
Our today.
Yard after yard, chain on chain,
Steel tyre on rail, clattering over fish-plated joint.
Descent into a new dale.
A vale?
Into Eden?
Paradise for a locoman -
Super Sprinter or Duchess of Hamilton?
Have not a care.
Relax. Marvel.
From this height you are in Heaven.
God's Wonderful Railway?
Not so far north.
By Dent in the National Park
Passengers alight into the evening sun,
White daisies their path delight
Conifers take over from hawthorn
Like crimped fronds of hair pointing skyward.
A tunnel
A child would jump in delightful fright on entry.
On exit, smile and laugh in relief.
Walls like ganglions,
Arteries running up the valley's sides.
Summertime beauty.
Winter wonder.

Wonder what it's like up here in winter?
Isolation.
Desolation.
The bulrushes stand in testimony to the ground,
The empty buildings to the past.
Who would live;
Who could live up here?

Travelling companions?
A painter sketchily recording our advance,
A group of day-trippers;
Settle and Carlisle buffs?
We've been; we bought the T-shirts!
Downhill; we can all sense it.
The speed; the anticipation.
The commuters from Leeds long-gone.
It's just us now;
Going home.
Purpose of journey; happy or sad?
The hills shrouding in; the sky darkening.
Cobwebs blown away by open windows.
No stuffiness here,
Soon the sandstone Citadel
Where once seven companies held hands,
Winging passengers east through the Tyne Gap,
Westwards to Maryport and Whitehaven,
North to Glasgow and Edinburgh,
South to . . . the south.
South-east to Settle.
Drumlins?
All manner of geological phenomena.
Botanical multiplicity.
Rabbits scamper away from railway track.
Rabbits run away when Sprinters pass.
Relax, marvel, enjoy.

Trevor Huntington, Emley

Yellow

Yellow is the sunshine,
Shiny and bright.

Yellow is hair,
In a bobble tied up tight.

Yellow is lemonade,
Sweet and juicy.

I know a person who will like it,
The person is Lucy.

Yellow is custard,
Lumpy and thick.

Yellow is a building
Made out of brick.

Yellow is a star,
Shining down to you.

Yellow is a card,
It might say thank you!

Yellow is a sunflower,
Tall and high.

Can you grow one?
Let's give it a try.

Yellow is shiny,
No doubt about it.

Can you imagine a world without it?

Asraa Hafeez, Cheadle

A Hot Summer's Day

The sun erupts like a volcano into the sky
Turning the night into day
Vomiting up rays of heat
Like a colony of migrated seals
People have come from everywhere
Like a barbecue we get cooked like meat
Basting ourselves with suncream
Like pterodactyls kites fly high
In the hot salty air

Oh what a glorious day
The sand is like walking on hot coal
The boats rock gently in the bay
White foamy frothy freezing water
Looks welcoming and inviting
Waves break against the rocks like eggs
Parents and tots paddle in the surf

Now the sun has gone down
Nobody is around
The day has died
Death comes like a thief in the night
He has stole the day away
It may have been and gone
In my memory it lives on

Michael McNulty, Runcorn

The Fortune-Teller

The fairground was in town and excitement filled the air;
It didn't happen often, so everyone was there.
The turn-out was spectacular - they came from far and wide
And jostled with each other for every single ride.
Myriads of neon lights were flashing all around,
While muzak blared out, making a cacophony of sound,
And the scrumptious whiff of onions wafted from the stall
Selling hamburgers and brandysnap - a temptation to all.
The stallholders competed for supremacy - so keen
To attract the most attention; so determined to be seen.
But I was strangely drawn to a corner of the field
Where a solitary tent stood, with entrance tightly sealed.
Intrigued, I ventured closer - by now I couldn't wait
To read the sign which hung outside; 'Let me foretell your fate'.
Unable to resist this enchanting invitation
I threw caution to the winds and succumbed to the temptation
And grasped the tiny bell, which swung gently to and fro
On its crimson satin ribbon, and secured with a small bow.
The tinkling of the bell induced a stirring from within,
Then a captivating voice called out: 'Come in, my dear, come in!'
I advanced into the boudoir, heart now pounding in my chest,
And, by the scene that greeted me, was favourably impressed;
For, what I saw before me was a grand sight to behold:
A dazzling profusion of purple, green and gold!
The tent walls were festooned with lustrous fabrics by the score,
And an array of sumptuous Persian rugs lay strewn on the floor;
And, as if these sights weren't quite enough to set my senses reeling,
A plethora of golden spangles hung suspended from the ceiling
And danced like fireflies on silvery, silken threads,
Flitting back and forth hypnotically just above our heads.
A small circular table occupied the central space,
Over which was draped a cloth of finest multicoloured lace,
And, placed upon the table - the most impressive thing of all,
Shimmering in the candlelight: the legendary crystal ball.
The gypsy beckoned me to sit in a gilded wicker chair,
So I complied, obligingly, and tried hard not to stare,
For she had a certain aura which fascinated me,
And I could hardly wait to find out what she would foresee.
'Let's start now - the time is right, as the crystal is so clear;
But first, it's customary that you cross my palm with silver, dear.'
The cash was duly proffered and, as she stretched out her hand,
I noticed on her finger an ornate golden band
Which matched the large, hooped earrings, glinting in the subdued light
Which radiated from the candles, flickering gently through the night.
She spoke in muted tones now, with an air of mysticism;
By now excitement had replaced my former scepticism

And I was quite prepared to hang onto every word
Uttered by this lady, no matter how absurd.
'The crystal ball predicts that your luck will soon be changing,
Though it won't be monumental - your life won't need rearranging,
But you'll come into some money before the night is out;
This *will* occur - of that there's no uncertainty or doubt.
The crystal also tells me that you'll get a brand new pet,
The nature of which I'm not quite sure - I cannot tell you yet.
There'll be a little accident, but you will be all right,
Take care, my dear, when you leave here in the darkness of the night.
And I see a romance looming: a chivalrous young man
Will sweep you off your feet and he'll be your greatest fan.
Sadly, though, there is bad news, I hesitate to add:
You'll sustain a loss which will cause concern and make you very sad.
But do not fret, for I predict that your sadness will be brief,
For you'll be reunited, and this will soon dispel your grief.
The crystal ball grows dim, so we must conclude, I fear;
But, one last thing I'll tell you before you leave, my dear,
Is that, by tomorrow, you'll find that you're bewildered and bemused,
Mystified beyond belief - perplexed and quite confused.
Mark my words, I'm never wrong - the crystal does not lie;
And so, on that note, we must part; goodbye, my dear, goodbye.'
I reluctantly arose and went out into the night,
With her words still ringing in my ears, giddy with delight.
As I made my way across the field, something caught my eye:
The slot machines were beckoning - I couldn't pass them by.
So I made a random choice and put a coin into the slot
And could not believe my luck when I hit the grand jackpot!
Spurred on by this achievement, I thought I'd try my luck
At my all-time fairground favourite: the tantalising 'Hook-a-Duck'.
To my complete amazement, at my fifth and final try
I raised my rod aloft, and the duck was high and dry.
Incredulous, I reached out to accept my well-earned prize:
A perky litte goldfish with bright, black bulging eyes.
So engrossed was I in my new aquatic pet,
(Already forward planning for the things I'd need to get
To make his life as comfy and as safe as I was able),
That I failed to notice on the ground a generator cable
Which had worked loose from the pegs that were designed to hold it taut;
And, before I could prevent it, my foot was somehow caught,
Which resulted in my falling to the ground with quite a thud.
I then became aware, as I lay there in the mud
Of the presence of a man, silhouetted against the moon,
Whose timely arrival on the scene was spookily opportune.
I grasped his outstretched hand without a second thought
And gazed into his eyes for much longer than I ought,
But I just couldn't help it, for he looked so kind and strong
And, as he helped me to my feet, I sensed our friendship would be long.
Thankfully, my goldfish had survived the whole debacle

And, although quite clearly dazed, his eyes had far from lost their sparkle.
It seemed the major casualty of the unfortunate mishap
Was my treasured antique bracelet, which the fall had caused to snap,
And the precious piece of jewellery had fallen from my wrist;
But I couldn't lose it now, for it would be too deeply missed.
So my new-found friend and I began a frantic search around,
Hoping to catch sight of it just lying on the ground.
But, beaten by frustration and the darkness of the night,
We resolved to resume searching the next day, when it was light.
So we embraced and parted company, both happy to have met
Under such romantic circumstances, which we never would forget.
The next day, as arranged, we returned to the same spot
Where I thought I'd lost the bracelet which, to me, meant such a lot.
We scoured the whole area, but all to no avail,
Despite our merciless determination not to fail.
Then, just as we reluctantly resolved to accept the worst,
And I began to feel that I was well and truly cursed,
The sun came out and cast its rays upon the ground nearby,
Which gave rise to my emitting an involuntary cry,
For the sunshine had highlighted something small, although quite bright,
Which lay glinting on the ground as it caught the strong sunlight.
It must surely be my bracelet, lying there upon the ground.
Having spent all night outdoors, just waiting to be found!
And, sure enough, this was the case and I could not suppress
The tears of joy I wept, brought on by pent-up stress.
Once I'd regained my composure, my ordeal now in the past,
We headed back across the field, victorious at last.
It was at this point a man approached, out walking his Dalmatian;
He stopped as we drew level and we engaged in conversation.
We chatted at some length, then went our separate ways,
But something he had said had left us somewhat in a daze
For, according to this man, the fair had not existed.
We questioned this, of course, but he had still insisted,
Maintaining that if there had been a fair the day before,
He would certainly have noticed it, for he lived just next door.
However, as we approached the corner where the gypsy's tent had been,
(Although now there was no proof of its existence to be seen),
I felt compelled to glance downwards and there, lo and behold,
I spied an ornate hoop-shaped earring, fashioned from finest gold.
In view of the foregoing I was, indeed, bewildered and bemused,
Mystified beyond belief - perplexed and quite confused!

Heather Pickering, Horsforth

I Speak To The Windy North

The wind sweeps over the wide moors to us;
Blanchland rides, bravely on cold, icy gusts;
Keilder sends the balm of pines and showers,
Hearts lift to Heaven and look down on bowers;
Gods spread their tepis on Cheviot Hills;
This beautiful land with spirits it fills:
Saints, bishops, shepherds, serfs just make a breeze
Over pathways, animals, birds and trees:
The salty deeps that gales tossed into banks;
Just children splashing and laughing at pranks;
They race and rest, now, Bamborough's serene,
Perfumed zephyrs stroke the harvests of green
That sway like troupes of gracious, dancing girls;
From ages of autumns in the richest of soils.
Where green leaves melted, in love with the land:
Ancient cliffs and rocks gave soft, golden sand:
Then, in grace and beauty, came forth treasures;
Breath of champagne; air of sea meeting forests;
Courtship unceasing; their love unblighted:
We leave, now, these scenes with hearts delighted.

Letty Linton, Sunniside

By The Sea

The blue sea and the smooth firm sand
With towering cliffs on either hand
The jagged rocks out in the bay
The rock pools where children play.
The lighthouse flashes its warning light
To guide ships throughout the nights
On stormy nights its beams shine bright
The clumps of sea-pinks are a delight
The seagulls give their noisy cry
As they swoop down from the sky
How exciting life would be
If I lived beside the sea.

Ruth Margaret Rhodes, Knaresborough

Thanks From A Dying Whale

I could have been washed up on a deserted beach,
Out of sight and out of reach.
Death would have come when I was all alone
Death would have found me when I was by myself,
On my own
But I was washed up at Redcar, on the sand
Where I found many a willing and helping hand
Crowds came to watch hoping I could somehow survive
Hoping against hope my rescuers could keep me alive

Those people watching prayed I would make it,
They all wished me well
Yet knowing as I did, I didn't really have a hope in Hell
My rescuers didn't give up, they did their utmost,
They really tried
They gave me comfort and support
As they stood by my side
Perhaps hoping I could be saved on the next high tide
All to no avail, my spirit fading,
I slowly and quietly died
And around and about me I knew people cried

When death comes there's always a touch of remorse
And a feeling of sadness
But at my death I was surrounded with so much goodwill
That I had a feeling of gladness

Thanks for making sure that when death came, I was not all alone
Thanks for making sure that when death found me
I was not by myself, on my own
Thank you.

David Sim, Normanby

Just A Natural Haven

Oh how I love to wander across the meadows green
with swallows flying overhead and minnows in the stream,
what peace I feel within my heart . . .
what beauty so serene.

The woodland now comes into view, beckoning me on
to walk beneath its canopy, which blends the trees as one,
my spirit is uplifted . . .
all cares and worries gone.

The earth is soft below my feet, the air around me cool,
I tread so carefully o'er the path, aware of each toadstool
that quietly marks this hidden trail . . .
towards a forest pool.

Sweet melodies of birdsong, flow from every tree,
while sunbeams filter through the leaves as if to welcome me,
'tis here I feel I do belong . . .
'tis here I feel so free.

I breathe the air, I smell the pine, I kneel upon the ground,
I touch the grass and send my love to everything around,
for deep inside this haven . . .
all nature does abound.

Out here within the countryside I am my own true self,
enriched by Mother Nature's gifts, I crave no greater wealth,
for through her natural healing . . .
I'm filled with inner health.

Oh how I love to wander across the meadows green
with just the swallows overhead and trees beyond the stream,
what peace I feel within my soul . . .
I close my eyes and dream.

Valerie Lancaster, Southport

What Is Easter?

Tell me what is Easter?
A greeting card or two
From a few well-wishing persons
And inscribed with 'Just for you'.

The spring flowers now are blooming
In park and garden bed
The nights are getting longer
And the warmer days ahead

Wildlife is awakening
The rabbits, birds and bees
And leaves again are coming
On bare and barren trees

Yet this is not the message
That Easter time portrays
It is something more reverent
And worthy of our praise

There is a cross outside a city
On a hillside bleak and bare
And a man despised rejected
Is hanging dying there

He's faced the taunts and trial
And the shouts of, 'Crucify!'
Now He hangs His head in sorrow
And sadly questions, 'Why?'

He came down with a message
From His father God above
How life should be conducted
Of blessing, peace and love

But they scorned, despised, rejected
And cast His words aside
And felt a sense of freedom
And liberation when He died

In the tomb they laid Him
And soundly sealed the door
It was the end of a troublemaker
He'd worry them no more

But there was a greater power
Within the realms above
That despite men's sordid treatment
Did care for Him in love
So the power of God upraised Him

And sent Him forth once more
With a stronger power and spirit
Than He possessed before

With the same resounding message
Yet with a mightier strain
That despite death's sordid climax
Mankind can live again

Yes! This is the message of Easter
That sadly men ignore
But demands their lives surrender
And bow down and adore

For the resurrected Jesus
Though returned to Heaven's domain
Still imparts His power and spirit
To the souls of men again

So please broadcast the message
All who profess His name
Of the meaning of Easter
For this is why He came

Go spreading the Easter message
And emphasise it is true
Its blessings are there for everyone
Not restricted 'Just for you'.

Arthur Aston, Townville

Paradise Mind

P icturesque scenes in your mind
A mazing adventure starts to unwind
R ainbow appears what a wondrous sight
A glowing with every colour bright
D elightful setting in your paradise place
I magination drifting far away from the busy human race
S ecret place only to you to suffice
E arth revolving revealing your paradise.

P Brewer, Cleveleys

A Seaside Summer

We're off to Scotland to see the sea.
Martin, Mabel, Mary and me.
To watch the crabs who live in a huddle
Inside a puddle, left by the sea
When it gets in a muddle.

We're staying in Oban, right by the quay,
And when we're called in time for tea,
We can sit by the window and eat egg and chips,
Whilst watching the ships,
From the dining room, with sauce on our lips.

Around the harbour gulls are screeching,
People meeting, with friendly greeting.
And all because it's summertime.
When we're nice and warm in the hot sunshine,
Feeling all in our sunny world, is sublime.

We're off on a ferry boat today,
To sail to the islands, come what may.
But it isn't as if we are going to stay,
We'll be back again at the end of the day,
To eat our supper off a tray.

Digging and playing in the sand.
Our imaginations to expand.
With rod and bucket in our hand,
Summertime is really grand.
With castles to make, and fish to land.

Time to go home now, we've had our fun.
Though it seems that the holiday's hardly begun.
Everyone's helping to pack up the van,
We've had a lovely time out here,
But it's time to go, Dad wants his beer.

Jacqueline Burns, Salford

A Rose In Calvary
(For Joy Hopkins)

The scented roses grow in a far off Calvary.
The dying rays of sun are slanted down
And fragrances are blown on evening zephyrs fair
To caress the slowly sleeping town
With essences of frankincense and myrrh.
The cedars rise from out the darkened soil.
Their roots are buried in the ruined rocks He knew
Where Simon helped the weary Jesus toil
To death and resurrection before the cockerel crew.
The blood-red thorns grew up to strangle holy blood
That spilled upon the ground
Where once the Roman legions stood.

Geoff Kendall, Chorley

The Swallow

Oh! Graceful lovely bird who heralds in the spring
With gay abandon through the air you wing
Now swooping low, now swiftly gaining height
You cleave the air with evident delight

Mouth agape, you take your succour from the air
Small insects on the wing become your fare
Dipping low with wings aquiver
You sip the water from the river

Alas the summer fades away
The time has come, you can no longer stay
To a warmer climate you must fly
For if you linger, you will surely die

So fly away the where the skies are blue
And when the spring returns we'll welcome you.

Jessie Horsley, Bolton

Maypole

Each small hand a ribbon holds
of pastel yellow, blue or pink.
They listen as their teacher doles
out orders not to break the link.

The music starts, the dance begins
and feet around the circle move.
Some feet skip out and others in.
Their actions are rehearsed and smooth.

As long as all the steps are right,
the children will fulfil their role
of twisting ribbons, colours bright
that form a pattern round the pole.

The purpose of the dance is clear;
to herald in the month of May,
a Pagan fest of yesteryear
when different gods were of the day.

No knowledge have the kids of this
but they will ever count their blessings,
for they are giving maths a miss
along with other boring lessons.

Gay Horton, Bollington

Greed

Roaming on my African plains
I survived floods from monsoon rains
Famines when no foliage to fill
Being a hungry lion's food kill
Droughts when dry season began
But not destruction caused by man
For I was an elephant wild and brave
Yet my freedom became my grave
For one day I was made
The target of an illegal trade
Poachers out hunting, I didn't see
Them hidden in grass tracking me
Just watching every move I'd make
Patiently waiting for those shots to take

No time to charge, too late to run
Their chance arrived, they fired their guns
And as I fell to the ground
My killers proudly gathered round
There they stood smiling above
No remorse or eyes of love
All they cared for was their need
So in their hands, my tusks, their greed
For your shelves more ivory to buy
And the circling vultures descended the sky
Now where my bones are laid
Let it remind the price I paid
So just how much was the selling cost
Nothing compared to my life lost.

Suzanne Beevers, Earlsheaton

My Garden

Sometimes when I'm troubled
and feeling rather low
I walk out to my garden
it's peaceful there, and so
I look at all that's happening
this bush is doing well,
that one wants some water,
so do others I can tell.
I think some need a little feed
might suit them all just now.
Oh how good these flowers look
they cheer me up somehow.
The grass is springy under my feet,
the blossoms scent the air,
and look the blackbird's having a bath,
his wife is waiting there.
The holly is full of flowers
will it get berries later on?
I'll fill these pots with pansies
now that the frost has gone.
Perhaps I'll sit a little while
upon the garden bench,
and now I notice weeds
are growing in that little trench,
I love my little garden
Life and beauty is all around.
It's helped to change my mood
Here cheerfulness abounds.

Vera Seddon, Gatley

This Summer

This summer I fell in love with a beautiful girl, hurling a radiant twirl,
This summer I saw a darling tempest, passing-by, smiling at me, sparkling a better sight than the moons of Jupiter and the rings of Saturn, which ignite the night sky,
This summer I met my burning flame passion as I fell in love with this colourful sprite, she rainbow across the blue sky sun shining highlighting blonder shoulder-length hair,
It was like she spread fire through a forest when she tenderly stepped towards her destiny, into her future husband's loving arms,

This summer I fell in love with a beautiful woman, as she whispered her name through a blanket of her cloudy tears,
This summer I felt a special twinkle it gave me pins and needles, with that dreamy wanted gaze sensitively in my heart.
This awaits every man.
This summer I felt a special tinkle providing me with my daily bread and water that provided me with rest and nourishment as long as you are holding my hand I will always feel your warmth,
This summer I fell in love with the woman who could change my life, my possible darling wife.

Next summer, we could cherish the time we spend together with our family resenting the time apart sharing our moments in our companionship.
In years to come, in the summer, we could cherish the time we spend together with our possible children grown up taking flight to bring up, the next generation,
In future summers we could be alone, in peaceful bliss, quiet and tranquil like the silent night air, there's just you and me alone again watching the clock ticking by,
During this present summer, I'm imagining and wishing that time would stop, framing us both in a passionate embrace,
Last summer you were sitting by the fire and this summer I gave you my heart, kissed your cheeks and tearfully waved you goodbye.

Gary Thompson, Whitefield

The Soldier Who Returned

No thought have I for those who stand,
Yearly round the cenotaph.
Carrying manmade poppies in their hand,
And pretend to make an epitaph.

What good does this hypocrisy do?
Who gives a damn, for all that?
You're better drinking a beer or two,
And thinking of those, who lay in plat.

It won't bring Sapper Berridge back,
A lad of barely twenty.
His remains we placed in dirty sack,
With tattered cross as sentry.

Nor help to locate, Captain Round,
Who vanished one hellish desert night.
His bones just mingled in the ground,
As dust of souls, crying to the light.

A thousand wreaths cannot still,
One haunting scream of death.
They do not save one, Tom or Bill,
Or bring back, British breath.

We knew it all, we knew it well,
We tasted blood and daily anguish.
Of course, we were scared to Hell,
And died in vain, to vanquish.

So I return from far-off grave,
To stare at medals you're wearing.
There's one small thing that I would crave,
Stop being so imperious and overbearing.

Please explain to me, why I had to die,
Forget your stupid mourning.
Stop selling symbols that lie,
Beneath a precinct awning.

Go gladly to your local inn,
And drink a toast to Tommy Mortal.
Forget the past, wars awful sin,
For my name is ever immortal.

'It's the soldiers of the Queen, my lads,
Who've been my lads, who are seen, my lads,
In the fight for England's glory, lads,
Of that worldwide glory, let us sing.

And when we say we've always won,
And when they ask us, how it's done.
We'll probably point to every one,
Of England's soldiers of the Queen.'

Henry C Culpan, Halifax

Stockport Market

I wandered down into the town
It was a bright September day,
Among the shopping crowds I went
To the market on my way.

Across the old Victorian bridge
That spans the chasm of a street
There went a crowd of eager feet
Into the cobbled market square where
Bright stalls were set around a handsome market hall
The parish church looked over all.

The stalls sold everything to pick and choose
From vegetables to jewellery or shoes
A cornucopia of wares displayed, the crowd did buy
Smallholders smiled, they did a roaring trade.

But time had flown, the clock struck four
I must not stay a minute more
So I turned to go my homeward way
And pondered on the many years
Our town had held its market day.

Margie Fox, Cheadle

The Green And Pleasant Land

Post-war the car-free streets
And rubble-strewn bomb sites
Where hardy weeds at will
Sprinkled their yellow suns.

Green fields aplenty in the days to come
With freedom to flourish
Except where airborne ball met boot
Or careering cork caressed the willow.

Now fields
Once smooth as the green baize
Snatched for supermarket chains
Greedy to increase their gains.

Reclaim the green
Where children can be seen,
Active and free
Happy to be
To run, to jump, to play
Open to the sky all day.

Confined to my room
Not unlike a tomb
Where flashing lights scream
From a silver screen.

Immobilised there
In my cushioned chair!

My mouth is dumb
My brain is numb
My zombie-like frame
Succumbed to the game!

L Growney, Crosby

Nightlife

Covered in skin, the soul cowers
From the burning light.
Counting down the hours
Until it's time to welcome night.
Amid the haunting darkness
The eager spirits careen
Flirting with the lustful stars
And the lovesick moonbeam.

Within the confines of emptiness
An echo replays a prose,
Melancholic collection of words
A servile whore's tale of woes.
On a saturated evening
Raindrops conceal the tears
And underneath the moonlight
Shadows steal the fears.

Only after a dark veil falls
Do mischievous pixies play
Shenanigans in the twilight,
Pirouettes in the month of May.
Candescent light scorches the blackness
When the fiery candles flare,
An opiate performance of dances,
As flames flicker in the air.

A seductive siren pouts
Upon the witching hour.
Casts her spell of silence,
You relinquish to her power.
Creatures of the night scurry
Just before dawn, as the darkness fades.
Sunrise emblazes the horizon,
Morning dew cascades . . .

Emma Simister, Morecambe

Brown Robin Nature Reserve

Sunlight and a gentle breeze,
My brother and I climb the hill,
Past grazing cattle, quiet, at ease
And clouds of frothing may, until
We step inside the magic wood,
That Otherworld of green and shadow.
We fuel each other's fantasies,
He tells me of the shining meadow,
Up through the tangling, sun-specked leaves.

Beech, ash and hazel flaunt their glories,
Sweet, piercing birdsong casts its spell,
A background to our laughing stories,
Hobbit and elves, an enchanted well.
Then, out through the gateway, there it lies,
Glowing with flowers, pink, yellow, blue.
Our eyes dilate, our chattering dies,
We gasp with delight, absorb the view.
The myriad blooms, the feathery grasses,
Fields, farms and bay spread out below.
Though memories fade, though long time passes,
The joy of this day I will never let go.

Ann Warren, Grange-Over-Sands

The Japanese Tsunami

The tsunami came rushing through, that awful day,
It thundered through, and washed everything away.
The warning came, but for many, too late,
The surge of the water was far too great.
Some got to the high ground, and watched in fear,
As it took the lives of their families so dear.
Then after the water came the fires so fierce,
The smell of the smoke the atmosphere did pierce.
The day after, the scene, was total devastation,
Nature destroyed a clever peaceful nation.
Remaining relatives, wandered through the debris,
Hoping and praying they're still alive, maybe?
People have lost everything, it's a crying shame,
Their lives will never be the same.
But now there's the threat of radiation leaks,
People holding their breath as the power peaks.
Nature played a nasty trick that day,
And now the people have lost their way.
The worst tragedy since time began,
But don't blame God, this wasn't his plan.
It's time for us all to treat this planet with respect,
Or more of this we will have to expect.
So our prayers must go to the people of Japan,
And help and support, and do all that we can.

Denise Clitheroe, Preston

Going Walkies

I'm Heidi the Westie and I've started to whine
Cos outside I see there's brilliant sunshine
When the weather's so nice I wish I could talk
Then I'd tell my parents it's time for a walk
Mam and Dad there's no time to lose
On with your hats, coats and shoes
I jump into the car I like the ride
I'm hoping we're going to Finchale Riverside

Down the steep hill away I go
These adults are really slow
They meet me at the riverside
It's rained a lot I hope they don't slide
They soon have worked up a bit of a sweat
I cannot believe it as I'm not tired yet
The end of the path is soon in sight
We spot some geese which have just taken flight

Two minutes rest I hear Dad say
Then we'll turn around and be on our way
As Mam turns she starts to slide
Down the riverbank on her backside
Dad puts out his hand to pull her up
The bank's so slippy she's finding it tough
After two more falls - we dare not laugh
It's third time lucky and she's back onto the path

The mud is so thick sticking onto her clothes
Leaving a path wherever she goes
I'm just thinking, *O what a day*
When we spot a lady coming our way
Just as she reaches us Mam stops her to say
It's dangerously slippy please don't go that way
She can see Mam is muddy from head to toe
So decides that way she will not go

I hear Mam say, 'It must think I'm a tree'
As the lady's dog uses her leg for a pee
This makes the mud all sloppy and smelly
Causing bits to drop off into her wellies
The lady then said the dog was a stray
Just as it ran off without further delay
If Mam had known she'd have given it a rap
Now she must get home and into the bath

Dad can be a bit fuddy duddy
Doesn't want his car seats getting all muddy
Mam has to sit on a mat in the car
Thank heavens we don't have to go very far
Once home she strips off her clothes at the door
Her trousers can stand on their own on the floor
Next time we walk we'll be giving Finchale a wide birth
As we don't want our Mam coming home covered in earth.

Margaret Robertson, Gt Lumley

Your Daffodils

(In memory of Heather Elaine Greenwood, died on the first day of spring 1995 aged 11yrs)

Every time you smiled my love, or helped a friend in need,
For your kindness and your sacrifice, for every special deed,
The angel who's watched over you ever since your birth,
Took one of Heaven's golden stars and sent it down to Earth.

And every golden star that landed in the fields and on the hills,
Filled the open landscape with a thousand daffodils,
And every daffodil that grew there showed a measure of the love,
That your special guardian angel knew would carry you above.

She's been there throughout your lifetime as your spirit and your guide.
She's watched you and protected you and has never left your side.
The breeze that rippled through the flowers was the rustle of her wings,
And she used them to surround you with the joys that living brings.

Then your guardian angel took you home to Heaven on her wings,
And left us with such memories of so many thoughtful things
That you had done, or you had said, we'd shared so many happy hours
And you've made those lovely daffodils your very own spring flowers.

Now every time we see a daffodil we know that it is spring
And think of all the precious things this time of year will bring
But nothing is more precious than thoughts of you and where
You are, in Heaven with your angel, her own shining, golden star.

Lesley Elaine Greenwood, Bradford

Golden Day

I sit by the river and what do I see?
Sailing ships maybe one of three
Their sails unfurled as they sail by the
Fisherman wave as they pass by.
A heron so tall and graceful stands on one leg
As he spies his dinner in the reed bed,
A frog toad are on his mind
The rustle of the reeds and the gurgle of the river
Soon there's a chill it makes me shiver.

So up I get to stretch my legs I wander on
Into a meadow of true delight of buttercups
And daisies all shining and bright.
A badger in his coat of black and white
Digs a hole with all his might
His claws are big and strong you see
He moves the earth so easily
He stops his dig as a fox crosses his path
But then he starts it's safe at last
Summer the fields look so good there's yellow
And greens all about
The corn with its ears stand tall in the sunlight
To make them sweet for us to eat.

The hum of the tractor is all around pushing
Up potatoes from the ground ready to pick
These are the things of June
Farmer calls his sheep from play to feed the lambs as
They hop and play.
Soon the harvest has begun with hay bales
Stand like soldiers in a row
Working till the sun goes down at eventide
With its golden glow.
Even the hens go home to roost and
The farmer so proud of a very good day.

Elizabeth A Wilkinson, Runcorn

Durham, My Durham...

The hill stands, nestled in the crook of a river,
Its hard foundations, standing rock, have stood forever.
Buildings that sit along the shore are timeless, so it seems,
Often wrapped in mist, occupants lost in dreams.
Atop the hill, its pinnacle, a testament to Man,
A castle proud, with a diorama of life on every hand,
Sits against a saintly cathedral, whose aura is calm,
A grotesque knocker offering sanctuary from harm:
Within their shadows, traders have plied their wares,
For decades and its seat of learning - student minds ensnared,
Millions of visitors arrive from all corners of the globe,
I wonder, do they pray at the cathedral in earnest hope?
They stand, entranced, by the reverence of Saint Bede's tomb,
Look carefully if you dare, at fading paintings drawn by . . . whom?
They hide upon the wall, high up, almost invisible,
Here peace is endless and time appears indivisible,
Durham, my Durham, oh so miss-able . . .

Helen Smith, Darlington

Our Flower Festival

The sixteenth of August was sunny and bright,
Our church was filled with colour and light.
We entered to see a profusion of flowers,
Tenderly arranged, taking hours and hours.
Everywhere was decorated and so pretty,
To think of them dying was really a pity.
The artistic arrangements, so beautifully done,
Obviously a combined effort of everyone.
For weeks the ladies had practised and learned,
The result was tremendous and truly earned
The praises and thanks from us all
Plus the interest it stirred for the silk flower stall.
Yes, indeed, it really was a beautiful show
Giving us a lead to the way we must go
To reach the total which we require
Before anyone can sit back or even retire.

Joan O'Toole, Blackrod

The City Awakens

Fumes rising and curling in the cold morning air,
their aroma intoxicating and sultry.
The sickly sweet stench of rotting waste as the refuse collectors do their morning rounds.
Last night's rain leaves a damp, dewy smell in the air, to dampen the spirits of any who stop by.
The aroma of strong coffee, rising from the polythene cups clutched in the hand of commuters on the train.
Close your eyes and breathe in the smell of the city.

Horns; honking, blaring, cutting through the groggy air like a knife through butter.
Snatches of laughter, the crinkle of newspapers, heard through the doors of the morning café.
The shriek of the sirens as the ambulances weave through the throngs of traffic.
Catch the tittering of the old ladies as they gossip at the bus stop, heads bent, laughter evident.
Hear the tinkling of the shop bells, the daily greeting of 'G'morning' and the usual polite exchanges.
Listen closely and you'll hear the music of the city.

See the glinting of the glass windows as they reflect the red light of the rising sun.
Glimpse the alley cats as they dart between overflowing bins, on the hunt for breakfast.
Notice the early start joggers, as they plod along in too baggy sports suits and flash trainers.
The rows of children, in bright yellow jackets, holding hands as they skip along the pavement.
See the paperboy whizz down the street, scattering newspapers like confetti as he goes.
Open your eyes and take in the true sights of the city.

The city like a beast rises from its slumber, it stretches and groans.
Its senses so alive, sparks fly, the heart beats; pulsating and throbbing.
Quicksilver flows through the veins, streaks through the streets, flashes through the sky.
The breath quickens, like mist rising or smog swirling, it dances and twirls.
Life whispers through its body, caresses its soul, infuses it with energy and light.
And so, the city awakens.

Qesma Mohammed, Manchester

Yesterday's Tomorrows

I inherited my sense of humour
From the proudness that is my father
My heart was a gift from my devoted mother
And I invented all the other

These mountains that we have climbed
Are only the memories of our minds
And all the songs that we have sung
Are just the symphonies for everyone

If it would take away all your pain
I would gladly take the blame
Yet I am just a mouse in life's field
And we only have nature for our shield

God if I wrote you a letter
Could you please make things a little better
Yet our children will be strong
Because we have gently guided them along

In the frostbitten ruins of time
No one is ever left behind
For when push comes to shove
No one and nothing can ever break our love

And now that the monster inside
Has taken away your life
And even though I miss you so deeply
You will forever be beside me.

Dean Beardsley, Old Denaby

Dream For The Deserving

(For Dad)

In verdant pastures of an unknown land
the bravest of brave arrive after battle.
Gone are all instruments and uniforms of war.
Golden rays play upon their naked skin
and bathe unshod feet with mellow caresses.
An arc of kaleidoscopic colours dips downwards,
filtering through emerald boughs and russet hills,
beckoning them to follow fields of scarlet poppies.
They stand beneath the iridescent canopy,
staring upwards to a cavernous, azure sky
whilst silver stars rain down,
gently transporting them through an ethereal galaxy of time,
in a dream, which will last forever.

Joy M Humphreys, Preston

General Synopsis

It has its own rhythm, peculiar to its content;
a measured voice, a rise and fall of cadences.

I think of those who wait and listen
Edging further westwards while filling?
Pushing slowly northwards? Heavy seas?
Reserved for the West and Southern Straits?
For whom and by whom bidding?
Millibars increasing from five to seven,
occasionally at first; good becoming moderate.

The mystery is enacted every night.
it is a recital I cannot resist,
rendered to the creak of timbers resisting winter's blasts.
It is a lullaby and I rejoice in a safe harbour.
Lows cannot reach me, highs elude me,
I set a *medium course prolonged, sleep induced.*
The best of brightness to the East tomorrow
. . . perhaps gale later.

Barbara Turner, Sale

Memories Of Summertime

I love the fading light of evening and the dawning of the sun,
the noonday heat, the wilting of a day half gone.
An afternoon of waiting until the dawn becomes the night,
I know the day is over at the fading of the light.

I love the wind in my face soft upon my brow,
footprints in the sand, life here and now.
Hedgerows full of blackberries purple, sweet on the tongue.
Buttercups that glow yellow held against my chin,
a day of promised sunshine warm upon my skin.

Walking down a leafy lane enjoying nature's charms,
daisy chains in bracelets that sway upon the arms.
Apples in the orchard that fall to Earth unplanned,
these are the memories of summertime, that this life has spanned.

Edna Sarsfield, Southport

Going To The Dogs

My home town is going to the dogs
What with 1 thing or another
Repeatedly telling Danny
To look after your wee brother.
Then in came acid, (E) and speed
And the flooding of smack,
Took over the hash and the weed
the young 1s don't believe
That taking this stuff,
This world you'll leave.
You can't say, that you just dabble
These drugs are really not worth the hassle
These drugs, you do not have to try
But, being a mum, I can't turn a blind eye.
The things I've seen throughout the years
Brings parents to their knees, in tears
All these drugs will make you ill
Then, they'll move in for the kill.

Caroline Connelly, Faifley

Born Without Consultation

He stood in solitude at the party
A glass of the finest vermouth in his hand
His back against the wall

Whilst the others congregated in small groups
 - Chatting amongst themselves

He tried to integrate optimism
But it was no use
They plotted against him whilst drinking fizzy squash

Coughing and spluttering, sinking to his knees
He tried to dislodge some offending obstruction
Face contorted; turning blue

The contents of the glass sent spinning

No one paid the heed to his distress
It was up to the chair-lady to cast the deciding vote
His body decomposing - rotting - a skeleton left behind
The partygoers ridiculing a useless corpse

He was glad his struggle with life was over
No more heartache; no more pain

Perhaps the almighty would keep his spirit safe in heaven
And not send him down again - to repeat the process
In another misconceived game of executive annihilation.

Alan Ernest, Sheffield

Seaside Revisited

The light is fading now, and I can see
Dark shadows spreading night in front of me;
Loose shingle slows my feet as in a dream,
My eyes are heavy and no longer seem
To recognise the beach I knew so well
So full of all the secrets it could tell.

We scrambled down the hill without a care,
Limbs seaside tanned by weather always fair,
And double summertime that gave each day
An endless, carefree roundabout of play;
We built sandcastles strong against the tide,
Too young to know the sea would mock our pride.

The bathing huts were few and often lent
A secret hideout for the time we spent
On stormy days avoiding windswept shores,
Untroubled by rough seas behind closed doors;
We little knew that one such day would end
Our childhood with the drowning of a friend.

On this my first return for many years,
My throat, constricted by my unshed tears,
Relaxes, as I turn and lift my head
And out of darkness see a crimson thread
Drawn from the far horizon straight to me
A pledge of painful memories set free.

Angela Butler, Allithwaite

Haunting Voices

I have heard the sound of wild geese
Flying overhead, in their almost air-display formation
Marvelled at their flight, their symmetry
Felt a stirring inside at the sound of
Their call as they pass overhead
On their long journey from the
Far northern climes of Canada
Maybe even from the wastelands of Siberia
To make their home, briefly, at the nearby bird reserve.
Their sound is almost primeval
A cry from the beginning of time
When we would have known such sounds
And lived our seasons in tune with
Their cry and flight
I have stood alone, in the evening shadows,
By a local lake
In the stillness I hear a duck skim across the water
It breaks the silence and the stillness
And then, as though the harmony is shattered
There comes the sound of other birds
Complaining, disturbed, even sometimes sounding quarrelsome
A brief cacophony of sounds
These fleeting experiences bring me
Closer to God
I feel as though I am eavesdropping
On His creation.

Brenda Hughes, Holland Moor

Mother Earth

Is Mother Earth but a speck of dust,
Spinning endlessly in space.
Will humans ever come to know,
Their true and rightful place.
Or are we an experiment,
To see how long we last.
From another time, another place,
In some far and distant past.
Maybe we are just a dream,
In someone's sleeping mind.
Searching for a peaceful world,
That we may never find.
Or maybe we have passed away,
Though won't believe it's so.
Reaching for a guiding hand,
To show the way to go.
Must we dwell here on Mother Earth,
Where her lands are soaked in war.
Is this a life that we must lead,
Until Earth exists no more,
It's in our power to put things right,
To end conflict and strife.
Mankind should put aside their hate,
And extend our Mother Earth's life . . .

E S Arries, Houghton-le-Spring

Whodunit?

'Why did you do that?'
Said the corpse to the killer,
Said killer to corpse,
'It's down in the plot.
In case you've not noticed
This book is a thriller -
I just had to kill you,
Like it or not.'

'But look at the blood on the carpet,
This stain on my shirt!
And what will my wife think?
We're off to a fancy dress party . . .
Between you and me I feel rather hurt.
I fancy a role a little more cheery -
Perhaps a detective keen on his beer.'

The killer retorted, 'We've got a good sleuth.
You can't in a book pick any old part.
Just comply with fictional truth -
You're the one to be stabbed through the heart.'
The corpse with effort got to his feet.
'My God!' came a wild yelp
From the killer, who retreating
With mobile in hand, rang for help . . .

From who else but that writer of thrillers
(Her of Whodunit renown).
'This corpse of yours, Ruth,' screamed the killer,
'Should be dead but declines to lie down!'
She thought of the cost, laughter in court,
Judge, jury, lawyers turned sour
By a corpse denied rigor mortis;
Ruth fled from her ivory tower.

Said killer to author, 'I've called in the doc.'
He was rather eager to please.
'This man,' said the doctor, 'looks like a crock,
But he's no corpse - just weak at the knees.'
'I do feel odd,' said the corpse, 'I admit.'
'Perhaps,' said the killer, 'you are going to die.'
'Not me!' said the corpse, 'not a bit!'
'O come on old sport do have a try!'

With murder in mind the detective,
Finding the corpse wasn't dead,
Decided the plot ineffective -
A thriller unfit to be read.
He dismissed himself, the judge and the jury,
Even the killer, the corpse and the doc;
Which provoked the cast into fury
And rendered the writer in shock.

Enter briskly Victorian nurse,
(Wife of corpse in fancy dress)
Saying, 'Darling you never looked worse.'
And, 'Who is this on the floor in distress
With stuffing that pours from her side?'
Said the corpse, 'I may be a fictional stiff,
But let's go - it's the writer who's died.'
Exit nurse and corpse with relief.

Epilogue
Those who witnessed her death throes
Barely audibly heard
The famous whodunit writer whisper
'All I am left with is *words*.'

Terence Smith, Sheffield

Lost And Found

The loss of a person, except in your heart
The loss of a sound, except in your head
The loss of a touch, except in your imagination
The loss of an image, except in your mind's eye
Memories never die!

Christine Pudsey, Cleethorpes

Vaisakhi

The beginning of the Indian New Year
Everyone united with nothing to fear,
Sikhs thank God for the foundation Guru Nanak laid
And the prayers written down in Sikh religion that he made.

Every year in April, a procession takes place in the cities
Which successfully brings together the Indian communities,
Thousands are attracted by the occasion
Everyone celebrating together as a nation.

Sikhs initially visit the gurdwara to pray
And worship God on this most prestigious day,
Then they set off down the streets eating Indian food
And listening to traditional Indian music which sets the mood.

A final visit to the gurdwara marks the end of the day's celebration
Where people are united for the end of an important occasion,
But a new start to the solemnisation of the New Year
That means so much to the Sikh community so near.

Ramandeep Kaur, Bradford

The Seashore Is Their Land

The smiling sand lights the beach
And the sea plays with the children.
Young hands build houses of sand
And give wonder to empty shells.
The seashore is their land.

Young hands set driftwood and seaweed to sail the deep
And the sea ebbs and rocks like a mother's arms,
Crooning lullabies from soft surfing waves.
Children gather smooth pebbles, strewn and patterned
Only to scatter them once again in heedless flight.
The seashore is their land.

The blue sky is motionless with knowing
For storms also roam its pathless heaven.
Fishermen seek and ships are wrecked
And restless death is abroad and yet children play.
The seashore is their land.

Ivy Bates, Lymm

Flower Power

Ivy is wild,
A wayward child,
Which clings with great tenacity,
Once thought to squeeze
The life from trees,
Compelled by its voracity.

Roses are found
Near to the ground,
And often, a great deal higher.
Sometimes they spread,
Way overhead,
From stock of a humble briar.

Foxgloves appear,
Year after year,
In hedgerows they stand quite apart.
Not for abuse,
Their leaves produce,
Digitalis, drug for the heart.

Buttercup bright,
Reflecting light,
With petals of vivid yellow,
Ranunculus,
Sceleratus,
Or a most unpleasant fellow.

Keep an eye on
Dandelion,
Their 'clocks' give children much pleasure.
Blown from small hands,
Where each seed lands
Brings problems gardeners don't treasure.

I'm sure we know,
If, left to grow,
That flowers, although quite pretty,
Before too long,
Become so strong,
May overrun town and city.

Harry Patrick, Carlisle

My Life

It's MC Haze from the strangest land!
I go to Morecambe Bay! - Near Grange-over-Sands!
My aim is to be in a successful band!
But life's stressful enough! - Maybe a change of plan!
I've got to stop dreamin'! - And get back to the mainland!
I've just caned that ganja! - I think I need a brain scan!
God it's hard! - Tryin' to be the main man!
The danger man! - I need a strategic game man!
God there's a paraplegic DJ making dough!
Taking hoes back home! - Doing famous shows!
I can't even compete! - What's wrong with me?
Now he's famous! - He don't wanna make songs with me!
Do I belong here! - They say I'm a waste of space!
A head case who sings Ace of Base!
Mayday! Mayday! - Can anyone hear this?
Bass in your face Madchester! - I'm the clearest!

I need power like one of those Rangers!
'Cause I cower! - I'm close to danger!
I'm an exotic flower who can't be touched!
Or I'll die - shrivel up! - easily cut!
I need to tower above the rest!
Bring home the bacon! - To the love nest!
I need good sex! - Rough sex!
I want success! - But I'm luckless!
I want to put to rest those negative thoughts!
Butts and breasts! - Now that's a positive thought!
Watch how she walks! - I need to be brave!
Stop being afraid! - God! Can I be saved!
I need to lead the way! - I need space!
This hectic lifestyle! - Has got me in a daze!
Please take away my aches and pains!
I need to break away! - Break the chain!

James Hazell, Rochdale

A Child Artistry

A thank you card
In all its brilliance
Lay upon the floor
A child artistry
Blessed me even more
For all kind of wonder
Showered me with myrrh
My Sunday walk
A treat for my soul
A window frame designed
With thank you words inscribed
Turquoise crimson, teal and jade
Were the colours that salute a rhyme
Each letter had their own special prize
Underneath a pink crown, wore a smile of grace
Expressed the hands that placed it there
Was tender and full of care
Either side of the tiara
Two pink stars gleamed with light
My satin heart beamed with treasure
A card in all its purity appreciation and wealth
This special gift should have been stored away with collectables
Not mingling with Jersey leaves
Then again if it wasn't
I wouldn't have gained such pleasure
I'll name this card Nicky
And store it away with my visionary friends
To the talented soul
Who made this work of art
I am sending you a telepathic thank you
With a smile of joy.

Carolie Cole Pemberton, Manchester

Unprecedented Water

Already knowing, he will hereby finish last
With mistakes made, will gain no second chance
You are the star of this show
Fear not you have the Midas touch

A strange journey to have been on
Brought to life for a day
Returned to a box
Remember this life

Where will love take them?
Where will the dream be?
The heart will take a rest
Before finding its beat

Sea rushed to meet the sand
Full of memories and drenched in experience
History floating back out to sea with renewal
Some is left behind in the sand

And yet, seeing the light
Feeling different this time
Salvation in a strange form
He will reap what he sows and embrace.

Jonathan Curry, Killingworth

Tranquil Scene

On an autumn morning I gaped beyond belief
Such beauty lay before me
Spellbound I could not speak
A sunrise of such splendour
That vision held my gaze
Nature's gift of colour
Surrounded by a haze

From sunrise to evening tide
The mist upon a mountainside
A waterfall cascading down
When autumn wears her golden crown

Changing scenes of red and gold
Nature's carpet will unfold
Upon a silver lake I gazed
Spellbound in a misty haze

In my heart tranquillity
Was this scene reality
Such beauty, so profound
This landscape I had found.

Shirley Temple Beckett, Widnes

Some Brighter Star

Scousers reach for distant dreams
And follow yellow brick roads
To everywhere and nowhere
They know what's what
And live to be alive.
Fomenting the experience of lighttime
Into words and songs.
Revolting into their own style
Playing upon thrones of clubs gone by:
Surreal landscapes
Brought in from abroad
And tied to visions of musicians
Lost in their own melodies.

They are apart and yet a family.
Raging against the machine
Steeped in chords of lean and mean.
Dropping out to secure a rising fame
Tracked to studio mobiles and tinsel town.
The damp cold stirring the void
On bananas, lambs and cotton,
Tailor'd to the distant empire
Of another country.
Talking up a storm in a tea-cup.
With free-parking at the end of the universe
With spit and polish
On wet pavement stones;
A wasted land of heroes and villains
Melted into slumtowns
And aspiring wonder.

But the rhythm is felt
Under all the surface twang,
Golden glows of paradise
Inching their way up
From all the doom and gloom
Down the Mathew Street river of life:
The beating heart of Liverpool
Exploding now and again
Into volcanic firework displays.
The two sides of the same coin
Soft and hard
Throwing tomatoes and roses
On to incredible magic
That oofledusts its charm
To down town letharios
And underground caverns;

Mythmakers in guitar-sewers and packed ice
Pedlars of grooves and gravy trains
Hitched up to some brighter star.

Peter Corbett, Liverpool

Abart Ar Shed

There's an apple tree at back o' our shed.
Planted a pip afore I wor wed.
Never thowt it would come to owt,
Didn't expect a tree or nowt.
It's about ten years old.
Standing there so tall and bold.
Its blossom in spring is oh so sweet,
Smells much better than your damn feet.
We've 'ad apples on but very small,
Not a really good harvest at all.
Here hoping afore I dee,
There will be a big apple for thee and me.

The shed is old and full o' muck.
Spiders and flies, an horseshoe for luck.
There's a hole int back, it's tatty and grim.
Darn't opent door and av a look in.
A robin lives in theer I think.
It's in and out for food and drink.
Robins bring bad luck it's sed.
So I hope mine keeps it in the shed.

I'm sat ere now wi' a pot o' tea,
So here's a toast to thee and me.
To thee good luck to thee good wealth.
To both of us happiness and good health.

Audrey Watson, Wakefield

Under The Crossbar
(The Legend Of Bert Trautmann)

Ability, agility, he left us all inspired,
He's still a famous legend though retired,
He reigned unequalled in his goalie shirt,
To every fan at every ground he was our Bert.

Made saves galore beyond our wildest dreams,
Those giant hands defied opposing teams,
He won the heart of every soccer fan,
Under the crossbar - football's biggest man.

Leaping, diving, driving forwards mad,
We had immortal Bert and we were glad,
Before or since and all the years between,
Bert still the greatest keeper ever seen.

A giant German goalie in our net?
He won the doubters over you can bet,
The finest football legend ever found,
They clapped Big Bert off every soccer ground.

For years he kept the City team alive,
Catching, punching, the daring dive,
One desperate lunge - he hit the deck,
Played fifteen minutes with a broken neck.

He was the main man At Maine Road,
Countless games - Über Alles he strode,
Opponents? Forwards? For all their kicks,
Bert unsurpassable between the sticks.

Tell all your children, tell the world,
Proclaim King Bert with banners unfurled,
Sportsman, ambassador, almost a saint,
Make him your hero, and use Sky-Blue paint.

So tragic he was never capped,
Bert kept saving, fans still clapped,
There's seldom been such magic on a field,
Give him a knighthood and a shield.

A sell-out testimonial for Bert,
That final time he donned his green shirt,
A crowd of 50,000 - hear the cheers,
I stood and flooded Maine Road with my tears.

He entertained all fans for fifteen years,
Bert so modest, did he hear the cheers?
His perfect status no one will eclipse,
Not even when we reach Apocalypse.

If just one memory ever stirs your breast,
It must be Saviour Bert - forget the rest,
Listen to the roaring crowd, then cry,
Bert's saved another shout up in the sky.

His famous life has now been on TV,
He earned the Iron Cross and OBE,
He served and saved with nerve, was always the same,
Bert Trautmann our hero deserves his fame.

Epilogue
The accolades are over, now I'm through,
Remember Bert forever - City Blue.

Eric R Sephton, Stretford

Autumn Harvest

Praise God for cherished autumn days,
with fields of glowing amber, and of burnished browns.
For harvest-time, when leaves fall
whispering gently to the frosty ground.

Give thanks for nature's generosity
of gifts of honey and of bread; for wheat and corn,
And orchards filled with purple plums, and
apples turning bronze and scarlet red.

Each flower now in autumn dress
no longer wears the frills of cheery summer gold,
But scarves of wrinkled taffeta
around their precious, heavy laden loads.

The beauty of this palette of delight
dispels the gloom of summer's slow and timely death.
And so, with ever grateful hearts,
we wake up to October's chilly breath.

Elizabeth Mason, Knutsford

Southport Beach, Merseyside

The sand stretches
to the horizon
with only a slither
of silver sea
now reflecting the
coloured sky.
The sea is
run dry
here in Southport
and I remember
the words of
Robbie Burns . . .
'Until all the seas
run dry my dear
until all the seas
run dry . . .
and I will love
you still my dear
until all the
seas run dry'.
In the arms of
one I love
here on the
Southport sands
the breeze
flickers my hair
and stings my face.
True love is a
test of faith,
we should cling
against all
storms and trials
and hold our
red roses
until death's
gate.

Mary Braithwaite, Southport

Memory

Memories are always there
Quite an amazing thing
To recollect a time or place
And the feelings that they bring
Sometimes you think a thought has gone
And it suddenly reappears
Bringing along the love you felt
The laughter or the tears
People long gone from your life
Pets that you still miss
They're in that box called 'memory'
Sealed up with a loving kiss
Now only you have the key
To that special box you own
You can sit, reflect and remember
And you will never be alone
The thoughts are filed quite tidy
In piles from A-Z
You can never destroy or lose them
For they are always in your head
Whenever you feel lonely
All you have to do
Is switch on that computer
That is built inside of you
And all the years will be returned
The sights, the smells, the sound,
And everything that you miss now
Will once more be around
Memory is amazing
And it is personal to you
You will never lose your memories
Whatever else you do.

Marie Greenhalgh, Burnley

It, Him, Or Who? (The Universal Question (Why?))

It, him, or who? Wrote all our stories, all our books
and makes us live them through,
sets all our clocks, knows all our lives what we are going to do,
Jesus, not being the only one to meet this Waterloo.

Free from this way of life,
we, may not wish to go to war and commit
to such strife.

What if, we find out we are no more than
his clockwork toy,
with no free will, a puppet that just tops his bill.

Our brains are made to last much longer
than this life going past.

Has he a library of lives strung out on film to see,
just, for what purpose would this be.

Does he just probe the universe because he is alone,
a member of some long-lost race, that's why he had to clone.

Made in his image like a mouse we would use in our lab,
whatever germs he needs to use his machines have us in a grab.

We're just big rabbits after all and we were made to say,
thrice a white rabbit on the first of each month,
what a day.

They found the graves of these fine beasts bedecked in finery,
His, sense of humour is quite good, it's still a mystery.

Jean Paisley, Hebburn

You Passed Friend, In The Summertime

(This poem is a tribute in memory of the late, great Michael Jackson (August 29th 1958 - June 25th 2009) and the love of God he shared with the world. I dedicate this poem with love to Michael's family and three children Prince, Paris and Blanket)

You passed friend - in the summertime, on the 25th of June,
Your star it shone across the world, but your light was Gone Too Soon
God bless you Michael Jackson, friend, we never will forget you
Your talent and your heart of gold, the man-star child, to not grow old.
Now a spotlight shines on an empty stage where you once did spin and dance,
With your 'moonwalk' feet, where you stomped the beat and delighted thousands fold.
You amazed, entranced with your song and dance, and your records - millions sold.
But they never knew who you really were, will the truth ever be told,
How you met your end on that morning friend, on that summer's day in June.
When your star was gone, and your flower fell, and your light was 'Gone Too Soon?
I believe you walk in Heaven now where the streets are paved with gold,
And your heart delights in those heavenly sights, and the Lord upon His throne
For you've danced your way into Heaven's home, where there's no more tears or sorrow
And now my friend 'You are Not Alone', we will see you in tomorrow,
I believe you were a gift from God, with a music talent rare,
And a child-like heart and a humble soul and a love from God to embrace make whole,
You never lived to see old age or watch your children grow
But we never will forget you friend and the love that you did show.
Your light shines bright forevermore in your music, song and dance,
In the man they called 'the King of Pop, of Pop and Rock and Soul'
The man they called the 'Peter Pan' who never did grow old
And now, you're in eternity, and the best is yet untold.
For you passed friend - in the summertime on the 25th of June
And your star it shone across the world - but your light was 'Gone Too Soon,
So, God bless you Michael Jackson - friend
For we never will forget you
Your talent and your heart of gold the man-star child who did not grow old!

Angela McLaughlin-Bolton, York

Sing My Praises To The Inner Eye

This straw of grass
dangling from my mouth
cares not for speed
looking up, lying here
on this finely flawed green carpet
outside in the sun
the clouds are not yet menacing
with their fluffy white cotton wool kindness
they conjure up castles
and happy monsters with tongues lolling
and eyes flaming
wielding swords and shields
to fight off the dragons
that no doubt exist
in everyone's misgivings
. . . if only they had the time.

The sudden drone of a scooter bike
interrupts my musings
with the insolence of a schoolboy
but means no harm
it has far to go.

I sing my praises to the inner eye
a cool breeze blows
a jet plane's trail slowly cuts the sky.

Gary Austin, Southport

The Event

Nobody does it better
Although the world can try.
A flypast timed to perfection
In the early April sky.

The practised song of the choristers,
In livery of every hue,
Through wooded halls of England
Come notes clear, as morning dew.

The land is laid to carpet,
Thick with leaf and bloom.
While golden crowns and trumpets,
Defy the evening gloom.

Butterflies do flit and dance,
Bound up with a nuptial string.
To celebrate their union
And the youth that it will bring.

The primeval urge to procreate,
To renew to build to be.
Is a gift bestowed by nature,
On show for all to see.

Forget the pomp and circumstance,
The English always bring
Enjoy the yearly spectacle,
The pageantry of spring.

Colin McCombe, Moreton

I Should Be So Lucky

Lust came to me again last night.
It came from a sea of musk
Caressing
Undressing
Inviting me to swim
It came stalking
On high stiletto heels
And long enamelled fingernails.
A lizard's tongue
Whispered a promise
Its lips did the grand tour
Of me,
Until the vampire teeth
Had found
All my undefended places.
It awoke
And aroused me
Then laughing
To the sleep
Not easily stirred.
Lust came for me last night.

Stuart Elsom Wright, Halifax

Winter's Veil

Ice and snow throughout the land,
salt and grit in high demand.
Stranded travellers in dismay,
as jack-knifed lorries block the way.
Aircraft grounded, high passes blocked,
city routes with some gridlocked.
Huge delays on route via rail,
by winter's white and silent veil.
Leisure seekers inclined to roam,
just enjoy the views from home.
Let's beat the frost and keep roads free,
other countries cope, so why can't we!

Snowman, Lymm

A Moment In Time

Poetry is the opening
And closing of a door
Leaving those to look through
To guess about what is seen
During a moment before

So poetry be my opening
As I sit and write my verse
This to all I see
It is the gift of nature
God has given me

A man's real possession
Is his memory
Wondrous thoughts prevail
To feel the sunshine
Amid a garden full of flowers
Spring and summer breezes
With all the Heaven sent showers.

Barbara Ward, Pickering

Pathways In Hulme

I love these old alleys, city paths free of crowds,
ginnels, snickets, film sets of Dickens.
Read the rubbish: syringe of an addict,
traces of costly, smoky parties.

I tap to rhythms of pop-songs-on-the-brain
past gravel where I see Zen abstracts
through a lonely square with one stone dolphin
behind ugly blocks to a white bridge for walkers;
backpack frees thoughts, while rain douses my hat.

I ferret out shady paths for rambling near
my canal, its marina, barging with other lives,
and a secret path thrusting holly, huge ferns -
my wild pretence at being elsewhere.

Arya Mati, Manchester

My Boy

He walks
head down, shoulders slumped,
laden with the cares of the world
in his kitbag.

He stops
and pulls up with slow
deliberance to take the weight
on his shoulders.

He turns,
the smile of a young man's
assurance on the face
of a son; my boy.

A boy
stumbling through life
as only boys do
with childish gung ho.

A son
rising up to be
a country's pride and
his mother's joy.

A man
hunched over with
the burden of our hopes and fears
in his heart.

He walks
with ghosts of the past
and ghosts of the future
united and alone.

This is a man
This is a son
And he is my boy.

Denise Jarrett, Leeds

Cist

Lay him low.

Cold stone sides
make hollow the earth,
provide the space
for his final rest.

Bowl for food,
band of jet,
placed carefully
from the living
amongst the dead.

And schist to seal
the kernel sown,
to cover the fruit
that from dust came
and to dust goes.

Slumber the dream
of immortality,
my lord,
until the day,
dawning on this Earth,
will raise the seed.

How quaint the customs of the old
gathered as sheep in to death's fold.
Capstone seals the ancient belief
of eternal joy from temporal grief.

And we,
denying life from death
in mortal frame,
while we have breath
would, after death,
too late to hold,
testify on headstones cold
a hope in a resurrection of the soul
when no escape from death's repose.

Lee Smith, Woodhouse

One Step Too Far

'You'll have to learn to dance my child,' said feisty Auntie May
'Those two left feet and matchstick legs we'll fix them right away.'
Pumps and tutu ready I joined the ballet class
Stomped around but never learned the mystery of the dance
Our teenage years were crazy as we chased the disco scene
To bop to jive and rock and roll with heartthrobs of our dreams
In pumpkin skirts with beehive hair around our handbags pranced
A shuffle here a wiggle there that really was not dance
Time moved on with handsome beau I trod the ballroom floor
To tango, waltz and cha-cha-cha in sequence round the hall
With poise and graceful elegance this really was my chance
Disaster struck I missed my step was asked to leave the dance
Mature but ever sprightly when the tea dance was revived
We tripped the light fantastic and did the palais glide
Stately as the galleon rigged out and under sail
Sadly we were ladies all not one single male
My dancing days now over I joined the grey brigade
A row of trembling walking canes line dance was all the rage
They hoe-de-hoed and doe-ze-doed like saplings in a gale
At last I'd reached my nemesis knew that I had failed
Musting my dignity I sneaked out of the hall
For just like Cinderella it was time to leave the ball.

Doreen Goodway, Airedale

What A Night

I couldn't sleep, I tried alright
Tossed and turned, was up all night
Plumped up the pillow, kicked off the duvet
Still couldn't sleep, no not anyway
I know, I thought, *I'll make some tea*
Did that do the trick? Well not for me
A nice warm shower, a hot milky drink
That's it my girl, now you're in the pink
Where's the crossword I started that day
Who thinks up the clues? A man, I dare say
A real good book, that will make me sleep
Oh! What the hell, I'll just count sheep.

Joyce M Chaffer, Yeadon

Friendship Is...

A phone call out of the blue
A natter and a brew
A card just to say I miss you.

Friendship is . . .

A smile that says hello
A hug when you have to go
A feeling only true friends know.

Friendship is . . .

A bond that time will not break
A faith in people you cannot shake
A relationship you should not forsake.

Friendship is . . .

A love that others don't quite comprehend
A reward you could never spend
A word that says you will always be my friend.

L E Marchment, Hathershaw

An Admiration

This ode is written in praise of you
Your presence in my world has pride of place
Don't shrug away my work, for so to do
Would only make me say, 'It is true.'
My pen must list your many virtues;
Pleasure taken in simple things,
Quiet reflection in the world around you;
Children, nature, birds on the wing.
With your constant optimistic view of life
Your motto should be, 'Nil desperandum,'
Problems, upsets, struggles, strife,
Nothing disturbs your equilibrium.
The picture I paint is of a paragon
But you are still of the same race, 'human'.

Olivia Barton, Balderstone

War Baby

When I had the age of two
And my brother, three months old,
The news that said the world's at war
Was starting to unfold.

Although so young, the memories
Remain so clear and strong
Some created by the trauma
All around us, for so long.

I recall the siren's warning sound -
Take shelter, danger near.
Then the noise of planes, the fires,
And all in constant fear.

This was followed by another noise,
A welcome sound this time,
The all-clear called, it's safe
Perhaps today will turn out fine.

Of all the tales I could relate,
About my early years,
There's one that always makes me smile
From memories still so clear.

The month of May, year '45,
Noise woke me from my sleep;
And shouting loudest, my friend John
Ran up and down the street.

He was still in his pyjamas
Calling us to join the fun,
And everyone was celebrating
VE day the war was won.

Mary Hoy, Bootle

The Magic Word

We are only human
With emotions that are strong
We remember many things
Having memories that are long

Eager enthusiastic
Excited by a thought
Hot-headed and impetuous
Quite often overwrought

We see, we hear, we taste
We respond to someone's touch
Of tolerance and patience
We can never have too much

When under stress we grit our teeth
We wince when scared or shocked
Tears like rain fall from our eyes
When hurt, insulted, mocked.

There are many, many words to
Describe our human traits
Sensations and experiences
Words can make or break.

But the word of which I'm thinking
Must have come from Heaven above
God gave the magic word to us
And that magic word is love . . .

Norah C Darbyshire, Daisy Hill

Remembering

He lowered his rucksack with a sigh
And gazed around with rheumy eye,
His breath was sharp within his chest
As he stopped to take a much needed rest;
His thoughts drifted off to long ago
When he walked much faster, he wasn't so slow.
Thirty miles then was an easy day's ramble
And less than twenty was merely an amble.
No aching muscles, no signs of strain,
Go that bit faster, we never complain.
Up at the front, ahead of the rest,
In the first twenty, one of the best;
Laughing and joking while climbing the hills,
No shortness of breath, no energy pills;
After reaching the summit, run all the way down
Jumping the streams, five miles into town,
Reach the last checkpoint, you're in the first ten:
Congratulations from the leaders, you've done it again,
Wait for your friends, fifteen minutes off the pace,
Handshakes all round, we've run a good race:
Retire to the bar, the drinks are on me,
And all thoughts are on what the next challenge will be.
Yes, those were the days, when we were all kings,
We flew over the ground as if we had wings,
No walks were too long, no rivers too wide,
For we were all young, took them all in our stride,
No thoughts of tomorrow, we lived for today,
What lies ahead was only a heart-beat away.
Alas time and tide for no man does wait
Slowly and surely you shorten your gait,
The miles seem much longer, the hills that bit steeper,
To keep up with the rest you've to dig that bit deeper.
Where once you were first, now you're way back at the rear
And though you try your best the leaders all disappear;
'Look sharp now, old chap, we're ready to go,'
He smiles to himself as he rises, little do they know.

John O'Connor, Little Hulton

The Children

I heard the voices again
Children's voices, subdued sometimes
Sometimes giggling
As if they were hiding from one another.

Then calling to one another
'Where are you?'
'I can't find you!'
'Come out wherever you are.'

The room was full of sunshine
Dust floating on the beams of light
As the wood in the old house
Settled in the warm sun.

I hear them running downstairs
And I step into the hall
'Who are you?' I ask
And there is silence.

I can feel their presence
As though they watch me
Then I hear their voices again
Giggling and laughing together.

As they run back upstairs
Their footsteps echoing
In the quiet house
Then all is still again.

The past is ever with us
As is the future
And one is enfolded in the other
Time is but a measure.

The happiness of the boys
Enfolds me
Are they in a time warp?
Or just shadows that come and go.

I will never know
Because I have to move on
To create my own impressions
Or shadows to leave behind.

Joan May Wills, Kendal

Time

There is a time to live,
And a time to die,
A time to laugh,
And a time to cry.

There is a time to go,
And a time to stay,
A time to think,
And a time to pray.

Time is something one can't buy,
But something one can save.
Time controls our every day,
From the cradle to the grave.

Time is such a precious thing,
Given by the Lord above.
So we can live in harmony,
With the people that we love.

Joseph Knott, Whitworth

Autumn

Autumn is coming with its golden days
Of sunshine filtering through morning haze
The fields are standing empty and bare
Waiting for new crops to be planted there.
The leaves on the trees will begin to die
And swallows away to the south will fly.
Creatures get ready to sleep the cold away,
To awaken again on a warm spring day.
Nights will get longer and time will slow,
Evenings will be spent by the firelight's glow.
Nothing can halt the rolling of the seasons,
And for each change Nature has her reasons.

Christine Naylor, Airmyn

The Old Brick Wall

God's amazing! - Did you know? -
This evening, in the sunset's glow
On looking out upon the park -
The old brick wall: though getting dark

There still was sun, a golden ball,
And in its light, the old brick wall
Was bathed in russet-red, and I
Knew lowering sunlight from the sky

Had caused the old brick wall to be
Quite beautiful . . . and, as for me . . .

I knew, anew, the wonder when
God's beauty touches hearts of men:

For even things mundane, and small,
When touched by God, are wonders all -

Like that old, beautiful brick wall.

Dorinda MacDowell

The Fairy Tree

You must see them, not just me
The fairies around the fairy tree
Dancing lightly not a sound
All this magic I have found

Look, oh, look you must see
The fairies around the fairy tree
Glowing, glistening in the light
Wings of gossamer so bright

As a feather, soft in flight
Blowing with the breeze of night
Don't blink, don't move, then you may see
The fairies around the fairy tree.

Cynthia Gibson, Ripon

Seize The Day

When you wake up from your bed of dreams
Tell me which plans are not profitable schemes
Tell me this morning of life's unpredictable themes
What about the dreadful storm it finally blew away
There was no choice other than seize the day.

Wounded by a raging war that was never yours
Why you fought for an answer or a cause
A reason to believe or to deeply grieve
What about the dreadful storm it finally blew away
There was no choice other than seize the day.

It was physical attraction and love at first sight
It was magnetic and energetic sheer delight
It was a story of hope of everlasting glory
What about the dreadful storm it finally blew away
There we were together prepared to seize the day.

So what the sun appeared not to brightly shine
Time and space is infinitely yours and mine
Cold moon's surrounded by glittering stars divine
Stars which we wish upon will never fade away
God granted me strength to boldly seize the day.

John Flanagan, Leeds

The Darkest Shadow

It's the best things in life that cast the darkest shadow,
but it's these we can't live without.
With love comes loss and with winter comes frost,
some things in this life we can't change.
For I have seen the good and I have seen the bad
and I have seen the thing in-between,
There's no escaping the fact that some things are just chance,
in this life best described as a dream.

Luke Greggain, Whitehaven

Dolour

Locked in dark chasms of memory
stir thoughts
and words yet unspoke.
Down cold cheeks run tears of despair
to form pools of sadness
on heartless slabs.
Rivulets creep 'twixt the marble
to a dark domain filled
with nameless parasites
that feed upon the salts
of my undying anguish.
In my dolour I will
grieve forever.

Kenneth H Wood, Ormskirk

My Garden

A patch of earth
Is mine to behold
A window of nature
Her story is told
Spring has arrived
The plants are in bud
Blackbirds in search of a tasty grub
A song thrush sings a merry tune
Blue tits display their colourful plume
Indian bean and birch stand proud
A sanctuary for birds away from the crowd
Relaxing and admiring the sights with a tea
The garden show is all for free!

John Fudge Jnr, Sunnyside

Seeds Of Sorrow

Let me sleep and dream sweet dreams
    That all this pain's not what it seems
That I'll awake to find it gone
    And the sun through my window warm as it shone
It's eight o'clock of the hour
    I'm helpless as I have no power
Evil devours me throughout the long night
    All dark and shadow - no trace of light
Muscle and swastika embrace and devour me
    Misery visits and I cannot break free
I'd toss and I'd turn but I'm tied like a knot
    All I endure will not be forgot
I can't see the sun - cannot see a flower
    The world is dark whatever the hour
Oh to see bluebells out in the wood
    I dream of this and the dream is good
But the dream is brief as I twist in pain
    Never to see a bluebell again
Never to see the blue of the sky
    As all I do is suffer and die
A wooden bed and freezing cold
    No warm blanket for me to hold
Harsh evil voices in the dark of the night
    Guns and whips ne'er out of sight
We're threatened and cowed with always a tear
    Constant terror - paralysed with fear
Cold slop for food and death at the door
    Its stench everywhere - more and more
All is grey - no green anywhere
    No sign of life and nought but despair
What is this creature performing such deeds?
    They call it man and on suffering it feeds
And it never changes except perhaps in design
    It feeds on blood and now it feeds on mine
Here in Auschwitz and all similar places
    One sees the same old crotchety faces
That lust for blood and the suffering it brings
    They steal all our teeth and diamond rings
They use us for lamp shades and turn us into soap
    There is no escape - there is no hope
Oh human kind you're the most evil beast
    In cold blood you dine and feast
'Twas always thus - will always be
    I wish someone would comfort me

But today is my last I am slipping away
        I am leaving the darkness I am happy to say
I'm touching the blue sky I once knew in the past
        In a life long ago afore shadows were cast
I'll smell no more burning of human kind
        All of that terror I'll be leaving behind
No more mountains of dead, naked, defiled
        Nor see human eyes manic and wild
See no more mass graves of skin and bone
        Emptied of flesh and muscle tone
Dark eyes staring into empty space
        All this courtesy of the human race
Now I'm slipping further away
        Glad to see the back of this day
A day so long - so grey - so black
        I'm speeding away down the railroad track
Into meadows and skies of blue
        I see sunrises and sunsets of every hue
Over there I see the bluebell as my train goes passing by
        A picture in the grass so green and nodding to the sky
Let me sleep now and dream sweet dreams
        That all this pain's not what it seems
That I'll awake and find it gone
        With the sun through my window warm as it shone
So make me a meadow in Auschwitz
        I'll be watching you, you know
Casting the seed of the bluebell
        Then watching this pretty thing grow
Let the grass grow free and the wild flowers blow
        In this hideous place of Birkenau
Give our tortured hearts something pretty to see
        From beyond the grave where we now be
Sow the seeds of sorrow with a kind gentle hand
        Scatter them lovingly o'er barren land
Shed a tear with each one and then declare
        'No more war forever on my heart I do swear'
Inflict no more pain for e'er evermore
        From coast to coast and shore to shore
Build meadows instead - let all suffering cease
        Hostilities over . . . We are now at peace.

Clare Marie Zeidrah Keirrissia Marshall, Langley

Victoria's Flour Power

Today's the day - it's baking day
Soon tempting aromas will fill the air
Ingredients are weighed measure for measure
It's always been half fat to flour
Greasing of tins - some are old family treasures
Sink full of bubbles, steaming away
Awaits the pots that are coming its way
From whisking - beating and blending
To mixing and rubbing in
Some of the tasks seem never-ending
The kitchen timer like the radio never stops singing
But soon the work - all will be done
Though the kitchen resembles a war zone
The table is groaning under pies and custard
Cakes - biscuits - muffins - the Victorian sponge
Might be a bit lopsided - but in our house it'll all get eaten
Be proud of what you've achieved
It might not all be perfect - who cares
Is a feeling that's well worth keeping
Now it's time for the washing up -
Then a well-earned cup of tea - a slice of Victoria.

David Charles, Lytham

Summer... Of The Wasp

Speed they put on with a spurt
yellow and black like a rugby shirt
flying in erratic zigzag formation
the Stuka of the insect nation.

Sudden stinging pain we fear
every time they fly too near
perfume really spurs them on
pheromones like a dinner gong.

Beer they also like to sip
from the cup or from the lip
where whirling dervishes abound
it's likely there's a wasp around.

People have been put to flight
preferring not to stand and fight
ice cream men and market traders
daily do battle with these invaders.

On sunny days beware the bin
it's sure to have these creatures in
they seem to know who fears them most
as they zero in on another host.

So finely tuned is their radar
we look to them like a giant flower
if these trials you would avoid
don't flap about and get them annoyed.

Adrian McRobb, Cramlington

Northern Bloke

My bloke Mike
Gradely, that's him
Strong, family man
Monochrome, no grey

We are chalk and cheese
You can trust him with your life
He does exactly what it says on the tin
Can be frustrating at times

He doesn't bend the rules
Straight as a die
There's no agenda with him
Transparent day in day out

There's a lot to be said
For his down-to-earth approach
Hands-on attitude
A brain and a tongue to back it up

None of that office work rubbish
Meetings are for wimps
Waste of time discussing
Get on wit' job

He's really a cuddly grizzly
A self-made man, proud
And determined, love him or hate him
You know where you stand

Mike the gradely husband, dad and best friend
Carer, disciplinarian
Black or white
I'm happy he's mine.

Karen Collins, Wrightington

Tanker

It settled its great black ballast,
Quenching as the ant man fled,
Grasping by the tides that whispered,
Gushing hot rasping breath,
Pulsing the heaving shingle,
Drugged listlessly it slept,
Dark bile slipped into green gold salt,
And the stealthy canker crept.

Stained the shadows unravelled,
Sealed in a sable mask,
Melting the tar borne serpent,
Spewing its ebony cast,
Pouring the endless ichor,
Strangled with coils of ash,
And swallowed the copper marshes,
Caressed with death all it passed.

Smashed in the bowels of the serpent,
Spilled on the silent shore,
Veins of hot jet grew shining,
With subtly poisoned jaws,
We yielded glazed and frozen,
Wrapped in the bitter pail,
While putrid leather tangles,
Grazed in the clinging squall.

The sickness was swallowed slowly,
Too weak to swim or fly,
We combed the withered grasses,
Scorched and blister dry,
Mourning our lifeless brothers,
Watching the brooding sky,
Lashed by the burning waters,
Waiting patiently to die.

Sue Hardy-Dawson, Harrogate

When I Am Dead

When I am dead
Cut me open you bastards,
See what finished me
Take what's necessary from me.

I know you will not think
You're cruel, the living part of me
Is gone, you'll be professional and say
He died of this and that.

Then sew me up
And take what's left and have the
Undertakers do the rest
And box me just enough.

I will not care I will be gone
The immortal part of me lives on
It was my time, the rest just bury
Or burn for that has died.

Robert Lockett, Bootle

Sheila

Sleepless the nights with misery and pain
Whoever thought I'd find love once again
This lady who came straight into my life
To help ease this pain left by my dear darling wife.

Sheila my love came from Stoke on the Trent
Blessed was I she was heavenly sent
So caring and kind so loving and true
That's why in this world I want only you.

When I fell so ill, knocking on death's dark door
Sheila gathered me up and my life did restore
Now we laugh and we sing we cuddle and kiss
This life we both share is absolute bliss.

My darling I cherish just love and adore
Our love for each other will last evermore.

Leslie Hogarth, Carlisle

The Comedy Terrorists

Have you heard this joke?
A good friend spoke,
And touched the screen
Of his phone
But who writes
The gags
To amuse the lads
Are they working
All alone?

Grey men in attic
Rooms scribble
All the time,
Awaiting the day
The papers say
Someone famous
Has died.

Before the news
Has hit the street
The wit has done
His worse
Using his gift to
Take the piss
He's texting to the
World.

Plastic keys
Pressed with ease
Send a withering line,
Nothing is safe
No sacred place,
For you to run
And hide.

The comedy
Terrorists are planting
Bombs to blow our
Tiny minds,

It's only for fun
So everyone
Can share in a
Mobile smile!

Philip Moore, Walton Village

The Lost Soul

I walked down the path of yesterday
I couldn't find you there -
No soul so spirit - where are you?
Do you really care?
Why did you ever leave me - tell me what to do.

I still feel your presence
I feel you coming through.
In time it might be easy - will I really know
Life is difficult without you -
Because I loved you so.

I'm walking in your shadow
I see you in my dreams
Will you reach out and touch me
Tell me how it seems.

For when tomorrow comes (it will be yesterday today)
Another day without - since you went away.
Yet the sun sets and rises -
Some things stay the same
And if I listen carefully -
I can hear you call my name.

Now I feel your presence
I know you really care
Thank you for everything -
For always being there.

Marjorie M Armstrong, Carlisle

Twin Soul Reunion

O my divine twin soul
We were once there in divine beauty
Of the magnificent whole
Living in God's divine essence
In golden goodness of our spiritual home
Vibrating in ecstasy and unison
With the purest form of love, flowing
Through our hearts, minds and souls.

The great divide arrived
Somewhere in divine space and time
Separating one another from each other
Tumbling down from Heaven to Earth
To come in and out of each other's lifetimes
Disguised and clothed in another
Dispersing more of our great divine within us.

As we keep plummeting further into darkness away
From divine light
Our hearts, minds and souls begin to know
They don't feel a perfect whole
There is something missing inside
An aching urge to be fulfilled again
We turn around go back towards the light.

Through many future lifetimes and spiritual fights
Ascending into Heaven's realms
We make it back into divine light
A reunion accured between twin souls
Divinity is restored
Living back in unison in a scared whole once more.

Jenifer Ellen Austin, Sproxton

The Midnight Bus

I'm leaving here
I'm heading north
on the midnight bus
I'm riding

To where the people are warm
where the people are real,
with hearts made for love,
not hearts made of steel.
On the midnight bus
I'm riding.

I was crazy for
what I thought was best,
so I headed south
where life was blessed -
so I thought . . .

But life was hard
and people were cold,
in their search for fame,
in their search for gold,
so I caught . . .

The midnight bus,
used my last few quid.
It was the best night's work
I ever did.
Now I'm riding.

When I left him flat,
him and the kid,
it was the worst day's work
I ever did.

If he'll have me back
I swear I'll try
to love them both
'til the day I die.
Now I'm riding.

I'm leaving here,
I'm heading north
on the midnight bus
I'm riding.

Went and bought a ticket
with my last few quid
it was the best night's work
I ever did.
Now I'm riding.

Maureen C Bell, Gateshead

What A Spectacle

When I was young
And learnt to read
The letters were so
Big indeed
I didn't have to
Wear no specs
Because the books
Were in large text . . .
But now I'm feeling
Old and grey
And squinting -
Order of the day
Most editors
Seem to enjoy
To print in small type
Is their ploy
It seems to me
To be a joke
That they should play
On us old folk
So please dear publishers
Please reverse
The order of
Your printed verse
And give us oldies
Much needed break -
So we can read . . .
For goodness sake.

Elaine J Seagrave, Woodseats

Dad You Said

'You're scum,' you said
'You're worthless,' you said
'You're not fit to live,' you said
'On my life,' you said
'I wish you had never been born,' you said
As you smashed my head
Then sent me to bed with no dinner you said,
'I'll make you wish that you were dead.'
'You deserve,' you said to my mom you said,
'To be beaten,' as you punched her in the face you said,
'I'd be free without you and all the kids,' you said
As you punched and punched her face you said,
'If you ever run away and tell the police,' you said
You would find her you said, and then kill her you said
As you rammed your fist into her face.
I was eight and crying, you said you were coming
As you climbed the steps of the stairs you said
You would show me how not to be bad
As you came in my room you said, 'Shut up,'
To my mother you said, as she cried and begged
You not to beat me you said,
'You should think yourself lucky that I only blacked your eyes.'
Then she said nothing.
'Don't hurt me,' I said
As you punched me, I said
'It wasn't my fault I was born,' I said
'Please don't,' I said
As I screamed as you took the belt from your trousers
'I'm sorry for whatever I've done,' I said
As you beat me and beat me and beat me and beat me.

Wayne Pugh, Brasside

Yorkshire In The Spring

The football season is nearly done
Now cricket is on the scene
Matches played at Headingley
Or on the village green.

Lambs are frolicking in the fields
Where lots of daisies grow
Birds are busy building nests
In trees and green hedgerow.

Yorkshire has some lovely food
Barnsley chop and Yorkshire pud
But if these two are just too hot
There is Whitby crab that tastes so good.

Daylight hours are longer
There is gardening to be done
Or else trips to the seaside
Enjoying the nice warm sun.

A ride out to the sunny dales
Can be a lovely thrill
Visiting village or market town
Or just sitting on a hill.

Lots of folk by car or bus
Enjoying life outdoor
Cyclists and ramblers
Over Ilkley Moor.

When evening calls it's homeward bound
As the sunlight fades away
Arriving back at home once more
And thankful for a lovely day.

Terence Leslie Iceton, Leeds

Loneliness

Sitting alone in splendour and state,
While the world outside rushes on past her gate,
With her stick and her shawl and her white crocheted hat,
She lives all alone in her house with her cat.
Sitting in the window behind curtains of lace,
She spins out her life at a leisurely pace,
Watching and wondering about this and about that,
Nodding and noting remarks to her cat!
But nobody sees them or knows they are there,
To hear her questions or answering purr,
For as the world rushes by past her rickety gate,
Looking neither left nor right but permanently straight,
They don't see the old lady in her white crocheted hat,
Nor her solitary companion a yellow barred cat!

Ed Collins, Southport

Freedom

Freedom is a wonderful thing
It can make your heart soar, like a bird on the wing
Your whole life means more, as hope starts to spring
Yes freedom is a wonderful thing

To do as one pleases with no cares at all
Seems only to happen when we are small
As we grow older and find our true loves
With soft chains to bind us we're happy as doves

To be locked away in a prison cell
To a few it's home to many it's Hell
Where no one hears you though loud you may yell
Oh yes! To be locked in a prison cell

Down through the ages our history books tell all
When armies do battle and many men fall
They live or they die for their freedom to win
Oh yes! Freedom is a wonderful thing.

Beryl Eastwood, Hull

Lover's Crime

Perfection is a word
that is somewhat overused
but when you've found the definition
you'll see the meaning can come true . . .

Stolen kisses on a grassy hill
the touching of hands, the danger the thrill
nervous smiles and racing hearts
upon this stage we all play parts

A silent whisper of three words
a rush of excitement our feelings a blur
looking deep into each other's eyes
an instant connection, but that's no surprise

This single moment, a fraction of time
breaking the rules, a lover's crime
Romeo and Juliet, so clichéd but true
the insanity of in a second, realising my one, is you.

Bianka Hannam, Ellesmere Port

Nosher

He drank dishwater daily,
With jam and eggs at seven;
Then dinners, teas and sundry snacks,
With a ferret fry at eleven.

An own-grub contest in the pub
Was won - Old Nosh came tops
By slurping pints of donkey's blood
And forty lizard chops.

Buckets of slimy custard
He licked off stones in the Row.
He was tucking into half a horse
One year at the Country Show.

Of course, his greed could never last:
With eyes too big for his belly,
His gut pushed out till his hat fell in
And he burst - all over our Nelly!

Howard Peach, Cottingham

The Last Word

'What is my place in time and space?'
asks the scholar in dismay.
'Such is my quest, I cannot rest
though weary of the way;
for whilst I cry unto the sky
and the Great God hears me pray,
yet I do fear I never hear
what the Great God has to say!'

'Nor me, nor me,' roars the restless sea,
(for she is seeking too!)
'My seven floors twixt crumbling shores
in deeper depths than blue,
I sound and chart and ceaseless start
to map again anew!
I plumb and probe round this globe,
and search the same as you!'

'I do not know,' gasps the wind as though
his breath were nigh deplete,
'For whilst I ride where gods abide
with mountains at my feet,
and chase each cloud-like chariot proud
from Heaven's judgement seat,
yet the only thing I have to sing
is my song of self-conceit!'

'At stardom's door,' shrills the meteor,
'Is the secret you must learn!
When passing there, I read with care
a message none may spurn -
See how I flame in dreadful pain
and how I wheel and turn?
How lest one word on Earth is heard,
to ashes I must burn!'

'He does not know,' says the Earth below,
'but fabricates a lie!
What chance indeed has he to read
a charter in the sky?
When thru the night in fearful plight
his fiery soul must fly.
Come rebel rock! - Far flung amok,
come hither child, and die!'

'I know a verse,' sings the Universe,
'and man is a note sublime!
A cherubim, a seraphim
who spans the dome of time:
I need him so that he may know
my rhythm and my rhyme . . .
Else I shall taste the bitter waste
of beauty left to pine?'

Bernard Shaw, Barwick-in-Elmet

Hiding In Plain Sight

Often you can see them,
drifting in limbo;
scattered on film sets,
throughout the world.

'Extras', forever on the move,
yet always going nowhere.
'Walk-ons', ordering their needs,
without a single word.

Who exactly are these people?
Minions making up numbers
or is nothing as it seems?

Perhaps they are aliens,
hiding incognito,
waiting patiently to pounce.
(is 'extra' a code word for ET?)

Perhaps soon they will rise up,
rip plastic from their features,
display antennas on their heads.

Perhaps then they'll screech
with laughter, as the lasers
from their ray guns, reduce
the rest of *us* to 'bit-parts'.

Paul Kelly, Walton-le-Dale

Seasonal Love

When spring is drenched green again
And salmon spawn on silvery rivers,
My new found love will flourish.

As starlings cut and claim the sky
And speedwell spreads its carpet
Passionate thoughts magnify.

When summer sun fires our faces
And seas glare burnished zinc
Tormented body will agonise and shudder.

On oven-hot nights with dripping stars
When world is hushed except for crickets
Desires and wants will be unchained.

On apple-ripe September mornings
When gorse shines butter-yellow
I will know eternal love has dawned.

When trees are heavy with growth
And poppies invade ripened corn
Heart will flutter as cascading leaves.

Winter, when antlered trees shelter robin
And winter winds wail in anger
Warmth of touch will excite inner being.

Alex Branthwaite, Sunderland

A Clear And Obvious Tale

An obscene tale of the obvious and ouroboros fiend of Chronos,
Is played in the dripping rhythm of pigs' trotters,
Under the solar glare of Athena's pet.

This world stage is played behind
Skull and cross-boned walls,
Which are closed to those without
The privileged scroll and the sardonic key.
It is shadowed by patriotic eugenics;
Given credence by a disturbed and violent sea.

From the top of this pyramidical panorama,
Osiris smokes his dried cigar,
Regarding his purged god child as it
Smears its glaring neurosis upon the
Blinding psychosis of public domain.

The serpents consume these syrupy and succulent specimens,
Wrapping their forked ever-seeing pupils around
The necks of barcoded fools.

This is an ageless tale;
Of a wooden boy's father, our father, our masters.
They eagerly abort genocide to taste the thick and crude treacle gold.
Rinse and repeat again, rinse and repeat without repent.

Andrew Gill, Chester

The Colours Of Childhood

Perhaps if I went seeking,
through a mirror looking back,
I'd find the place I lost,
my yellow, gold and black.
In old and dirty cobbled streets,
I'd find them wet with rain,
I'd dry them and shine them,
and take them home again.
And all the joys of childhood,
will sit upon my head,
I'll peel the layers of life away
and wear my heart instead.
My tools will all be toys again,
and all my words will rhyme,
I'll shrink the world to rainbow size
and make it beat in time.
Pale yellow mornings,
skipping rope skies,
seeing plain horizons,
all the rest is lies.
Backyards filled with golden days,
brimming with content,
shining, shadowless, halcyon time,
a total innocent.
The gentle black of childhood sleep,
a small death in itself,
every waking reborn,
no guilt and no regret.
My colours are all blurred now
and only looking back,
will I ever find the clarity,
of yellow, gold and black.

Yvonne Valerie Stewart, South Shields

A Fool And His Sin

Only a fool makes light of sin
It is part of our lives each day
But we have a god who forgives us all
In everything and in every way

The pure sinless lamb was sacrificed
It was God's plan from the beginning
His name is Jesus, God's only son
To atone for all our sinning

Don't turn your back upon the cross
You'll regret it when judgement is given
God sees everything in your life
From Him nothing is hidden

Be humble before Him
Be patient and kind
Love everybody
He will give peace of mind

Put God first
Give to the needy
Help a stranger
Try not to be greedy

Give thanks for each day
Without God you can't live it
Trust and be faithful
With God there's no limit

He will give and keep giving
Wherever you turn He's there
On cloud nine
Or in the depths of despair
Saying, 'You are mine'

So cherish each moment
Don't let it pass by
Thank God for His giving
Lift His name high.

Alma Taylor, Manchester

Eclipse - A Tercet

Earth is plunged in depth of night
as sun's gold disc is out of sight
depriving mortals of its light

In midst of day the eerie dark
even silences the lark
leaving landscapes cold and stark

Gradually sun and moon
become entwined as one - in tune
encircled by their fire festoon

All at once the diamond ring -
then the longed-for glow it brings
when muted birds begin to sing

Warmth rejuvenates the Earth
spreading love and joy and mirth
giving creatures second birth.

Jennifer D Wootton, Bradway

Dance With The Bees

The sweet scent of jasmine
wafts through the open window
as I sip my tea
and watch the bees dance upon the white petals.

Each rhythmic move
resonates with the beat of my heart.
The bees shiver, shimmer,
hover and vibrate,
their buzz sending me into a misty swirl.

My spirit lifts and soars,
sweeping through the summer breeze
and I dance the Dance with the Bees;
the Dance of Life.

Jacqueline Zacharias, Naburn

Retrospection

(Looking back - but not in anger - and not nostalgic.)

Nostalgia pure and simple, is surely pessimistic,
The past was not a universal bed of roses,
Change always comes, man proposes, God disposes.

Each era brings changes, some good and some bad,
If we want more change we must take stock
But remember, there is no way to put back the clock

This retrospect covers over ninety years
Since I came upon this earth
A gift from God to my parents, just the miracle of birth.

Faith in God I have, and shall have until I die,
To live my life without His love,
I would never even try.

I am grateful for all the help He gave me,
Throughout the years I have spent on Earth,
No money could ever buy what to me it had been worth.

Of course there were ups and downs - life was ever thus,
Tragedies brought a sadness we often did not understand
But this Earth was never going to be the Promised Land.

Life on Earth was never meant to be easy,
It was never intended to be stress free,
But help is there if you ask - for us He died on a tree.

I never prayed for miracles nor selfish desires,
But I prayed for Him to show me the way,
And never ever have I been sent empty away.

A darling wife and five wonderful kids
Loving grandchildren and great grandchildren galore,
Could any man ever have asked for anything more?

I believe that life is what you make it
Each day God sets some sort of task,
And if you run into trouble you only have to ask

So I am grateful for my life and loves
First as a son, then husband and dad,
Believe me, the good times, have far outweighed the bad.

Robert H Quin, Knutsford

Divorce

Why does it have to happen to me?
I fall in love
And think I am free.
I pour out my heart
And expose my soul
Instead of joy
I find a black hole.
I thought it was time for me to connect
To be protected
Not rejected
To be valued
To be honoured
I thought the time was right
I forgot about free will
That bitter pill.
Even contracts can be broken
That are made before God
Even though I find it odd.
I just want to be loved
I never give up hope
I know how to cope
I can walk the lonely shore
I have trod this path before.
One day I shall be happy
One day I will be free
And as always
I trust in love eternally.

Janet Rocher, Wirral

Some 21st Century Events

Remember our efforts now.
We will see things through your eyes:
Nature's flourishing meadows
Flaunt their abundant flowers,
Wild birds winging back again to
Fertile welcoming wetlands,
Endangered species have now
Settled and procreated
In safe places chosen by man.
Improvements by law changes
Have been long in coming about;
Our charities' donations,
Our perpetual letters
To people of influence
Paid off eventually.
Firms' attitudes regarding
Humane animal treatment
Were outlined by them for us.
Sponsored people's events,
Also special appeals helped
To offset our expenses.

Most satisfying of all,
Improvements by mankind when
Dealing with things of nature:
Showing compassion towards
Its creatures, trees and plant life,
Caring for its provisions
And Earth in all its beauty.

E Joan Knight, Great Houghton

No Nonsense Knickers!

Alice was in the ATS in the Second World War
There she met her friend Sally
Opposites attract that's for sure
Sally wasn't either thrifty or mean
But spending brass to Alice was something obscene
Even after the war she painted her legs
And made Yorkshire puddings from powered eggs

It's almost 60 years since the war came to an end
Since the war there were lots of letters to send
Sally was in Sussex, Alice was in Leeds
By letter friendship always succeeds
But now there's been a reunion at last
Two ladies nattering about the past
Sally suggested a shopping spree
Alice went white and said, 'That's not me!'

Sally said, 'Come on and spend some money -
- You can't take it with you when you die!'
Alice said, 'I know this sounds funny -
- but am going to have a jolly good try!'
Alice said, 'Come on let's go to Leeds -
- I want some new knickers, they're essential needs!'
Alice thought they'd go to a market stall
But Sally was used to the shopping mall!

Down Briggate there's an arcade so very posh
Shopping at Harvey Nicks costs lots of dosh
Sally was used to shopping up west
- and going to Harvey Nicks when she wanted a vest
Alice thought she'd give it a try
But when she saw the price tag she'd surely die
Charging thirty pound a pair, how could they dare
With the market for Alice this couldn't compare!

For that price she'd want a gusset of gold
But if they had she couldn't darn them if they got tatty and old
Alice told Sally that she, 'Didn't feel right in here,'
She was going to the market she made that quite clear

Pink flannelette was the order of the day
And they'd last her ten years or more I'd say
After that she'd make a duster or two
I think they'd be value for money - don't you?

Anthony Gibson, Hartlepool

Peaceful Day

To be inspired . . .
The sun has to shine its warm light . . .
to drench pale winter woolly covered up skin
in sensual yellow glow . . .
To walk and hear the little birds about
their day . . .

To be inspired . . .
To have eyes that see only
beautiful things . . .
Spectrums of shining angels
that dance over trillions
of fragments of perfect delight . . .

At the riverbank I sit and watch
I am inspired . . .

D Ritchie, Roseworth

The Fundamentals

The fundamentals never alter . . .
Change or falter,
The river running by . . .
This river that is I.

Forever has been the same,
Yet, unable to name,
In bliss contemplate,
And imagination slake.
As in awe - wonder and quake,
At the man it make . . .
Servant of our Lord . . .
Who can only put word,
To some of the things heard,
Come from the woodland
Songbird . . .

Michael Riley, Farringdon

Memories

The room lies quietly dreaming
As I creep softly down the stairs
The rain tap tapping upon the windowpane
Winds whistle down the chimney, embers flare, then die
Deep shadows embrace me, sweet and warm,
A treasured box of memories whispers in the night,
The moon smiles at me as he goes on his way,
The stars peep shyly, from a deep dark sky,
Tick-tock, says the old clock
Proudly, standing in the hall
Now I grow old the memories fade
Of long forgotten days of sunshine and love
Now the dawn will soon be here
The night will slowly slip away
And I give thanks that I'll see another day.

Ann Warner, Prestwick

Nathan

One tiny soul as pure as a pearl
Kept safe within his mother's shell
Waiting for the call to live, unfurl
His limbs, to breathe and yell
With us at last on Earth to dwell
But none of this to be.

God took him home and set him free
Leaving all this pain for me
Precious darling, second son
Your brother asks why you have gone
To live with the angels in the skies
And then he cries.

What would I give to have you by
The world on a plate for a baby's sigh
But don't look back, don't wait for me
You were just too good for this world you see
Just one little thing we can give of ours
Your name to write amongst the stars.

June Knight-Boulton, Newton-le-Willows

Our Festival

There's electricity in the air.
It's infectious. Thousands of voices resonate together.
We fill entire landscapes with our spirit.
We bond with strangers over trivial things.
Maybe we make friends for life, that's half the fun.
Maybe we fall in love.
We wander, not lost, just looking. We lose things. We gain things.
We spend money we really don't have.
We dance like we don't care, a thousand bodies moving to one beat.
Everyone's here for the same reason.
We watch rock stars on the big screens and sing their lyrics back to them.
We're part of it. Guitar chords thrash. Electricity surges.

Even when the rain comes, it won't stop us.
We'll only dance faster, hold each other tighter.
We'll pass around a hot chocolate to dispel the cold and laugh
when our hair goes frizzy and our clothes stick to our skin.
It won't matter when that one band we've been waiting for takes to the stage.
It's only us and the music.
No one has jobs here. No one pays bills or goes to school.
We laugh here. We play here. We love life here.

Erin Fitzgerald, Liverpool

Untitled

There a phrase in my vocabulary
And it's called 'sporadic sleep'
I lie awake for hours -
When I should be lost in slumbers deep.
Eyes tightly shut, I toss and turn
Longing for sleep to come
Willing myself with all my might
To have, for once, a 'sleepful' night.

S D Sharp, Stockport

Relax Dear

Relax dear
The battle's over
Got my old seat
Back again
Somewhere to
Put my bum.
The garden's
Looking a bit
Shabby we need
A gardener for that,
Will put a claim in
I know dear.
It's us that makes
The rules don't
Have to keep them.

Frank Oldfield, Hackenthorpe

The Sandmartin

Stroll through the park beside the riverbank.
Stately white elephant, the sum of all
its capabilities, cash cows and sheep,
unfolds dramatically before your eyes.
Offside the model village built to house
those dispossessed who spoiled this perfect view.
You reach the bridge, arches where waters part,
reluctant as sweethearts at knife point, keen
to re-embrace first chance they get. Love nests'
dark button holes in banks of gold, will-o'-
the wisp, jumping jack flash, zigzags of shade
and light, watch martins slip and slide this way
then that, like careless skaters on thick ice,
kiss mirror images in shallow stills.

Peter Branson, Rode Heath

Bubbles

As usual, without a second thought
Put powder, conditioner in the washing machine
Pushed the start button
Then! Changed the setting to
Time save.
I had a quick look around
Before going out for the day
When I reached the kitchen
I stopped in amazement
I was flabbergasted to say the least
Masses of soap bubbles
Were seeping across the floor slowly
Towards me
It looked so strange I had to giggle
I've never seen such an eerie sight
I couldn't see the top of the tub
Nor the dirty bedding laying close by
It took a few seconds for common sense
To kick in.
Before I remembered to dry my hands
Because of the electricity.

Christina Batley, Rochdale

Drift, Drift, Drifting Off

Sinking into the crisp, cool sheets
Resting my head on the pillow
Pulling up the thick duvet
Closing my sleepy eyes.

Drinking in the fresh scent of lavender
Relaxing every muscle - every limb
Awaiting sleep just around the corner
Wondering what dreams will follow.

Rachel Wilson, Silksworth

Summertime

Summer's day in the month of June
when most of flowers start to bloom.
Smell of grass
and new mown hay
and sun shines bright
for most of day.
Bees and butterflies
flying around
up in air
and on ground.
A trip to the seaside
with children in hand.
With buckets and spades
to play in the sand.
A swim in the sea
and an ice cream cone
and after a while
We're ready for home.

Dorothy Jessup, Keighley

Sea

The velvet sea keeps
on moving
and crashes against the shore.
When the storm brews
in the grey silky sky.
Covering the cool sands
as the tide rises.
Must be the biggest form
of liquid.
Doesn't dry up when the
rain stops.
Boats float amongst tidal
waves.
Ripples under tranquil sky.

Rachel Van Den Bergen, Levenshulme

To Glenys, A Free Spirit

(For my sister)

On a day in September
She passed out of our lives
But where has she gone to?
Why did she die?
For the mystery of death is a puzzle to me
Though her body lies here
Her spirit is free
Where did it come from, where did it go?
The answers to questions we may never know.
Of one thing I'm certain,
A spirit can't die,
It can't be explained
But I don't know why.
Where should we look for it?
Where can it be found?
I believe, it is all around -

It cannot be seen
It cannot be heard
It's in the song of a tiny bird.

It's in our dreams
Before the dawn
At sunrise, on a summer's morn.

It floats on high
O'er wind and wave
Not in the depths of a lonely grave.

It's over the hills,
And far away,
But it's in our hearts,
When to God we pray.

It's in the cloud
With a silver lining
At the end of a rainbow,
When the sun is shining.

A star in the sky
The wings of a dove,
A candle burning in the night,
Lit for those we love.

Carol Taylor, Wakefield

To Attenborough's Meadow

A day of blue and pure sharp light.
I cross the stile into the field, where
The meadow-brown butterflies are alighting
On the rose mauve knapweed flowers.
Near the old stag oak by the hedge,
The butterflies dance almost in tandem
In the pure sunlight, barely skimming the grasses
All flowering full blown with summer.
Grasshoppers make a short dry song of summertide.
A yellow hammer joins in, making his little ditty
From along the hedge, music indeed to reap the sward by.
And yet the hedge becomes full of cheeky, chirping sparrows
Making their sorties forth into the ripening corn
Of the second field.
An English summer day
When the mind feels good to be alive
And all the butterflies dance among the grasses,
Carefree as children at play.
The great oaks now metal-green, are barely
Stirred by the breeze fanning the old meadow,
Shaking the sward into beauteous motion.
A wren trills from the hedge and for a moment, the
Silence of the fields - though so near
London - steals upon the soul . . .

John Sears, Congleton

One-Eyed City

Delving deftly into the lyrical kitty
to ponder and pen an affectionate ditty
for the one-eyed city
that never seeks pity
is the abode of the wise and the witty
and even the odd sage with their bunions.
A town blessed with wondrous parks
King Paxton, Queen Arrowe rule
Victoria and Mersey gaze mistfully across the river
to the other side, the pool.
Prenton Park, the theatre of seems
seems we're going down
seems we're going up
seems that one day we'll win a cup.
Sepia memories of cattle sheds and steam trains
newlyweds and lashing rains.
And always the ships ebb and flow
a shipyard, hopefully afloat
ready to build many a boat
as always the ships come and go
in a world ever so topsy turvy
good to live in a town so worthy
no mean feats from these keen streets
Birkenhead bred, born but never fed up.
Always end on the up.

Allen Beit, Birkenhead

A&E

At A&E, I sat on my chair
Awaiting attention, like everyone there
I was facing reception so I had a good view
Of all of humanity joining the queue.
With time to observe, it was illuminating
As all sorts of people arrived - fascinating!
A youth in a wheelchair clutching pad to his knee:
A girl in tall, platform shoes limped heavily:
A child in arms with face flushed and red:
A man with dried blood on the side of his head.
There were all shapes and sizes:-
Fat, thin, short and tall -
Young, old, well-cared for, dishevelled and all
In a wide range of fashions and choices of dress.
Some were quite tidy but most in a mess.
I was amazed at the insight
That visit afforded.
It was worth my split lip to feel so rewarded,
By an outsider's view of good hospital care,
And the varied work of all the staff there.
Of course, I'm not saying it's an ideal way
To study cross-sections of people, all day!
But if you were an artist and needed a place
To sketch lots of humanity, face-to-face,
There's so much material in an A&E
Enough for your paintings till eternity.
You'd have to ignore the pain and the grief
Of some of the patients and just grit your teeth(!)
But it opened my eyes and it would yours too,
To see so much of interest and so much to view.
A hospital waiting-room on ordinary days,
Is full of drama and life, in all kinds of ways.

Joan Evans, Upholland

Intrepid Me

The moon was shining through the cloud, wispy thin like a silver shroud
I stood there quietly surveying the scene, knowing I was going where few had been
then I started walking up past the wood, completely unperturbed
I heard the rustle of night creatures, scurrying from being disturbed
I was walking very steadily now, going for miles and miles
crossing the silvery countryside, through gates and over stiles
tendrils from the spiders' art, snagged my hair and quickened my heart
the gentlest caress upon my face, far more delicate than the finest lace
with a mighty swipe I set myself free, nothing this night was going to stop me.
The sky was bright and I felt so good, I was humming a marching song
but as I took my next big step, I realised something was wrong
I knew instantly I was in trouble, I felt I was beginning to sink
frantically trying to keep my head, as I wallowed in the drink
I thrashed around wildly, thinking this was not good
but as the water chilled me I grasped a piece of wood
I clung fast to it dearly, screaming hysterically with all my might
when I heard the sound of Mummy's voice say,
'What are you doing out at this time of night?'
The relief I felt was very profound, Mummy was kneeling full of concern
as I did the breaststroke down on the ground
I started coming to my senses, saved by the fickle hand of fate
the piece of wood that saved my life, I'd ripped from the back garden gate
as I lay there on the soaking grass, I'd really had a scare
thinking that I was going to drown, whilst gasping to get some air.
'You silly goose,' Daddy said, 'you've been walking in your sleep
we won't bother sending a lifeboat, it really isn't that deep.'
My brother and sister stood there smirking, so everybody knew
that I'd been fighting for my life, in the early morning dew
we all had a jolly good laugh at me, and then Mummy said,
'Get out of those wet pyjamas, and up the stairs to bed.
My intrepid little hero.'

Michael Harrison, Aintree

Where Is The Pride?

This world on which we humans dwell
Has beauty unsurpassed,
So why do people mess it up
With paper, tin and glass.

On every hedgerow, tree or field
The litter can be seen,
Obscuring the natural beauty
Of leaves and grass so green.

Bridlepaths and right of ways
Are strewn with household waste
Tiles - bricks and even beds
And some things not so chaste.

Cans and bottles smashed apart
A danger to us all
Be it wildlife, dogs or hikers
Or children very small.

Where is the pride of Britain
Sunk without a trace,
The streets and hedgerows once so clean
Are now a real disgrace.

Dot Young, Durham

Bliss

What a privilege to view life objectively,
Not one minute detail forgotten or obscured by any feeling of guilt,
Or desire for the creation of obscurity.

It's there, a documented history never to be replicated:
When can this kaleidoscope of living be seen
By the one who lived and perpetrated that existence?

Only during the epilogue of life, the short prologue to death,
Can all subjection vanish,
As one floats through the liquid of reflection
Propelled by a faltering heart.

The urgency for rectification of misdemeanours.
The aching concern for the health
And fortune of family and friends . . .

The entrapment of one's spirit
By an unremitting frame . . .
All these are lapsed.

When drifting unrestricted through the noiseless span of time
Cushioned against the counter-buffeting of duty and desire,
Bliss comes . . .
As the last filament of vision is finally severed.

Kathy Denton, Horwich

The Family

Tee-hee, I am better than you.
I have more money than you.
I have a bigger house than you.
I have a better car.
I fly in aeroplanes
And pollute the environment.
I have a caravan
And travel round the world.
I teach at Toppers
And live in a stately.
I have married thrice
And know Anneka Rice.
I am the great one.
But hail; head supreme,
Greater even than you.
Bow down before him,
Come and adore him.
He is the greatest of them all.
Tee-hee!

P Mitchell, Morecambe

Earth And Heart

E arth and heart
A re never apart
R emember they spell the same
T error cries on nature's ride
H ere on planet game

A s we spin round
N ew life is found
D estiny shapes our frame

H ands on heart
E volve takes part
A nd man Mother Nature gain
R esolve is pride all worldwide
T oday Earth's hearts beat . . . again!

Nick Pearson, Gipton

Midsummer's Eve

It was midsummer's eve in the forest glade
All the woodland creatures were stirring
Tonight would be the midsummer's dance
An evening for all to share in

The toadstools were set in circles
Where the fairy folk would sit
The spiders spun their lacy webs
And the glow-worms' lights were lit

The fairies in their gossamer gowns
Arrived on the moon's silvery beams
The sandman swung his lantern
Spreading light on the magical scene

The bees provided the nectar
And all drank from acorn cups
Tall grasses swayed in the summer breeze
And the beetles' band tuned up

The fairy king then bowed to his queen
A sign for the dancing to begin
A hush fell over the forest glade
And the nightingales started to sing

The king and queen led the dancing
The fairies and elves followed suit
The stars twinkled in the heavens
Whilst a gnome played a reeded flute

They danced until the sunrise
Bathed the glade in its first pale light
Then quietly, all went their separate ways
Disappearing out of sight

You'd never know they had been there
They try not to leave any clues
Only a toadstool ring remained
And a spider's web covered in dew.

Carole Revell, Hull

Tortoiseshell Bay

She stands on the grass as proud as can be
Watching the sun caress the deep blue sea
Her hooves first attentively touch the soft, warm sand
The owner eagerly guiding with sunburnt hand
Her mane and tail sway to the summer breeze
She moves with the grace as a goddess would tease
Small ripples rush, tapping against her hooves
Gracefully lapping her every move
A chorus of foam sings around her legs
Like the froth building in her mouth as she gently begs
The shiny bit so silvery and cool
Sparkles in the ripples of after pools
The tide recedes and she's ready to catch
Bold body and long strides are no match
She thunders along the sandy shore
Racing the waves as her eyes hunger for more
Her coat mingles with shingles and sand
As she steaks like lightning along the shore land
She comes to rest at the end of the sun's rays
My goddess!
My beauty!
My tortoiseshell bay.

Linda Gray, Ashington

The Roman Road

Purple light seeps through bare trees,
in the deathly hush of Christmas
no sound cracks the silence,
no bird nor man, nor beast
the deserted road is left untroubled.

But then, back then, it was used,
by the citizens of Empire,
who walked this cobbled road,
with carts and goods and children,
the soldiers who marched in ranks.

Now mist creeps across it,
the light fades into dusk and
the ages are still as they were,
nothing has changed much at all,
though the stones are overgrown.

No one treads this road but
a few hikers now and then;
the trees at either side are charcoal
but if you stand, take note
an echo will yet reach your ears.

The dusk will evoke ancient Rome,
strange shadows lurk where
no man brings money or commerce
cast in twilight, the time worn track
is here forever, indelible as ink.

Peter Cardwell, Keighley

Pursuit

A pursuit is more exciting with eyes closed.
A pursuit will eclipse any evergreen edge of vision
With a phantom ghosting its path past shades of laughter
As, coincidentally, the little moth flirts with the flame.

Pursued, our haunted figure seeks reason,
Suppressed in flowing sands, amongst the cries of lost souls
Which cajole the hand to unfurl the stream between
Evergreen shades of laughter . . . and treason.

Just as embryonic fingers glow precociously around curtains -
Calling in zeal, in zest, towards pleasured pursuit -
A blood rush again resounds in nearby callow ears
And a blood lust rises rigid in fear of failure;
A pursuit is more exciting with eyes frozen.

Just as enthusiastic fingers of anticipation
Start to tease proud the pink of petitioned prospect
And scare away the shadows of yesterday's erratic steps,
The urge, steeped in falsehoods and mistaken expeditions, springs forward:
A pursuit is more exciting in rapt indolence.

Through serial motions, a broadly practised modus operandi,
The core gilds a flower in the wild . . . assuages soul in sole purpose . . .
Gilds metaphysical indulgence on the other side of the fence;
Gilds hunger, urgent pressure, and so to amnesia where
A pursuit is more exciting with foreboding closed.

A crested pride clears a channel in the daunting mists of yesterday,
To fear nowt but the verve itself: forcing false colours and strained sounds
Which are not of design, not of knitted cognisance, and which engender knotted revolt,
Voila de quoi te doper, mon vieux taré, mon pauvre mec, mon semblable:
A pursuit is more exciting with reason unbounded.

The decrepit bridge which from the bank of tactile whispers -
Where the act is prematurely spent out of anticipation, out of time,
Out of fear - spans the flow of opposite but equal forces
To a bank of blossoming indulgence beyond the measure of its own length:
A pursuit is more exciting with it ardour unconstrained.

Equal forces in equal hearts - in equalised hours and equalised parts -
Discharged the foremost terror . . . the yang is on the prowl for generalised excess;
Excess which stops one step short of revolt . . . in equalled expedience,
For only a fool hungers again once he has tasted his nectar.
A pursuit is more exciting with moulded boost.

For he who has smelt the reaper's breath, cold as steel on the throat,
Will not readily glance the shoulders to risk a stench of forlorn fervour;
For he who has drunk through charmed lips,
There only remains to savour further, further and further fermented ideals;
A pursuit is more perfect . . . more perfect per se . . .

A pursuit is more exciting with eyes half-closed;
Peripheral vision plucks evergreen sight
From the flowing, suppressed cries of lost souls,
Then compels the zealot to trace the quest.
A pursuit is more exciting with mind closed

To petitioned pink obscuring the little moth's dance.
A pursuit is more exciting when the degenerated posture
Of realised dreams resounds a blood rush in callow ears
And when a blood lust rises rigid in fear of impulse;
A pursuit is more exciting with mind closed to reason.

A pursuit is more exciting with lids consciously dropped
A pursuit will eclipse any evergreen tones of melancholy
From a phantom ghosting its path past the edge of fusion
As, coincidently, the little moth dances in the flame.

Pursued, our haunted figure seeks reason,
Suppressed in flowing sands, amongst the cries of lost souls
Which cajole the hand to unfurl the steam between
Evergreen shades of laughter beyond the measure of their own length.

Straddling the fence of coveted paradise, legs treacherous beneath the weight
Of history, of foreboding, of cyclical palpitations . . . de la joie de vie, quoi!
The wavering to apprise, with port realisation before the eyes of Diana . . .
To behold the jaded abandon and live in the wild prospect where
Pursuit is more exciting with eyes opened.

Ian Lowery, Upper Denby

Love Is

I know what love is
It's tender . . . it's true
It's just being honest
Relying on you
When the chips are down
It's you being there
Showing that you love me
Showing that you care
It's touching me tenderly
Or holding my hand
It's you backing me up
On those things I have planned
And if my dreams should fade
And I'm feeling low
It's you saying
There will be other dreams don't you know
Love is knowing all of my faults
But overlooking them too
Yes I know what love is
Love is just . . . you.

Joyce Hudspith, South Stanley

Ben Lomond

Just for you
I'm Ben Lomond look at me
I command the skyline
I'll change my colour
Just for you.

I'll change my moods
Through sun, wind and rain
Just for you.

Because I'm the loveliest
Mountain in all the world
And I'm here
Just for you.

Norman Mark, Carlisle

Always By The Window

Discretely from my casement shyly peeping
I ever watch my loved one come and go
And that my aching heart lies in his keeping
This sacred secret he must never know
Although my frail and failing flesh is stricken
And grows yet weaker with each passing day
Always does my feeble heartbeat quicken
Perchance it seems a glance he sends my way
Devoid of locks and bars my lonely room
A stonewalled prison might be nonetheless
A well-appointed fashionable tomb
A sepulchre of pain and loneliness.

N G Charnley, Blackpool

Canadian Rockies

Tall mountains reaching upwards to the sky
Peaked with sparkling snow to catch the eye
Cascading streams of water flow
In a shimmering flight to land below

Fir trees fill up the flanks with green
For miles and miles they cover the scene
A haven for the wildlife living there
Sheep and goat and the grizzly bear

Glaciers creep along the crevices
A crystal blue from their long recess
Among the ice fields, where nature is bold
An impressive picture to behold.

Through the valleys rippling rivers run
Where the salmon return one by one
To the former place where they were born
Proceeding then to breed and to spawn.

Margaret Whitaker, Brighouse

The Stand-Off

They came sweeping down
Low over the treetops.
Firm, forceful, focused.
Dismaying to watch them land.
So 'Lords of the Universe'.

Others gave way
Unable to defend their territory
Heads down the onslaught began.
Bird food disappeared like magic.
The pigeons had arrived.

Watching from the window.
I hatched a crafty scheme.
I'd deprive them of their wherewithal.
It seemed a perfect plan.
Other birds might suffer too.
But not for long I thought.

An empty table met their next assault.
But undeterred they came again and again.
Until they finally gave up.
With relief I thought I'd won.
Food in hand I sallied forth.
Unbelievably a lookout had been left.
And the pesky pigeons were there again.

With dark thoughts I glared my feelings.
Surely the human brain could match a bird's.
But battle had been fairly joined
And the challenging sides evenly matched.

Betty Graham, Whitefield

In Memory Of Oscar, My Beloved Collie

He was such a friend
For years and years
We shared so many things
Long walks and talks and secrets
We shared everything.

Over the years, we'd seen so much
Our journeys went all over
England, Wales and Scotland too
We were habitual rovers.

So much to see and do
Life just went on and on
No change would come
Or so I thought
But I was very wrong.

Came the day my dearest friend
When you became so ill
No more walks, no more talks
I watched you slip away.

No human friend could take your place
No truer friend I'll find
You'll never be forgotten
You're always in my mind.

Leila McLeish, Carnforth

The Birds Are Back

Down the face of the high-swinging nuts they abseil
With insolent ease,
Chittering huge bravado,
Swelling their brawlers' chests, rat-tatting
Bodkin beaks. The tits are back!.

These little yobbos, pied scrappers, yellow and blue,
Unshakably confident, send
My cosy behind-the-window world
Topsy-turvying.

And last year's robin is back, close-hunched
Against the cold around his red-hot breast,

Short-tempered, ageing and famished,
He is grounded, a helpless watcher
At the aerial feast.

Even the farm moggy pussyfooting by,
Ostentatiously aloof,,
Knows when he's licked.

Blue tits rule! OK?

Jim Spence, Dufton

That's Racing

O'er hill and vale by iron horse
Along the tarmac bridleway
Equine pleasures to resource
Could this be our perfect day?

Sunlight bathes the battleground
Fences hurdles dotted round
As gladiators prance the ring
All bookies' satchels start to sing

Drumming hooves go hell for leather
And our 'pony' looks well placed
Every fence he pings for pleasure
At every ditch he's not outfaced

The big black gelding jumps for fun
The bookies think their money's done
Never ever count your plunder
For your charge may make a blunder

Race in bag, and never in doubt
He hits last a mighty clout
Out goes the jockey from the plate
The racing gods have sealed our fate.

Ernie Graham, Millom

Flowers Of The Wilderness

Our last wilderness is the loveliest place
Where peace and solitude mark the hours.
Here are whispering streams and windswept fells
With the birdsong at dawn, and the glow of wildflowers.

The silver-pink grasses, the blushing wild rose
By riverbank or beneath the trees.
Each flower has chosen its own special place
Petals turned toward the sun, heads a-dance in the breeze.

All the colours of the spectrum
Daisies bob and poppies sway.
The Pyrenean lily, curled and gold
Breathes scent to take my breath away.

Examine closely one small flower
So delicate, detailed, perfect, pure
No human hand could reproduce
Such a masterpiece in miniature.

Magic names of magic flowers
Columbine, heartsease, alkanet,
Too many to recall by name
But, far too lovely to forget.

Mere words can never justice do,
Mere mortals barely understand
When we stop and gaze, enchanted
At this wild and unspoilt beauteous land.

Edna Mills, Riding Mill

Island In The Sun

I once went to a little island
The name of which escapes me now
I know it had one pub
They call the Old Brown Cowl
They say it never rains
The sun shines all the year
So on the plane I climbed
Without a mac, just suntan gear.
I was really looked forward
To laying on golden sands
Eating and drinking as much as I liked
And hoping the money would meet the demands.
We arrived about on schedule
It was raining at the time.
You ask what I thought to that.
I'll not tell you, it would not rhyme
The hotel has not been finished
The builders hammered all day.
Hoping it would be finished
When next year's tourists came their way.
The next four days it rained
Had to buy myself a mac
The next three days were cloudy
Then it was time to pack.
I climbed on the plane
Could not see the way to my seat.
Because the glare of the sun
My eyes could not compete.
In some ways I enjoyed the holiday
Though not seeing the sun till coming back.
So if you go to an island in the sun
Do yourself a favour and take a mac.

Jenny Bosworth, Louth

The World Of Me

The day starts, as all else does
Only this one starts
There is no you
The sun came up as yesterday
But, somehow there's little warmth
In the ray
Why has so much changed,
Because suddenly I'm alone, and in a strange
And vacant way, there is no time
The world stands still today.
For so long it was always we
Now and from now on - it's me
I have health and wealth and friends
And what am I to do
With all these gifts,
Will they make me happy
Will they fill the void
The moving space, the busy space
The space that's really me
Will I ever feel the same
Find the person who was me
Perhaps she's gone, never to return
Who knows?
Weeks and months have now slipped by
And I'm still here you see
Now I have a busy life
And I can see a light

Six months ago I could not see
Beyond each waking day.
Now I live and move and breathe
In my individual way.
I have a bank of memories to
Fill any empty space.
I have known love and happiness,
Will he, could he, ever be replaced,
Sometimes in my quiet heart, I almost
Feel the joy of loving arms and tender
Lips, dreams impossible to destroy
I've had my share of that I'm sure
But who knows what life will send

But I have had his arms, his lips
His love,
These have set me free
To be happy
To be me.

Maureen Dearden, Keighley

Is There Still Time?

Is there still time to save the world
from the final degradation?
Is there still time, on the very brink
of complete annihilation?

Is there a way to save the world
a path unknown, untried
back from the edge, is there a way
to stop the rot - to stem the tide?

Is there a man, a saintly man
larger than life or nation?
Is there a man and could such a man
excite, ignite Man's imagination?

If there is still time, a way
and the man to say, follow me
with time and the man
but, would we nail him to a tree?

Ed Gardner, Boston Spa

The Brook

Rays of golden sun
Peeping through
A tangle green
Where the waters
Of the brook
Creep along the mossy banks.

All the pathways intertwine
Often when the day is ending
And the sunlight fades
Sleepy willows bend their branches
To rest gently
On the water's sheen.

Now the gleaming brightness
Has gone
Finds it way
To a shady nook
There the moonlight
Softly beams
On a darkened brook.

M Noad, Thornaby

The Forecast

Quite early in the year,
When the weather was severe,
A songbird took us by surprise.
We thought he must be telling lies
By making it appear
That spring would soon be here.

Later on we found that he
Had forecast spring unerringly,
A setback to our self-esteem
But Mother Nature is supreme
In giving little creatures powers
At times more accurate than ours.

Kathleen McGowan, Newcastle Upon Tyne

A Moment In Time

Anniversaries are like old clocks
time marches on
and every tick of the moment
leaves a tock to go on.
Tick-tock, tick-tock and
the whirling of the old clock's
mechanism makes justice
to our lives
and our special days
remembered as time ticks slowly on
so happy anniversary to you
Forward Poetry
may you prosper day by day
and each sent immortal poem
belongs to our UK.

Margery Rayson, Daltongate

Universe Of Harmony

Is it summer
On a distant planet?
Does the sun shine
On another moon?

Is it winter
On a distant planet?
Does the snow fall
On another moon?

If there is life out there
Will the echo ride the solar breeze
Bring an alien form to wake our dreams
Help us live . . .
In a universe of harmony
Together . . .
Forever.

Lyn Crossley, Burnley

Time And Space

Can you get your head around what time is?
It can weigh, drag, stand still or whizz!
When did it begin? When will it end?
Sometimes it goes backwards! It can even bend!
Time slips through your fingers, like grains of sand,
Yet we still waste it when it's on our hand.
Intangible yet real, both present and past.
Cutting and saving it leaps to first from last.
It lingers, it waits, it can come and go,
And today becomes yesterday tomorrow!

Space is an imponderable dimension,
In essence, a concept without comprehension.
Its end is its beginning with a beyond, beyond, beyond,
Onwardly ever expanding with a cataclysmic bond.
A complex plethorific void,
Unexplainable by God or Freud.

John Masters, Marske-by-the-Sea

Stop And See

Nobody sees the pain inside
The constant feelings I have to hide
If only they would stop and see
Maybe they would understand me

Nobody hears my lonely cries
I hide my tears in my eyes
If only they would stop and see
Maybe they would understand me

Nobody feels the pain I bear
All I want is someone to care
If only you would stop and see
Maybe you could understand me.

Maria Jenkinson, Blackpool

For A Sad Friend

Be not downhearted for I have been there too
For such a long time I didn't know what to do
Then I looked up to see the heavens one night
And everything seemed to come to light
For God loves us each and everyone
He made the Earth the sky and sun
He is in every living thing
And when our prayers to Him we bring
He listens to us as we pray
And gently guides along the way
On Him we really can depend
He is our saviour and our friend
You too will have strength and courage one day
And see a new road to a happier way
And all at once you will find
The heavy load will leave your mind.

Margaret Bate, West View

My Poppy

When the poppy blooms again I'll remember you
So much like the poppy growing wild such as you
You're alive so deep in colour
Like your affection, your personality, so tender so true
Like the poppy I hold against my heart
Yet even as I hold it so gently as I treasure our love
The breeze blows the petals away
Just like life our love drifted away with you
Into the evening twilight never to meet again
But next day when I pick the poppy from the roadside
I will hold you in my loving hands
And kiss each petal with tender care
Till we meet again in Heaven above.

William Nicklin, Widnes

Poetic Signals

This poem arrived unexpectedly
It knocked hard on my door
Demanding to be let in
At first I refused
Not really wanting to write today.

The poem became angry
And began emitting
High frequency sounds
Which vibrated my door
And rattled my window.

Suddenly the sound stopped
My door and window still intact
It attempted to climb down the chimney
Got covered in soot, then got stuck.

I have never seen a poem
So determined to be born
It escaped from the chimney
And started rapping on the window
The insistent rapping of unwritten lines.

'Unborn poem, leave me alone,' I cried
But the poem was insistent
Demanding its right to life
'If you abort me you are cursed,'
It cried out in a desperate reply.

Then rolled a pen under the door
So I had compassion on the poem
And proceeded to give it life
I opened my heart
To these poetic signals, and now my story ends.

Ian Bosker, Leigh

Ghosts Washed Up

(Beachcombing - West Loch Tarbet)

Porcelain handle, smoothed by sand and water, lying proud 'L' shaped
How many fingers have caressed you before you were discarded?
How many lips have kissed and drank from your beauty?
How many lives have you been privileged to know?
Blue and white pieces of many patterns
Still vivid blues of various hues
The glazes washed away without detergent
Just the harsh maelstrom of life, sand blasted
Royal Doulton, England - just the maker's mark lying in the silver sand to catch the eye
To say that you were once a sought after piece of china
Pick me up now so I shall not be forgotten or ground into the fine sand
Est 2 Phillip's 1760 - stood out as the tide came in
Pale blue on both sides - must have been a rather special prize
A tantalising jigsaw piece in the riddle of the beachcomber puzzle
A rich Prussian blue piece with an intricate pattern of crazed glaze
Striking against the sand, both sides totally different in their crazed patterns
Earthenware shards, beautiful intricate hand-painted pattern
Not glazed yet paint has remained deep in its form
The pigments still so striking - saying - yes I was beautiful before my demise
Raised petals of two flowers tantalise the thoughts of what was a lovely piece - someone's special object of love
How many years ago the potter crafted those dainty petals to show his love to someone?
How many hours of hand painting of each brush stroke lovingly placed to make someone happy to see
Yet now after all this time hands can still caress the softness of the hard china
Caresses again and admires the colour and design of artist's eye
To capture too late
Before the elements again destroy their beauty
The sea gives up her ghosts of the past
You jewels of the sea.

Hilary Jean Clark

Crystal Healing

Crystals are minerals with magical vibrations
And power to manifest healing transformations.
Crystals can uplift your mood,
Rose quartz helps to calm and soothe.
Wear aquamarine to promote compassion,
Or turquoise for eloquent self-expression.
Quartz can bring light into your life,
Re-energise your aura and heal toxic strife.
Amethyst can help ease migraine,
Bloodstone cures stress and strain.
Wear jade to bring you inner peace;
Ruby's passions never cease.
Pyrite can help to stop snoring,
Keep it under your pillow until morning.
Tiger's eye can improve intuition,
While sapphire helps fulfil your ambition.
Jasper helps you achieve your goals;
Sodalite heals fears of anxious souls.
Fluorite is conducive to meditation,
Lepidolite improves mental concentration.
Agate stimulates emotional security;
Jet may attract financial prosperity.

Wendy Anne Flanagan, Rishton

Wilf's Boots

He'd come steady up that trodden track,
adjacent to every plot.
With his trusty walking stick,
and the ruttled cough he'd got,
increasingly fragile,
as the seasons came to pass,
for all those 'King Edwards'
and the caulis to amass.
'Twas a joint venture with . . .
our Henry, tending that patch,
if Wilf, the 'overseer'
of stepdad, raising each batch -
on occasion, friction,
as to whose allotment it was;
but to whom was a quota,
a claim on carrots because . . . ?

He left those boots behind,
for his 'garden' in the sky,
ones well worn and designed,
where ashes would come to lie,
a worth more than each welly,
alas, a bonfire did cremate,
if the smoke was smelly,
and we chuckled at their fate . . .

Andrew Gruberski, Dewsbury

Congratulations

Twenty-three years is a long, long time
spreading words we write in rhyme.
There it is before my eyes,
'Write a poem and win a prize'
Choose the subject and the tense
try to rhyme and still make sense.
It may have to be within a theme
or maybe just an idle dream.
What e'er it is you have to choose
appropriate words you wish to use.
If when you feel that you have done
it may not appeal to anyone,
the only thing that you can do
is tear it up and start anew.
You know the things you wish to say
express them in a different way.
Some words perhaps can be left out
but retain those that have the clout
When you have done and sent it in
just sit back and hope to win.

Robert Hogg, Guisborough

My Loving Mother

My dear loving mother
Has now gone from my life
And also this world of pain and sorrow
But even though she has now gone
From my life
She will never be gone from my heart
Or prayers of both today and tomorrow
So please, dear Lord above
Watch over the one I love
Please keep an eye on that dear old girl
For she was the best loving mother
In the whole wide world.

Donald John Tye, Wallsend

Taj Mahal, Agra

We crossed Jumna River
in a leaking boat,
and saw three camels -
a train through the water.

I felt something, like
a lump in my throat
to see radiant marble,
brought by elephant porter.

On her deathbed she asked
for something to show the world
- what true love means,
its intricate shapes.

Floating above the surface
where dark waters swirled
and the night spreads out
vast, glittering capes.

A paradise garden
for the palace jewel
who died giving birth
to their fourteenth child.

Life and death
must often seem cruel
but in subtle splendour
their passion smiled.

Paul Judges, Leavening

Walking Through The Bluebells

Walking through the bluebells wild and free
Is somehow down inside how I would like to feel
Warmed by the sun
Fed by the rain
Blown by the wind and they don't feel any pain
Each year they will flower as beautiful as the last
And they do not remember painful memories of the past.

Sandra Meadows, Lymm

Geordie Ghosts

The river Tyne flows a real magical spell
Working a mighty fine magic incredibly well
It flows of history of memories and all
Whispers of hard workers proud and tall.

Like the soup kitchen, it leaves eerie chill
All the old history gives hearts a thrill
So many ghosts walk alongside of us all
It's only true Geordie hearing their call

Tell the world Geordie how strong we all are
Spread it abroad globally worldwide and far
Tell them all too that Geordies have real hearts
Whispering ghosts Geordie history imparts

Make sure they all see Geordie ever lives on
In all the new buildings Geordies are shone
As far as all the oceans' sea shores ever meet
A Geordie's a great heart no one will ever defeat

Whisper to hearts histories long gone old days
Reek of hard workers endless many ways
Let them all know Geordie history will live on
In the hearts of you all is where it's best shone.

Christopher Robin Slater, Newcastle Upon Tyne

Are We There Yet?

Grandma's yard was four times bigger
When I was young and little
Then, it was always sunny in summer
And it always snowed in winter
But Christmas took so long to come
- At least three years
And summer holidays took forever to arrive
- Everything was further away then
Now, Christmas comes twice a year
- Where did it go - is that the time?
Please . . . Don't let me be there yet!

Ann Eddleston, Worsthorne

Two Moments

I saw you in the dreams again . . .
Was that actually you, or was it a ray of light?
Was that actually you, or was it a smiling flowerbud?
Was that you, or was it the rain of dreams?

Was that you, or did a cloud of joy pass overhead?
Was that you, or did a flower bloom?
Was that you, or did I find a whole new world?

Was that you, or was it a scent on the breeze?
Was that you, or was there colour bursting in all four directions?

Was that you, or was it some light in the road?
Was that you, or was it a song echoing in the atmosphere?
Was it you who made the star twinkle in the night's sky?

Was it you who blew me away?
I saw you in the dreams again
Calm and mellow . . .

In the droplets of the rain I see you
In the night I see your shadow
In the light I see only your face . . .

I see you and only you
I agree you're crazy
And I'm zany for you

Catching a slight of a glimpse only for two moments.

Kiran Ali

Perplexity

I seem to have lost the ability
To rhyme with a piece of wittility
I think, it's the whine of I-podic swine
That deprives me of my gentility.

Eric Prescott, Southport

Cockney Knees-Up

Fetch me pipe and slippers
Cook me up some kippers
And we'll have a cockney knees-up
In the hall
With some bread and luverly butter
The mother-in-law will mutter
That kids today
Have no respect at all

Grab a sandwich, plum and peach
And we'll head off to the beach
And we'll have a cockney knees-up
On the shore
With some buckets build a castle
The mother-in-law will hassle
That kids today
Are always wanting more.

Rodger Moir, Allerton

A Penny For Your Thoughts

She finds a quiet moment alone and deep in thought,
Her head is full of turmoil and her shoulders very taut,
Her husband breaks her silence like he always does,
She tells him not to worry and not to make a fuss.

'A penny for your thoughts,' he says, she looks him in the eyes,
She needs a little time to come to terms with her demise,
He says he wants to help her and not to shut him out,
But she's afraid to share her burden with reasonable doubt.

She suddenly finds courage and tells him of her plight,
'Your car is in the river dear and almost out of sight,'
He finds a quiet moment alone and deep in thought,
His head is full of turmoil and his shoulders very taut,

'A penny for your thoughts dear . . .'

Pauline Walsh, Blackburn

DFDS

Denmark bound my Scandinavian Seaways.
Ticket control and check-in.
Without a better shirt
might not be allowed in.
Old lady prodding
to get an earlier check-in.
Companion against this urging
will have to give in.

Top bunk
Bottom bunk
Engine urging throbbing.
Sleeping sleep a trial.

Breakfast time a-coming.
Cabin hot shower first.
Out of digital-keyed door
to a cup of coffee first.

Stateside extroverts converse
visited 50 states in all.
Tour European started 1989.
What a holiday divine.

Escaped their romantic clutched
To get to Kroner before 11 o'clock closure.
Divined a ship board coffee
to have with our breakfast steal.

Girl with ship's wheel earrings
sits writing in the sun.
By her look of happy experience
she's certainly had her fun.

Sun beats down on sun deck.
Sheltered aerodynamic design.
Remembered the ozone layer
but forgotten the sun lotion again.

K Chesney-Woods, Sacriston

La Primavera

(In memory of four girls who were killed one warm, bright March day)

The March winds ceased to blow,
The daffodils stood high and proud,
New life took a hold down below,
As winter lost its grip of the ground.

The sun shone as bright as May,
Blue skies with flowers displayed,
Tempted the girls out that day
To drive with caution mislaid.

Four flowers with young lives to live,
To blossom, to grow and give pleasure,
Were crushed as none could forgive,
And became - four friends together forever.

Vivienne Fitzpatrick, Bradford

A Vision Of England

A leaping English wind
A bright summer morn
A clear blue sky
A rainbow after a storm:
An English country lane
Daffodils in full bloom
Birds nesting in hedgerows
Church clocks striking noon;
The herdsman driving cattle
Laughing children at play.
Quacking ducks crossing
Shadows of the day.
The love of England beckons
To all those far away,
Many will never return . . .
But the vision will stay.

Arthur Pickles, Waterfoot
.

Going Places

Going away where shall we go
Look in the brochure for sunshine, not snow
Going abroad will it be dear
Should it be summer or spring, come next year
Look for a bargain, a free place for the kids
You must shop around to save those hard-earned quids
Let's go all-inclusive they give you free beer
I hope it's John Smiths that they serve over there
How much is the pound worth when we travel abroad
Should we change our money early, to burden the load
You may need injections, so please heed beware
When travelling by sea, or by coach, or by air
All year saving, just for two weeks
Just to show off our tans and look like the Greeks.

Paul Hough, Barnsley

Love - A Four-Letter Word

What is love? Is it just a word?
Does it conjure up thoughts or feelings
Or is it just a word?
Imagination, inspiration, tenderness
Words to make your heart glow
Or is each an empty word.
Affection, fondness, devotion
Words to make you think it's love
Or do you deceive yourself into
Thinking you are in love?
Passion, ardour, desire, do these words
Put romance in your mind and heart
Or are they all just words!
Love is an interpretation of you,
Of how you make others feel
Or is love just another four-letter word.

Joan Lister, High Pittington

Childhood Memories

I remember, I remember, oh so long ago
a blazing coal fire on the hearth our faces all aglow.

How our father would make us laugh
in the early evening just after our bath.
We'd sit and listen to his stories and songs
with worshipping eyes and silent tongues.
How our mother would scold him and say
come on, they're tired, it's the end of the day.
You put such nonsense into their head
come now, I've told you it's time for bed.
But her gentle smile would soften the rebuke
and of course we all knew she was listening too
Steaming hot cocoa she'd pass around
and then we'd persuade her to come and sit down.
It was a wonderful ritual which filled us with joy,
Those precious moments we'd happily employ
in carefree enjoyment and family fun,
a natural repose when all work had been done.

I remember, I remember, oh so long ago
those times that sowed the seed keeping our hearts aglow.

Marlene Jackson, Wath-upon-Dearne

Summer

Church in bloom
The cherry tree stands proud
Sombre graves below
Angelic voices raise in praise
Organ's crescendo grows
Seagulls fly Heavenward
With angel's wings
Down the lane the children cycle
Laughter in the clear air rings;
Near the trees the brook flows gently
Tinkling music as it sings
Blackbirds and song thrush in chorus sound
As the church bells ring.

Irene Patricia Kelly, Bolton-on-Dearne

The Allotment

He prunes and waters
And pulls out the weeds
He plucks off the dead heads
And puts in more seeds
He sows and mows
And cultivates
He talks to plants, and pests he hates
His boots are muddy
His jacket's torn
Dirty trousers and hands well worn
His hard cracked fingers
And weathered skin
With embedded soil sunken in
Webs cover corners inside his hut
There are rusty scissors
That no longer cut
Lemonade bottles filled with
God knows what
Plants and bulbs, once growing
Now rot
Bundles of canes and dirty string
Broken panes lay from spring to spring
Different size buckets lie on their side
Where hardbacks and beetles
Creep and hide
Weed killer has spilt
Upon the floor
Old jackets, and cleaning cloths
Hang on the door
Slugs and snails and rusty nails
A hose pipe drapes the wall
His compost heap where hedgehogs sleep
And leaves stay where they fall
The day has gone
The light is low
He gathers up his tools
He locks his hut
Making sure it's shut
And now it's time to go.

Lynette Coote, Harrogate

The Fruit Of The Seasons

I would not eat the fruit,
Which appears so juicy and sweet,
What seems to be a thirst quenching, delicious treat.
I would always think twice,
Before I purchased the fruit,
Always at the most expensive price,
It is pure poison, not worth the temptation,
Of this gorgeous, thrilling sensation,
With which my heart and soul and mind will
Be filled with so much vexation.

I must be kept away from all harm,
To be sure I am calm,
So my good omen, my good fairy, my lucky charm
Can comfort me, so I am not alarmed,
As one bite of that apple becomes a lovely temptation
I may only know a wonderful sense of peaceful contemplation.

A lovely bunch of juicy red cherries
Will always keep me so merry,
As this wonderful fairy tale
Keeps me healthy and well.

Those gorgeous wild berries,
Which are in all the hedgerows,
Could be oh so precious, so always be wary
Of picking any wild treats,
There is the bitter, but also the sweet side of life,
So this could get you into a state of utter confusion,
Do not be under any delusion,
I would not eat these berries
No matter, I must always think twice
As I am always enticed.

With wholesome, delicious mouth-watering fruit
I always experience a wonderful sensation,
Life is all about these juicy, sweet treats.

Linda Hardy, Southport

Not A Chance.Com

I am not at all conversant
With the computer age
And have no idea whatsoever
I would do on a Facebook page!

I hear talk about Twitter
Whatever that might be
I know nothing about the Internet
It all sounds Greek to me!

I know people who send emails
And buy goods online
They assure me that by doing this
It saves them lots of time.

I prefer to put pen to paper
And send correspondence the old-fashioned way
To me this is much the best method
And that is the way it will stay.

Yes I'm well aware that regarding technology
I am totally out of tune
And can say without hesitation
I will not be logging on anytime soon.

Jackie Richardson, Underbarrow

The Sea

I don't like the sea, it makes me feel infinitesimal
That vast expanse of omnipotent liquidity
Those waves lapping along the shore endlessly
Make words as the Chinese say inadequate
And make me a staunch friend and advocate of terra firma
Goodbye Mr Briny
Maybe there are people that like you
But not me.

Philip Corbishly, Rossendale

Taken From The Masters Of Surprise

After-all . . .

The mist dispelled, dilutes the landscape of another dreary day,
Windbleached shadows solidify out of the backwash of pouring rain;
Along the streets of this grainy, grimy city it proclaims
Enough of its plasma of tiny souls, squeezed along concrete arteries and veins
To give semblance to a preference of these transparent remains
. . . after-all, they say, as the world turns undisturbed on its way
It offers such hypodermic relief; of antiseptic souls awry,
Of relics scattered like failing hail along every street and byway.
. . . for now, let us sit upon the ground and watch the sad decline of things,
Of all honourable intentions and the reputations of future kings,
Of dubious regal prizes, and usurped queenly duties,
Of princes compromised, and crownly confessions sold to the highest bidders!
The great questions of Mankind are wheeled out from time to time,
To be debated by conscious idiots, oblique in matching ties;
Whether Man invented God, or whether Jove strove to weather
The storm of his petulant offspring and make things a little better.
Would you crack a boiled egg on the narrow side or the wide?
How many times must a man ejaculate to avoid the spermicide?
The biggest number in the world, indivisible but by itself
Will change both sense and nonsense, to cancel each other out!
The time before time where angels in union sang,
Or what was the universe like before the Big Bang?
A rose by any other sweeter name, a language incomplete,
What will women clergy be wearing when they stand up to speak?
Generations of the listless ill-born before their time
Wonder whether work is something more perhaps than a social plebiscite!
They litter the streets, an aftermath of waste and toxic dust
Craving a few meagre coins to stem the rising tide of superfluous
Creeds; Heaven and Hell are joined in tenuous matrimony
And the difference between good and evil becomes another mumbling theory!
Do you have to be that anxious, to scream with aberrant rage,
To smash everything around you and send us back to the Dark Ages?
Your uprising will quell this gross distemper, and in your best attire
This hell will turn such a ragged existence into a fathomless quagmire . . .
So . . . say goodbye for this, and bide your uneasy time,
This living Camera Obscura moves its all-seeing eye a little further down the aisle,
Soon the wedding feast will hurry to heal this petty rift,
This ship of stranded souls, keel-hauled and set drift,
Onward, into civilisation's beckoning furrow,
Though bondaged now, we'll all be free tomorrow!
Scarce solace my friend, for those whose cry unheeded, for whom
A shallow future awaits only on some scanty European . . .
Death to this latex strangler, this ripper of mosaic souls,
I'll write him grisly fan letters, and send him all my love!

But you, you grip the armchair and worship at the rail;
Hours of mindless drivel is the bread and wine of your faith,
'Quiz' and 'chat' are the holy relics of this worthless creed;
Smiling, catatonic faces nailed to the symbols of their greed
Serenade you with sermons of how excessive their lives have been,
And there you sit, and share some portion of their excess
While all around you your dull existence collapses.
Vetted positive, that the game was fairly played,
No favours dubiously bought for heavy subscriptions paid.
You angelic sot! Blinded by the light of sheer depravity
Your smile, vacant-like, misses the whole point of its sleight tenacity . . .
Oh . . . rant on, my friends, you'll never change that much,
And all your vicious ravings will surely vanish into dust.
The twilight protracts another day of indecent exposures,
Of failed promises and blithe, indifferent confessions.
Night descends, and refutes these smothered graves;
The masters of surprise, kings of all they survey
Turn the page,
And all their faults and favours drift silently . . . away.

Christopher Hayes, Bolton

Before We Go

Before we fall into the void
Before we sink into the abyss
Let this wall between us be destroyed
Let us taste a final kiss

Before we fade into eternal dust
Before we drift into nothingness
Let us listen to the ways of lust
Let us feel love's gentleness

Before we disappear without a trace
Before we're swept 'neath the undertow
Can we share one final embrace?
Can we take this love with us when we go?

Wayne Barrow

Thistle Down

Floating in the summer air
Thistle down is everywhere
Where it settles on the ground
With nature's help the thistle's found!

She dresses in a shade of green
With an armour of spines that can be seen
She grows in splendour strong and stout
Till her purple flower blossoms out

Living her life in the sun and rain
Till nature takes a hand again
Making seeds of silver grey
That the summer breeze can whisk away

They float o'er meadow and babbling brook
Where some may stop to take a look
At the tiny fishes swimming there
And then again they take the air

Once more to land upon the ground
From where they grow without a sound
To majestic thistles with purple crown
That changes again to thistle down.

George Gutherless, Withernsea

A Dream

The darkness came and it became bleak across the lands
Everything had changed and not for the better
As they gave the final command
Strangers met in the dark watching the midnight sky
Waiting for a miracle to save their sorry lives
So without any warning, along came the shadows
Not a trace of light, only the sound of breaking windows
Time was running out and there was no saviour in sight
'You must run for your lives and run to the light.'
Remember these words and try not to scream
'Wake up now it is only a dream.'

But you do not wake and you soon realise
You cannot scream
Nothing will ease you and your tears run clean
In a motionless state you plead to be free
But it will not let go it will not let you be
You know the feeling of drowning as you try to grasp at breath
You are just somewhere in the middle
Between life and temporary death

Driving headlong and crashing feel the burn feel the wall
If I wrote you a letter you could not read it all
These emotions never leave you, not until the break of dawn
When you awake from past journeys and
Dance on the circled lawn
Darkness begins fading and daylight slowly returns
The sun rises across the sky and birds take fight in turn
Remember these words and do not scream
'Wake up now it is only a dream.'

Denise Evans, Thornaby

The Best Thing Around Our End

The white strip painted on the pavement around Mrs Daycroft's corner wall.
Walking past it and feeling peculiarly happy that Mrs Daycroft lived on our bit: our own witch.

No, the best thing about summer evenings on Arthur Street was to walk by her corner and up the cobbled backs,
find a bit of tar that had softened in the hot day sun and hold Grandad's magnifying glass over the top to help it melt.

Or was it playing 'Buzz Off 1-2-3' with the kids from Maple Street and Poplar Avenue, even Alexandra Road if we were short:
pegging it back to the lamp post to yell, 'Buzz off!' without being caught?

No, no, it was 'ring-a-bell-and-run-away' but never at Mrs Daycroft's house . . . no, of course, the best thing of all was Mrs Scamell's corner shop: going in for two-penny-worth of rainbow sherbet, the doorbell ringing loud and Mrs Scamell's big husband coming out in his vest –

unless that is Mrs Scamell came herself, disturbing her early evening news on TV for my ½p sherbet dip, telling me, 'Do you know, the paper bag costs more than this?' – and me staring back at her: almost not flinching.

Jacqueline Bulman, Great Harwood

Pleasant Sunday

As the sun shines brightly to welcome a brand new day,
The village being woken by Sunday newspapers posted through the door,
Busy housewives preparing breakfast as newspapers clatter onto the floor,
Kids moaning that they are bored and nothing much to do,
Father gets them to tidy up their rooms and make their beds,
Recite their homework till it's perfectly stored in their head.

Clean washing being hung on the washing line to freshen and dry,
Housewives chatting over the garden fence passing the time of day,
Discussing the school summer holiday starting in two weeks' time,
The extra money needed for new uniforms is certainly going to bite,
And the noise kids will make later in the evening whilst they are out at play.

Fathers out the front tending their garden and mowing the lawn,
Hoeing between the flowers and pulling up the newly sprouted weeds,
Filling up the bird bath with fresh water for the early morn,
Raking up the litter from under the privet hedge and flower beds,
Finally putting all the tools away and lock the back garden shed.

Late afternoon tables and chairs on the back lawn for afternoon tea,
Platefuls of different types of sandwiches laid there on display,
A pitcher or orange juice with matching glasses sat there on a silver tray,
As assortment of biscuits and a large cream filled home-made cake,
Which finishes off a really nice pleasant sunny summer's day.

As late evening closes in for the kids' bath time and an early night,
They have to be up for school in the early morning nice and bright,
Mum and Dad wash and dry the tea things and tidy them away,
Relax with a nice hot drink watching television for an hour or so,
Then retire to bed in readiness for a brand new working day.

Bryan J Holmes, Wheatley

The Late Bloomer

There's nothing wrong about oldies holding hands in the street
It's possible one needs support and if they're quite discreet
And it isn't for support, who other than their business can it be
Declaring their love towards each other is something with which I agree
Younger people assume that the right to show affection will pass
But what if they're still caring and he still loves his lass
It isn't as if they're billing and cooing and trying to make a show
When they just exchange a look their faces seem to glow
They're not love-struck youngsters wondering what next to do
Each knows what pleases the other, she's not a harpie or a shrew
He doesn't think he is Superman, she knows he won't fly away
And she knows he's not a ladies' man, he's balding - she's grey
He has a happy disposition and is always ready for some fun
But also decorous and well-mannered and when all's said and done
He is really intent on caring for her which most women would like
They've known each other from schooldays when he was a 'tyke'
Even during National Service he knew she was the one for whom he'd care
And with persistence and patience her heart he would ensnare
'They are made for each other' though once their paths did separate
Now all their wandering is over - they're happy and life is great
They accept with aplomb the funny looks they sometimes still get
But the time apart - time they wasted - that is what they regret
She loves him with a childlike trust - on him she can always depend
And he knows she is always there for him - his true love and his friend
They laugh at each other's jokes, others don't understand their humour
They trust each other implicitly - their love is just a late bloomer.

Florence Broomfield, Ashton-in-Makerfield

Before You Came

My life used to be simple
With each day just the same
With nothing to write home about
My life, before you came.

I never knew how lost I was
Now isn't that a shame?
Not knowing just how lonely
I was, before you came.

Until the day that you arrived
When I could call your name
I never knew a love like this
In the days before you came.

And now you're here my heart's alive
Love burning like a flame
Indifferent and cold was how
I felt, before you came.

You are my world, my everything
A bold yet truthful claim
Cos nothing made me feel such joy
In life, before you came.

And now my life feels so complete
Not boring, weak or tame
So full of laughter and delight
I'm very glad you came.

Elaine Sands, Standish

Remembrance

I have gone away from here,
I've travelled on before you.
Weep not for me, my precious love,
No tears of grief, no sorrow.

I'm just absent for a while,
Yet with you, hand in hand;
My fragrant presence by your side,
In everything you do.

Remember me in springtime, love,
As snowdrop's pearly head
Offers up in pale sun's gleam,
Its kiss of sacred innocence.

A full-blown rose of summer,
Its heady scent a message
Blown on the wind, to tell you,
I'm waiting here for you!

Children blossomed from our love,
Flourished from our garden;
Mourn no more in autumn's shades,
No falling tears, summer's leaves.

My laughter's in a playful breeze,
Sad tears in April's rain;
Midday's sun a warm embrace,
A melting kiss, a snowflake's form.

Hear my whisper in the trees,
My distant voice in ocean's roar;
At night, look skywards to the stars,
I'm waiting here for you, my love!

Jillian Minion, Millom

Square Eyes

John Logie Baird
Is the man to blame
For inventing the box
Full of pictures and fame
John Logie Baird gave us
Square eyes

We rushed in from nursery
To 'Watch with Mother'
But after school
It was 'Blue Peter' and others
That's when we began to get
Square eyes

In our teenage years
It was music and soaps
Kept us glued to the box
Interest in the news no hope
Even more hours spent with
Square eyes

As the years progress
Afternoon TV cookery and quizzing
Keep the grey matter burning
And our brains are fizzing
Now we need specs for those
Square eyes

So John Logie Baird
Look what you started
With that box of yours
We can't be parted
But what would we do without
Square eyes.

Dawn Williams-Sanderson, Newbiggin by the Sea

Dreaming

We dream it is good, we are dreaming
It would hurt us if we were awake
Since it is playing and not subtle dower;
Dreams are well, but waking's better.

If one wakes at down
Derived its confronting
Adds the gladdened hour
That's how we can be bode of dawn.

Leading its prudenter to dream
Into the precinct raw;
That makes as rich an hour sweeter,
I wonder if this so true, the way we dream.

Heather Aspinall, Heaton

Blessed Moments

Sweet those blessed moments
When life's so charmed and kind
Lock those treasured moments
Safely in your mind
Enjoy those happy feelings
Keep them close at hand
Never let them slip and fade
Like snow upon the sand
Blessed precious moments
Imprinted on our hearts
Ours to love forever
Never to depart.

Kathleen June Jinks, Eston

Remembering

How well do I remember
Those dark satanic mills
And the clatter of a 1000 looms
Now forever stilled.
Their hooters and/or whistles
That pierced the morning air
Threatening we shall close our gates
If you don't hurry here.

I remember too those cobbled streets
Well worn by plodding hooves
And spotless little back-to-backs
Whereby lay my roots.
Our lasses then wore pinnies
Dust-caps adorned their heads
They could conjure up a meal from 'nowt'
And bake the finest bread.

I remember too those summer times
When kids could safely play
And mums then didn't worry
If out of sight they strayed
When skipping ropes and bully-hoops
Were always close at hand
As was the football (back-street) style
A battered old tin can.

I remember too those old cloth-caps
Perched on the heads of most
And when our wash-day tablecloth
Was a well spread 'news' or 'post'
But thankfully there are some things
That time will never change
Like our Yorkshire pud, fish 'n' chips
And a pint of superb ale.

Austin Baines-Brook, Gomersal

Grandma's Arm

Poor dear Grandma's in a state
Her arm is but a bother
'But never mind,' we all say
'You can easily use the other.

Grandma can't do a thing with it
The arm's strapped up in a sling
'Leave everything to us,' I said
'You mustn't do a thing.'

The arm needs rest to recover
From this sprain it has got
It will heal in a few days
It certainly won't rot

The doctor says stay warm and cosy
You must do as you're told
To us you're very precious
Even more so than gold

So stay indoors warm and rested
And take the tablets given
You will feel happy and gay
To enjoy future living.

Alison Scott, Heaton

Tadpoles

a tangle of commas
will morph into full stops
and migrate from this page
to another
as a strident coda
to a summer travelogue

Geatana Trippetti, Heaton Mersey

Untitled

It rained as I walked up the valley;
The hillsides were crowned in white mist
Which clung to the dense wooded slopes.
I walked near the shallow river
In which white mist was reflected,
An unreal and curious vision.
I walked through the lonely village,
On the rough and uneven main street
Where dogs and the cattle roamed free,
The street deep in mud in the winter
And dusty and dry in the summer;
It was boarded by old wooden dachas
Enclosed by crude primitive fences;
A grey concrete building peered down,
The old and the new thrust together
This century imposed on past ages,
A coerced unnatural union.

Nigel Miller, Sandbach

Unsuspecting Heart

Unsuspecting heart, beware what he is telling you
For he will kiss you, just like you want him to
And he'll know he's got a hold on you.

Poor unsuspecting heart, tell yourself,
This feeling's much too fine
And your heart is getting out of line.

Poor unsuspecting heart, so let your feelings know
That you have felt this kind of thing before
And if you fall you must be sure.

You would think by now, I'd know the score
Well I've thought and thought within
Till my head is in such a spin
And I tell you, I'm falling in love again
With my beautiful wonderful unsuspecting heart.

Shirley Gray, Sheffield

A Saturday Afternoon In Summer

A pleasant lunch disposed of,
the sun-bathed garden calls.
A haven of tranquillity
within those sturdy walls.

Dig out the ancient deckchair
and find a shady nook.
Wrestle with its woodwork
and settle with a book.

The head begins to nod
and the book just slips away.
All is peace and happiness
but it is here to stay?

The peace is rudely shattered
by some very loud guitars
as next-door's wireless thunders
like the sound of fifty cars.

A word across the wall
achieves some slight relief,
So it's back to the reading,
though it's probably brief.

Another annoyance!
A great cloud of smoke
from a barbeque fire.
This is way past a joke.

No sooner we're settled,
when, from nowhere at all,
right onto the book
lands a large rubber ball!

On this beautiful day
is there no peace at all?
'Can I have my ball please?'
Comes from over the wall.

Having duly obliged
then it's back to the chair.
But just wait a minute,
what's that in the air?

A further disturbance?
It just cannot be true.
It's a huge swarm of midges
right out of the blue!

Fast action is called for.
The shed is the spot
to find that old fly-spray
and get rid of the lot.

A glance at the sky
to see that they're gone
and despair fills the air.
Black clouds hide the sun!

As rain starts to spatter
rush in with the book.
Then return for the deckchair
and curse the bad luck!

So it looks like the telly
instead of the sun.
But it might be more peaceful,
and possibly fun.

Peter Roebuck, Prestwich

Diversity

Diversity.
Diverse.
Diversify.
What is diversity?

I have a	D	ream
I have an	I	dea
I enjoy some	V	ariety
I enjoy some	E	nrichment
I try to	R	each
I try to be	S	trong
I try to be	I	nnovative
I try to be	T	houghtful
I try to be	Y	outhful.

I'm black and I do all these things.

Nicola Karunaratne, St Helens

On Leaving West Somerset

I'll remember your green hills and lush countryside,
The pale-gold of spring mornings and fall's eventide.
I'll remember your people with their West Country burr,
The warmth of their greeting and the friends we've made there.
The castle at Dunster on its wooded hillside
Will in my memory forever abide;
A 'come to life picture' from a child's story book
This medieval village begs us, 'please come, take a look'.
And we succumbed to its myriad charms,
Its tea-rooms and gardens and delicious cream teas,
Its enticing gift shops and cobblestone streets;
The bells that tunefully chime from the ancient church tower,
And the 'Old Water Mill' that grinds grain into flour.
On Minehead's Quay stands 'The Old Ship Aground'
And little chapel of St Peter, where a moment of peace can be found.
The Lifeboat Station is manned by a valiant crew
On call day and night, all the year through.
While oft from the Channel strong breezes blow,
And safe harbour is found as tides ebb and flow.
Selworthy's white church can be seen for many a mile;
Within its sacred walls I've oft lingered a while.
Lunch in Periwinkle's tea-garden beguiles;
We'd choose from the mouth-watering menu,
Sip tea from a china cup; drink in the glorious view.
Porlock High Street is full of character and charm;
Steep Porlock Hill a breathtaking climb.
Then a drive over beautiful Exmoor
To Lorna Doone Country and the old church at Oare.
Maybe wild ponies we'd see; perhaps a red deer,
Then savour the view o'er the bay to Porlock Weir.
When winter comes and the north winds blow,
I'll remember the spring blossom trees on which cider apples grow;
The heavenly scent of pink roses in bloom
In the early summer gardens at Hestercombe;
The banks of primroses when we took a steam train ride;
And oh that lush green countryside!
These are the things I will never forget
On leaving the green hills of West Somerset.

Anita Cooling, Boston Spa

Incarnations

I looked and saw
Through many times
The lives that I
Had led
How a man I'd been
Though now and then
A woman I'd become

I felt the pain
Of burning
And saw the scars form
On my arm.
I felt the wild joy
Of ancient warfare
And the price one paid
A thousand times.

I'd practise at an art
One, two, three times
And more
To improve my skill
Through many lives
To win or paint or sing.

Mistakes I made
Not once nor twice
But many, many times
Though promises I kept
Across the years
That centuries forgot.

Some think to reach
Perfection
Across this span of lives
But it is a roundabout
With ups and downs
That's lasted through
All time.

Ian Lennox-Martin, Carlisle

A Homely Scene

A cottage small a happy, homely scene
Table laid with strawberries and cream
Home-made cakes tasty, fresh bread
Families sitting round table, grace is said

Time to eat enjoying this lovely meal
Love is obviously living there, we feel
Cosy off teapot Mother pours the tea
Then hands it round to all her family

Meal over, time to clear china away
Thanks to our mum is what we say
For the lavish meal, the spread you lay
We all agree it's been a wonderful day.

Elizabeth Mary Dowler, Bulwark

Let's Be

Let's be strong in each other
Let's care for no other.
Let's be as we should be.
Let's not be blind, as we can see
Let's be strong in our strength, and safe in our hearts.
Let's be each other and no other.
Let the fire in our hearts not burn the flesh or skin,
If we're sure we can't lose only win
Let's be apart together, come whatever the weather.
We'll unite together, come foe or friend united to the end.
The world is controlled, yet we've unrolled the symptoms of ourselves
We're not hundred percent, we're not ten percent
we're not Heaven sent.
Let's be mortal, let's go through the portal of life.
Let's cut the air like a knife.
Let's weather the storm, and awake in the dawn.
Let's be strong in our head and let's awake in our bed.
Let's be here instead, feeling, growing, yearning
Knowing, encompassing all, and as we grow so tall -
not feeling small.

T McFarlane, Wavertree

Untitled

There are moments that I treasure
And moments that I dread
I love every minute
Spent with you
We can argue and fall out
But I always love you
You take care of me
Like no other man could ever do
I know you appreciate all that I do too
The respect is deep
The friendship kind
You are the one constantly on my mind
I cannot imagine being without you
That is the big dread that fills my head
You're deep in my heart
No more to be said.

Elaine Briscoe-Taylor, Shipley

Change Of Heart

Sun and sand and seashore
Rain, sleet, snow and hail
My childhood at the seaside
I thought forever would prevail.
When summer sun was shining
Scantily clad we played
On shining sand in sun-warmed pools
For hours on end we laid.
The vast expanse of sea and shore
Spoke of places far away
We laughed and joked and chatted
Here forever we would stay.

But now we live in the suburbs
Inland and far from the open sea
With access to culture and learning
Which now mean everything to me.

Marian Williams, Davyhulme

Long Day - Again

I sat alone for many hours,
Spoken to no one, only my flowers,
They pass, shop and go to church,
Sitting alone, I'm left in lurch,
When you pass by, pop in and see me,
I'll give you welcome, coffee or tea
We can sit, have a little talk,
Even plan a short walk.
Recently, my best friend died,
I could have done more if only I'd tried
100s turned up to see her go,
Those friends of hers, could have done more?
Eyes now closed, she's at rest.
Lots of relatives, but her friends were best,
Don't wait! Just knock on a door,
Before family and friends are no more,
Youngsters! Don't need to call in for a chat,
They, truly believe when gone, that's that!

Sheila Donetta, Swansea

The Hill Climb

Cycling is one fine way,
To spend a lovely summer's day,
Grandad rides along the track,
Little grandson
Not too far back,
Grandad then decides to say,
'Right now son!
Here's a hill that we must climb,
Just follow me and take your time.'
At the top,
The winner stands,
With cycle cap in his small hands!
And then he shouts,
So full of glee,
'Come on Grandad, keep up with me!'

Sylvia Joan Higginson, Timperley

Gross Injustice!

Ladies waken up!
You've 'slept' for centuries
And whilst you've 'slept'
You've been chained to slavery
By the middle-class and by the gentry.

Property landlords
Have it worked out to a tee
Female tenants
Shall maintain their properties
Work a lifetime through and all for free.

Yes we women are
Expected to work for free
Cleaning, repairing, gard'ning, washing
Daily for thirty-hours all constantly.

A whole lifetime's work
All unpaid, unthanked, unpraised
How women are exploited
Taken for granted
While males are left all lazed.

If something gets missed
Seems it's the woman's fault
The cry from the males - 'Make her work overtime'
It's far past time it was all called to a halt.

Where would landlords be
Without women, all is another story
Landlords' lives remain cushy all ending
With them, taking all cash, and all glory.

What a shockingly
One-sided situation
Not one man on this Earth
Would work for free
Yet a woman! - It's a foregone conclusion.

Wicked, wicked how
Women are pathetically viewed
By the inferior male population
Of whom ev'ry last one should be sued.

Women do all donkey-work
While all landlords do is shirk.

Barbara Sherlow, Preston

What A Plight

Oh dear, dear, what a plight
The dentist's chair, I had in sight.
I broke my plate, then I couldn't eat,
I was missing out, on my special treat.

It was fixed but, it did take time,
I couldn't eat, so I wrote this rhyme.
For forty years, I'd had my teeth,
And when they broke, I came to grief.

It was bread and milk and soft food then,
Soup, rice pudding, over and over again.
When I got my new teeth, they did cost me quite a lot,
But I was happy, when my plate, I'd got.

I was very young, when my teeth came out,
I had falses but a good many, were in doubt.
They looked like mine, a lot thought they were,
They'd done very well, to last forty years.

But I got by, I had a new set, one afternoon,
And at night we had a picnic, under the moon.
I'd been missing out, on my toast and jam,
Bacon butties, apples, carrots, lettuce and Spam.

William Jebb, Endon

She Left With The Summer

As the sky dipped in a redden'd sky,
Sinking southwards to the warmer climes,
She laid there in a troublesome sleep
And dreamed of distant happier times.

She turned awake to a darken'd wall
And watched pictures in the candle light,
Shades of the night sidled in on her,
Waiting for the finish of the fight.

She looked back over the years past
With a little sadness and regret,
All the things she should have said and done
They came to haunt her as the sun set.

Faint memories drifted back and forth
'Mong flickering dancing shadows,
She relived again many memories
As the thin waxy taper burnt low.

The wind rose and wailed as the light fled,
Beating an old tune like a drummer.
Once more she turned her face to the wall,
Closed her eyes and left with the summer.

Gwendoline Douglas, Hull

Always Spring, Forever Summer

Leave behind the cold, dark days
Of wearisome worries and never-ending strife
And enter my world where
It is always spring and forever summer.

Leave your travel bag of burdens
And bitterness behind on the homely tree stump
To be forgotten forever.
Commit memories to the past for
Here there is no yesterday to haunt you

Only the ever-warm sun of today
Touching you with the glittering golden
Rays of a bright tomorrow.
There is no autumn decay or
Cruel, harsh winter here for
It is always spring and forever summer.

So open your eyes,
Step forward in life,
Step forward in hope
To where the waltzing, weaving wheat
Whispers excitedly about your arrival;

While the kindly, worldly-wise beech tree
Bristles to attention and prepares to bend
To shake your hand, ready to
Embrace you as you journey onwards.

Flying by is the colourful Red Admiral, who
With military precision, ensures that
You walk in the right direction
While trumpeting your arrival here where
It is always spring and forever summer.

Soon the bright red poppies of peace
Are curtseying at your feet,
As the dazzling daffodils dressed
In their Sunday best, sing
A glorious welcome to you.

And watching from a distance
The timid field mouse scurries
So as not to miss a thing, for
He has to report to all
This excitement of this day.

You may not be able to stay forever,
But this land is always here,
Simply open your eyes and visit,
Again the place where
It is always spring and forever summer.

Sue Gerrard, St Helens

Sports Day Memories... 1952

Hop, skip and jumping,
Hurdling too.
Three-legged racing,
Shove and push through!
Hundred yard dashing,
We get a bashing,
From Standard Two!

Relay team tripping,
High jumpers slipping,
What a to do!
Egg and spoon racings,
Get a right pasting,
Best we can do?

Relay team flapping,
Standard Four lapping,
Long jumpers queue.
Standard One slacking,
No time for cracking,
Half mile at two?

Shoving and pushing,
Heaving and pulling,
Tug of war through!

Heart stopping, gruelling,
Best bit of schooling,
Four classes duelling,
Back in fifty-two.

Betty Lightfoot, Swinton

Reflection

Today it's impossible for anyone to tell
That thousands of miners and families did dwell
In long rows of houses that all looked the same
New Delaval Colliery that was the name,
Today no trace to be seen
It's now a golf course pleasant and green

Each house had a long garden where folk grew their own veg
Leeks, potatoes, cabbages and peas
Round every front door climbing rose trees

The houses were cosy with roaring big fires
Brasses all polished for friends to admire
On the floor a home-made proggy mat
Armchair at the side where Grandmas sat
They looked after their old folk
Were no old folks' homes then
Just the district nurse who would come on her bike
To deliver new babies or such-like.

They would bath in front of the fire
The toilet was over the road
Which wasn't very nice on a cold winter's night
With no light in the street you would get mud on your feet
The least noise would give you a fright
The grocer and baker came with horse and cart
The milkman would measure you a pint or a quart

Sometimes a beggar would sing in the street
Rags on his back no shoes on his feet
Some might give him a halfpenny if they had one to spare
I think in those days it must have been rare
A trip on the bus was a luxury to many
The fare down to Blyth would cost you a penny

There were three little churches full every Sunday
Two schools where they taught to read and to write
Given the chance most children were bright
The Sunday school trip was a treat
At the end of the street friends would meet
To wait for a bus that would take all of us
For a lovely day out by the sea

Holidays were unheard of people didn't get far no one then had a car
Miners worked hard for a living
Long hours underground every day
Their wives worked hard too
They had plenty to do, certainly earned their pay.

Today horizons are vast
Wonder how our children will reflect on their past.

Doreen Tattersall, Cowpen Blyth

Angel's Wings

The gigantic limousine pulled up abruptly
At the royal show gates

Immaculately-clad chauffeur opened the gleaming door
Revealing the exit of three teenage beauty queens
All decked with tiaras, sashes and flowers
Clutching my hand she looked up bewildered
As the flouncing skirt of a teenage beauty
Brushed against her wheelchair
Only to be pulled away in arrogant pride
'I can't wear anything pretty; my legs and arms didn't grow
I will never be pretty like that'
She sobbed as a small hand wiped the tears
'You are always pretty, my dear child,' was the reassuring reply.
'True beauty comes from within; that makes you a little angel
One day you will have angel wings'
'Then I can fly home,' was the quick reply

'I won't need my wheelchair anymore'
Her eyes sparkled with incredible charm
As a shawl was tucked around her frail form
Closing her eyes, whispering, 'Angel's wings some sunny morn.'

Frances Gibson, Beragh

Take Me Away

There's noisy traffic and road rage.
Supermarkets that take your wage.
People passing in a hurry.
Workers' faces etched with worry
Why should I let this spoil my day?
Someone please take me away!

I finally find I have the fare
And travel to France by air.
I arrive in beautiful ancient Brittany,
My favourite place being La Gacilly.

Soon dreamy visions come into sight.
Houses painted brilliantly white
With wooden shutters in pastel blue.
Flowers abound in a delicate hue.

My eyes take in endless fields of corn
Standing erectly in the windless morn.
Each of my cheeks is planted with a kiss
By friendly locals who I'll truly miss.

I hear birds sing and the rustle of trees
Then nothing more than the buzzing of bees.
I'm totally re-energised by the beauty of Brittany
And my favourite place being La Gacilly.

Claire Gordon, Mottram

Behind Closed Doors

Nobody sees the evil that goes on,
After the blinds are pulled,
Friends never realise our problems haven't gone,
When fake smiles have them fooled.

Behind the walls that drown out the screams,
People's true colours are painted,
Those elegant houses of their dreams,
Where love and hate get reacquainted.

See the shadows when the curtains are drew,
Pointing and pushing under the stars,
Emerging the next day black and blue,
Dressed to the nines hiding all scars.

Hear their doors bang and slam,
And the smashing bottles of scotch,
Hear someone say they don't give a damn,
During the meeting of the neighbourhood watch.

And when the lessons have all been learned,
We'll try our best to sound surprised,
We'll give you the impression that we are concerned,
Our sorry speech so often revised.

Ian McNamara, Belfast

Summer Sun

The sun is shining the birds have appeared
The garden is blooming and the sky is cleared
It looks like summer might have arrived
Another cold winter we have all survived.

The winter was long the days cold and dark
The snow kept falling; it was passed being a lark
The roads were impassable all slippery with ice
And the children grew bored it wasn't very nice.

The spring was deceiving it was grey and cold
But the sun tried its best, the clear skies to hold
Then suddenly a warm day would appear
But this isn't guaranteed at this time of year.

Now the dove is cooing it wakes me up at dawn
The sun greets me at daybreak and the days are warm
The bees are humming, their honey to collect
Summer is here that's what we expect.

But our summers are brief and soon they are gone
The weather changes and the nights turn long
Autumn arrives and the sun loses its heat
The winds return and the outlook is bleak.

Winter is now also back on its way
The weather turns cool throughout the day
The sun tries to shine in quiet relief
But the nights are cold and the days are brief.

Our summer now has been and gone
The year has flown it didn't seem long
Now we look forward to this time next year
When the summer returns and gives us good cheer.

Sheila Storr, Gargrave

The Supermarket

Molly the trolley, has definitely got it in for me
Tim, my grandson is sitting good as can be.
I want to go straight down to where they keep bread
But - Molly thinks otherwise and takes it into her head
To crawl sideways across the whole of the floor
We travel fast hitting the gents' toilet door!

Molly now travels at an alarming pace
My legs can't take it and I'm red in the face
We rush into the cereals and to my obvious dismay
A box has burst, Tim loves it and in glee shouts out hooray!
But - I have cornflakes in my hair
They surround me simply everywhere.

Now Molly heads for the bottles of squash
I'm now bathed in orange and people rush
To help me in all my various troubles
Timothy loves it and blows beautiful orange bubbles.

I've no control and Molly pushes me away
I think I'll go home - I've no wish to stay
When I get to the check-out forlorn and aghast
I can't find my purse - oh! Here it is at last.

The things are checked out and my bill is so high
What a day, I feel any minute I might cry
I've got dog food and cat food - Tim's been helping himself
From animal food on the very low shelf
I've no dog and no cat and I'll have to confess
But knock six eggs over in my great distress
Now an omelette is forming round an old lady's legs
The box is empty, I've lost all of my eggs.

I pick up my things and I start to depart
When I find Tim devouring the lady's jam tart!
It isn't my day - I'm not at my best
I need aspirin and whisky and a very long rest.

Jacqueline Bartlett, St Martins

Two Little Birds In Love!

There they sat on our garden fence
On a sunny bank holiday morn.
The year is two thousand and eleven
Sixty-seven years since I was born.

This little couple live in the wild
They depend on nature for food.
They met in our garden of wild flowers
And what followed was extra good!

She sat on the fence so contented
He loved her time after time.
Just lighting so gently upon her
And the sun it continued to shine.

Those two little birds are God's creatures
Like all of the others he's made.
I thank him for health and my eyesight
And pray that my memory won't fade.

It really was lovely to watch them
Unaware of the presence of me.
He! even chased off a rival
Then continued to enjoy their love spree.

Lorna Hawthorne, Armagh

A Tear

A tear is like a jewel that falls from someone's eye
It sparkles on the cheek as the soul it starts to cry
These tears they form rivers from hearts so filled with pain
For in this land of live and loving you must give before you gain
Oh I believe that all those rainbows that are formed way in the sky
Gain their lustre and their colour from the eyes of those who cry.

Robert Bannan, Townhead

I Will Sing Of Islay

I will sing to you of Islay
And the Cullins of Skye
And the Hills of Ardmorn
I will bring you by and by
When we walked the Haughs of Cromdale
Our battle plans we laid
And when we came to Killiekrankie
A different song we played

The Flowers of the Forest
They have not lost their bloom
And the castle keep's still standing
Where we wandered in our youth
Ae Fond Kiss and then to sever
By the Dawning of the Day
And cruel was that parting
Which stole our time away

Now a man can be a soldier
A poet or a saint
And a man can be the hero
Or choose the quiet way
He may make his mark with money
He may travel far and wide
Still a Man's a Man for a' that
And he'll no' away to bide

So I'll Weep no More by Atholl
Those days are in the past
And this ship so long-a-sailing
Comes safely home at last
The Chevalier lays down his claymore
Now the fighting all is done
And by the Roses of Prince Charlie
We two shall stand as one

The Chevalier lays down his claymore
And the day will surely come
When by the Roses of Prince Charlie
We two shall stand as one.

J Williams, Swansea

On Its Way

When days are chill and evenings dark
and the wind blows cold and drear,
then thoughts of brighter days to come
fill the heart as it wishes summer near.

Curtains drawn tight, telly on,
last year's summer retakes showing,
these things draw the mind to summer ahead
whilst outside the sky is snowing.

When summer's come and evenings light,
and the kids go out to play,
get out of the house, share an evening stroll,
make the most of each new day.

For summer days are soon enough gone,
the season's all too short
and thoughts of winter are not far ahead
when we in its 'web' again get caught.

Time in the park, garden or beach,
or rambling country lanes
can relax the mind so the body refuels
to cope with inner angst or pains.

So, boost the body's Vitamin D
from each treasured summer's day,
then thoughts of this bright season last longer
to cast winter's gloom away.

Summer - have fun, awake and enjoy it,
British summers never last long!
Summer - days to laugh and bring joy to our hearts,
share in Nature's long-awaited song.

Ann Voaden, Nantymoel

An Invocation To The Forest

The sun trickling like honey
Through the canopy of ancient trees
The wise ones
Warm up the ferns, the moss, the bark
And the leaves
Their scent envelopes me

I grew up '**á** la lisiére des bois'
The Forest of Yvelines, France
It is why my mother called me Sylvie
So that the forest could whisper my name

Entering the forest was like
Walking in a prayer
A cathedral of trees

Oh, I hope, when I cross the veil
At the end of my days
To walk back in the Forest of Yvelines
To tread lightly on the emerald-green moss, so soft

To dance at the top of the trees
In dapple green and gold light
With the spirits, in the gentle breeze
Maybe to curl up and sleep as a dormouse
Or, growing roots to become a tree
In the blessed forest of the land
Of forever dreams.

Sylvie Alexandre-Nelson, Swansea

Hope

When I weaved through the passages of scripture
Each word each line I define
Such nuggets and jewels I find
The words bring healing to my heart and my mind
God's word helps me grow in knowledge I know
I have found a new friend who is with me to the end
He died on the Cross for those who were lost
He is Jesus my saviour He is saviour for all
To know His great love and pardon from above
We must call on His name there's so much to gain!
With hope for the future, forgiveness for the past
His promise is eternal for the first and the last
His kingdom is not of this world but sited above
His world is above filled with joy and with love
He said in His word He is coming back soon
So there is much to gain free from sickness and pain
For all who will know Him and believe in His name
Come and join us in eternity forever
With the Father and son and the spirit endeavour.

William Waring, Belfast

Spring To Summer

Back and forth, back and forth,
Busy as the bees,
I watch them from my window,
Building nests among my trees,
The sparrows chirping cheerily,
Some feeding on my lawn,
Bringing hope of better days,
Now that winter's gone,
The flowers have started blooming,
A colourful display,
A little bit of sunshine to brighten up one's day.

Annie McKimmie, Portsoy

I Love

I love the way you still love me
when I sing out of tune.
I love the chicken sandwich
you make me at noon.
I love watching you cook
and when you make me a cup of tea.
I love you so much more
when you smile at me.
I love the way you hold my hand
and the way you caress my face.
I love the way your heart
is always just in the right place.

I love the way you love me near you
and the way you hold me close.
I love the way you kiss me
and the way you touch my toes.
I love that when we're walking
you will stop to look in my eyes.
I love the way you tell me
all your dreams, hopes and desires.
I love being in bed beside you
and watching as you sleep.
I love the way you love me
and I pray our love's for keeps.

Barbara Rodgers, Belfast

The Quietness Of Nature

You do not hear a snowflake fall,
or the tide turn in ebb and flow.
The clouds in the sky bump
without making a single sound.
Each morning rises the dew
up from the ground.
This is the silence of God
found only in the natural round.

John Harrold, Bettws

Cleopatra

Oh Cleopatra Queen of the Nile
After years of searching they still cannot find
Where time has not touched you
Your last resting place
Yet there you still lie, serene in your case
Sceptre and orb rest in your hands
Somewhere under Egyptian sands
Envied by women, worshipped by men
No woman has matched your beauty since then
Bedecked in jewels, bathed in milk
Groomed and pampered dressed in silk
Your love was Mark Antony, but it wasn't to be
So with a bite from an asp, you set yourself free
And oh how the gods wept that day
As they watched your life slowly ebb away
Men have pillaged defiled and stole
And what once held beauty, are now empty holes
Barren now is the Valley of Kings
Gone are the mummies and all precious things
Over the years they have found quite a few
But where, oh where Cleopatra are you
Are you under the Nile, or maybe the sands
When they search are you far or close at hand
Do you look down upon them
Laughing with glee, saying, 'Fools I'm well hidden
You will never find me.'

Maureen Cole, Felin Foel

My Life - A Candle

Let my life be like a candle
Let my smile be bright
Let me give out warmth and comfort
To those who have no light

Let me be a light that brightens
Sorrows darkened road
Let me always shine for those who carry
Illness as their load

Let my light be there to guide
The children in my care
Then when grandchildren appear
Still, let my light be there

Let my brightness never darken
Let my love shine on
Let my life be an example
To those who follow on

Let me prove that I was given
A precious light to show
And when my life on Earth is ended
May I leave behind a glow.

Margaret Non Williams, Saundersfoot

A Changed Man

O God we thank Thee for the joy.
Of saving Thomas and Janet's boy.
Jordan Neill is the young man's name.
And he as a sinner to Jesus came.

He found no pleasure in his sin.
When God's Holy Spirit convicted him.
But he gave them much delight.
When he trusted Jesus Christ one night.

Young Jordan's heart is now on fire
And to see his mates saved is his desire.
He wants to please his Lord and master.
Who saved him from spiritual disaster.

My friend what will you now do?
With Jesus Christ who died for you?
You will your precious soul neglect.
If you God's salvation in Christ reject.

His precious blood was freely shed.
And with it sin's awful debt was paid.
My friend Christ Jesus loves you too.
And wants to give you life that's new.

Salvation in Jesus, that is a promise.
Which God gave to Jordan, Janet and Thomas.
The promise is also extended to you.
Trust Christ as your saviour, for His promise is true.

Samuel McAlister, Carrickfergus

December In Belfast 2010

Snow is here
Snow is scary
Snow is shocking
Snow is insensitive
The footpaths are impossible
The council is not responsible
For gritting
DRD is not responsible
For gritting
Nobody it seems is responsible
For gritting
The cost would be unreasonable
The effort would be impracticable
Meanwhile old dears trip
On the treacherous pavements
And the shopping falls
Out of their Tesco bags
But as least it gives
Men the chance to be Sir Galahads.

A man phoned into the Nolan Show
And said, 'You are all a pack of whingers,
Buy cat litter in B&Q and scatter
Upon your footpath.'
Stephen Nolan says the situation
Reminds him of The Magic Roundabout
And now he's playing the theme tune.

Brenda Liddy, Belfast

The Dog On The Motorbike

In 1910 a 70-year-old man who had a family of 13 was very frisky
He was a great musician and very jolly
His wife was 50 years of age
Both of whom lived in Carrive
While out for a walk with his wife
He seen a young teenage girl on the road
He whistled and yodelled and ran after her
She passed no remark and walked on about her business
However, his wife was very embarrassed
She didn't say anything to him.
Later that evening she went to the parochial house
She told the parish priest her trouble
She says I'm ashamed of my life
My husband is 70 years of age and every time we are walking out together, as soon as he sees a young teenage girl on the road, he whistles and yodels and runs after her,
I don't like saying anything to him at his time of life.
Ah, says the priest, pass no remark on him
I have an old dog and he is almost blind and every time he hears a motorbike going up or down the road he runs after it and barks.
And even if he did get up on one he wouldn't be able to ride it.

Michael McGuigan, Carrive

The Weeping Willow

The weeping willow sways and bows majestically
Her anthem whispering on the breath of the wind
As it journeys, revealing her natural loveliness
Languidly she drapes her billowing green attire
Which gently caresses the sweeping grassy slopes
Above the arched bank of the chattering stream

As the wind subsides she sinks into quiet slumber
Her stillness brings a haunting, deep silence
Which the sun seeks to disturb with dancing beams
Sending shafts of golden sunlight to warm earth
Casting reflections on the quietly moving water below
Capturing the beauty and magnificence of each moment.

Mary Leadbeter, Beaufort

Seascape

All shimmering bright, this island paradise
Jewels the skyline of a summer day,
Pinned to a radiant, rainbow-hued array
Of rippling satin called the sea.
As though once laid aside by nature's hand
Carefully, in a scarce-frequented nook
Of this her orb; fashioned in true likeness
Of her sketches; textured to display
Her matchless skill;
But torn, in second thought; from out her book
Too rich and glorious for every day.
This is no palm-fringed coral shore.
Reflections in the silver-sequinned rocks
And subtle sounds merged in the breaker's roar;
The homely bleating of the Machir flocks
And peat-smoke drifting over Castle Bay,
Betoken Barra's Hebridean Isle.

G Aldsmoor, Broughty Ferry

Fields Of Heather

Fields of heather brush together,
Like fluffy clouds in summer weather,
Flowing effortlessly in the breeze,
They almost put your mind at ease,
An evergreen shrub of many regions,
That stand together like Roman legions,
On alpine slopes they flourish and sway,
In the grip of snow that approaches their way,
And when the sun shines through the morning mist,
Their colours sparkle like they've been kissed,
A beautiful fragrance fills the air,
As they greet a new day without a care,
In the fields of life where these hardy shrubs grow,
May they thrive forever and fill the fields row after row after row.

David John Hewett, Dyfed

Scotland

I am the soul of highland
I am the heather's bloom
I am the sound of freedom
I am in clans a tune
My soul will not forget them
For blood to run like rain
In history 'tis written return I will again

Behold I have a flower
My country's emblem proud
Devoted to my nation
Scotland cried out loud

The thistle grows in memory
Of glens and clear clean air
Just stand and look around at
The stag the tall green fir
Tell me as you stand there
Your heart it will not race
Tell me when you stand there
Scotland's not the place . . .

Paul Kurt Lockwood, Welshpool

Skye

The sky on Skye
Is blue not grey
It takes its colour
From sea below -
Cliffs have stories to tell
Of pirates in the years gone by
A wondrous place
In every way.

Violet Burggy, Kilmuir

Look For Gold

I'm going to find me a rainbow
See there's one there where flies a swallow
I'll get the spade and go dig for gold
Where it will end there's a pot I'm told
When I reach there it's in a new place
Disappeared not even one trace
Only makes me go now look again
To follow where I can see it plain
And then there thought so had touch the ground
Like also has it still can't be found
Off once again now moves over there
All day I've chased, looked everywhere
It's playing this game of hide-and-seek
That's made me walk I'm now getting weak
And then the sun stops showing the way
It must set so that to end this day.

Roger Paul Fuge, Llwynhendy

Finally Found

The love I found
Is found in you
Now that I found someone
Someone to believe in
I feel so complete
Complete by your side
I just want you to know
How much I love you so
From the moment we spend
Spend our time together
I feel so completely alive
Alive from your love
I finally found
My love in you
And am glad that you love me too.

Angela Cole, Llangunnor

The Village Fete Remembered

Merry-go-rounds on a village green,
The prettiest flowers you've ever seen.
Competitions to find who's best
At growing big marrows and all the rest.
A silver cup to the victory grower
Is presented beneath a flowery bower.

Children's smiles at Judy and Punch
Then off to the tent for a home-made lunch.
There's a marching display by the local Armed Forces
But hurry - it's time for judging the horses.
The local vet is the main judge here
And the winner of the prize won last year.

Ice cream vans with queues abound
Little kiddies running around.
There's a prize for the scruffiest dog as well
Which is won by a small terrier dog named Belle.
Her eight-year-old owner is really quite pleased
And jumps up and down with Belle on a lead.

The stalls are busy with lots of trade.
They have toys and china and things home-made.
Cakes and jams and chutney too
All yummy things just made for you.
There are trees and plants in pots for sale
And hay for pet rabbits sold by the bale.

The sun has shone upon this scene
The fete upon the village green
Now only seen in rural parts
But remembered forever within our hearts.
The setting sun now calls us home
So back to our cottages we do roam.

Gaynor Evans, Bridgend

Forest Reflections

If I ever find that life is really stressful
And I would like to have some time to be alone
There is a special place I love to visit
It's the lovely forest park close by my home.

The birds sing in the tall trees in the springtime
And rooks caw loud and clear at nesting time
The rabbits scamper round amongst the soft grass
And busy bees the honeysuckle find.

Bluebell time for ever long remembered
In profusion there they grow from year to year
Their brilliant blue an endless stretch of colour
A sight the saddest heart would surely cheer.

The River Bann that flows so swiftly sea-ward
The stately swan that swims there in its tide
The cattle grazing in the luscious meadows
These memories in my heart will still abide.

The cuckoo's call is heard amid the stillness
The lark's sweet song soft in the evening air
The smell of pine trees in the gentle breezes
The perfume of the wild flowers everywhere.

The brilliant colour of the trees in autumn
Gold and brown and russet tan and red
The fallen leaves have made for me a carpet
Upon the paths my feet have chose to tread.

In wintertime with snow upon the branches
The trees look like a fairyland sublime
And berries red against the dazzling whiteness
God's provision for the birds in wintertime.

When we look around at God's creation
And see the wondrous things that He has made
We must thank Him for the special gift He gave us
When Jesus died on Calvary our souls to save.

Doreen E Todd, Portglenone

A Touch Of Beauty

Snowflakes fall in soft abundance
Clothing everything in white
Even places drab and dingy
Soon will look a wondrous sight

Roads and houses trees and hedges
All will share this winter coat
Suddenly the place looks different
Making it a scene of note

Heavy snowfall stops the traffic
The setting sun gleams on the frost
Lighted windows shine so brightly
The sounds of twilight hushed and lost

Looking through the open window
At the silent scene outside
Can't believe that it's so quiet
Like living things have gone to hide

Comes the dawn, now wet and windy
Normality is back again
All that beauty lost so quickly
Washed away by falling rain

Then the slush, the mess, the traffic
Reminding us that life goes on
That fleeting glimpse of nature's beauty
Has touched our hearts and now is gone.

Graham Thomas, Llanelli

First Footing

Here am I, once again, feeling the rub of age.
Woken by the pulse and beat
By the bellows and the bloody weir.
By life inside my shell
Riotous with its frantic spell.
Thro' this crumbling well, fresh waters swell.

On a whetstone fate has sharpened time
To cut December's anchor line.
Free the sun from its pouch of night
To charge the January light.
Stunning my senses, as I hear
The shrill cry of the new born year.
The first day's table has been laid
With plaits of breath and golden braids.
Upon this frosted cake of land
This layered earth of clay and sand.
Green tipped nibs of crocus pens
Stab the vellum lawn.
And all that winter scourged and tore
Is healing now - fields lie supine for the heavy plough.
Life dances in the womb of mare and ewe and sow.
Feather and fruit and fur and fern
Wait their eager turn.
As all about me bait is hung to catch the errant Spring.

In the distance, on the air
The exclamation of the bells,
Urging me, this New Year's Day
To live, to love again . . . to dare.

Philip J Mee, Kinmel Bay

Africa The Song Of Soul

A man like fire,
In the eternal mind,
No less the chant
Rips the eardrum,
And the gazelle
Grazing, cognisant
Of taste, chant and soul.

Heat, red and drums
Are one.
Like a jigsaw,
Fitting together.
A nation,
Not solemnly, yet
Joyfully
Smiles.

What is there?
The remnants of
Survival, famine?
No, it's not that.
But culture, soul and
Tradition override
Famines with
A mind laden with
Knowledge of life.

Suffering,
'Tis it right?
Shouldn't each
Person receive serenity each night?

But underneath the
Famine,
Lies a nation much stronger
Than we care to believe.
So unleash Africa!
A plethora of joy
On the soul.
Smiles never cease,
So that is the song.
Let our admiration for Africa
Be no longer prolonged.

Joshua Peters (12), Redbrook

Heritage

Scattered on the pavement,
tossed into the air,
scudding round street corners,
rubbish everywhere.
Litter hung like washing
caught on bush and tree,
bottles with sharp message
spiking grassy sea.
Armchairs slumped in lay-bys
blind to nature's scene,
bedsteads resting in canals
slowly turning green.
We make the world a dustbin,
failing to understand,
our heritage lies in the care
we take of sea and land.

Shirley Johnson, Falkirk

Summer Day Break

Infant day breaks through my window
with a ray of summer sunshine.
The night has sailed quietly slowly
sleepy like an ocean voyage.

My window looks like a Christmas decoration
dotted here and there with
Slithers of summer rain
glistening gleaming like a thousand fairy lights.

Warm and cosy am I tucked tightly
into my bed blankets.
Sleepily staring at my summer window
wondering do I dare emerge!

After careful consideration I curl up
tuck my nose under the bed blankets
and take great delight that it's Saturday morning!

Elizabeth Phillips Scott, High Valleyfield

All Sunshine

Night unto day, gone far away,
The sun coming here, to warm,
Some of the night, in our delight,
Will keep us from all
Earthly harm.
With the weather that's rough,
It can be so tough.
If we have to fathom our way.
Through the waves, wind, ever braves.
With nothing, but ere to say.
Gone far away, in alas of a dream.
All of partaken.
That alone, comes to mean,
We are all sunshine, whatever the rain
Fall away backwards.
To come sweeping again.
You know you've said it, then been told,
Forever in time.
That we never grow old.
Brighten our day, with each sunny ray,
Will all of tomorrows
Be the same as today.
I've known its source, from within its course.
And future will come, so along
But that of today,
Just come on away,
Bringing all sunshine, to beyond the dismay,
We will find, it knows of mind.
The water runs deep, will ever be kind.

Hugh Campbell, Lurgan

Pick Not

Pick not at another's scabs,
For you don't know,
What has caused their wounds
Nor how deep the blade was thrust,
Do not try to conceal their hurt,
Underneath bandages of lint,
Nor ignore their wellbeing,
For it was their very soul,
That has bled,
Yet they still walk,
Among the living,
Baring all the scars,
Of those who are dead,
Dress first your own sores,
So that they might,
Get time to heal.
Before the fate of others,
You try to reveal.

Pauline Uprichard, Lurgan

A Promise To My Dog

I will keep you, for as long as we live,
in my home and in my heart,
I don't care if you make a mess, growl at me, or pull
you are family too, we'll never move to a place where
pets are not allowed,
a palace would feel like a shack, without your furry presence,
so this is my promise, I make it to you, won't ever break it in two,
'cause I don't want you to end up like some others do,
with baited breath on death row, losing their lives,
'cause their owners broke their promise.

Samantha Forde, Magherafelt

The Thirteen Days Of Glory

They gathered at the Mission of San Antonio de Valero,
For freedom they would fight 'gainst any force.
One hundred and eighty-eight had to buy Sam Houston time -
And history recorded such a course.
Men like Davy Crockett and Jim Bowie were legendary people,
Their friends looked up to them with sincere pride.
Crockett's presentation rifle called 'Old Betsy' in his hand:
Jim Bowie's 'Iron Mistress' by his side.

Co-commanded by Jim Bowie and Colonel William Barrett Travis,
Brought together in this crumbling fortress' ruin.
The year was eighteen thirty-six and liberty at stake,
The battle for freedom now ensuing.
On Tuesday, February the twenty-third, the siege began at last;
Santa Anna's troops had rested long enough.
They had ridden from Laredo to San Antonio de Bexar,
Now found the Texan stronghold more than tough.

The legend of the Alamo began that very day,
So called because of cottonwood trees there.
Day two saw Travis send out his 'Death or Victory' appeal,
In his heart he had a solitary prayer.
Fate dealt a bitter blow that day to a man they all looked up to,
When a cannon slipped and fell from 'neath its rest.
Colonel Travis took command of the fortress on his own,
As the injury had crushed Jim Bowie's chest.

On the twenty-fifth of February - day three of the Alamo siege -
And earnest shots were fired from each side.
No help from Colonel Fannin, trapped at Goliad, forthcoming,
The Texan stronghold dug in with fearless pride.
There were Tennesseans, Texans - men from Louisiana too,
A Scotsman and an Irishman as well,
Men from old Kentucky and Virginia also fought in battle there,
For liberty and freedom 'midst the hell.

Further skirmishes ensued on day four of this great battle;
The weather cooled, and cold had now set in.
Santa Anna's red flag hovered - high on San Fernando's tower,
Indicating that 'No Quarter' would be given.
Day five was cold and windy, and the Mexicans exposed,
The fighting lulled beneath a dark grey sky.
A party of soldiers made a futile attempt,
To block the Alamo's precious water supply.

No help from Fannin yet arrived on the sixth day of the siege,
On the seventh, Travis sent out two more to try.
By the eighth, they were encircled by the massive Mexican force,
Perhaps the time had come for them to die.
But at midnight thirty-two more volunteers joined the mission,
Texans all to stand and fight for freedom's name.
On the ninth day came the build-up, of Santa Anna's army -
The Alamo would pay the price for fame.

On the third day of March, now the tenth day of this war,
No help from Colonel Fannin would ever come.
Captain Bonham made it through the ranks of Hell to bring the news;
The men of Alamo went grimly numb.
Colonel Travis drew his sword, made a line scored in the ground,
'Not death, but immortality!' he said;
All but one then crossed the line, for Jim Bowie still lay there,
So they carried him across the line instead.

On March the fourth, they were bombarded by the troops of seven-thousand,
Hour-after-hour from morn till night.
The North Wall was breached that day, tho' the men were fighting strong,
They were weakened under Santa Anna's might.
On the twelfth day of the siege - like the calm before the storm -
Things were quiet, only token shots took place.
The men of Alamo, holed up inside the crumbling mission,
Had fought boldly, never losing faith or face.

On Sunday March the sixth - the thirteenth day upon them,
They were roused at dawn by gunfire and cannon-blast.
'Midst the acrid stench of gunpowder and the clash of swords and lances,
Men were dying in the mission, thick and fast.
In three hours it was over - all bar the non combatants,
From whose lips the world learned of the story;
How the men of Alamo fought for liberty and freedom,
And the legend of the Thirteen Days of Glory.

When Sam Houston heard the news, his face turned deathly pale,
Men, who died there, were friends in times gone by.
Six weeks later he attacked, at the Battle of San Jacinto:
'Remember the Alamo!' was his war cry.
Santa Anna was defeated, his army dead and slaughtered -
The Texas boys gave them Hell in one go.
'Not death, but immortality' said Travis, not long past,
Nor defeat, but resurrection, for the men of Alamo.

Ian L Fyfe, East Kilbride

Brown

Brown is the colour of summer I say,
Brown is the colour of sand.
Brown is the hat on the old man's head
and brown is his wrinkled hand.

Brown is the colour that flows from the peat,
Brown is the colour of earth.
Brown is the spoonful of chocolate ice cream,
And brown is the oak tree's girth.

Brown is the colour of suntanned limbs,
Brown is the colour of chips.
Brown is the globule of Daddies sauce,
and brown too round children's lips.

Brown is the colour of summer I say,
Brown is the sparkling ale.
Brown is the colour of sausages hot,
And brown too the ice-cold pail.

Hilda Marjorie Wheeler, Llanon

To My Unborn Child

Soon I welcome you my little girl or boy
Though the waiting months seemed long,
They were always filled with joy.
I've watched your growth impatiently, your little life I've felt
Through movements slight, then stronger,
From the womb wherein you dwelt.
When you arrive in this world of ours, the season will be spring
The most wonderful time of any year for every living thing
But this year the birds will sing sweeter, the trees wear their brightest green
The sun's rays feel much warmer, and the flowers the most beautiful ever seen.
And now you too will blossom forth, but a richer flower from above.
Your earthly life will ever be guided, your years filled always with tender love.
I pray for the wisdom and the strength with which to guide your life
Along the path the future holds of happiness and strife
Someday I will tell you of the wondrous months we shared
Whilst your spirit and your body were being tenderly prepared.
But my eager heart awaits you with abundant love and joy
So welcome soon to this happy home, my baby girl or boy.

Glenys Allen, Pendine

Poppy Wars

There are some fields - not far away
Which are green or ploughed or given to hay
These are the fields of Northern France
Where assorted troops once made a stance
To stop a foe that sought more ground
By ignoring borders all around
The country in which they were born and bred
Their quest for land spread and spread
So battle was joined in World War One
With rifle, bayonet and big field gun
Soldiers fought and soldiers died
Mothers grieved and widows cried
Limbs went missing and blood was spilled
For four long years men were killed
Then came the day that peace returned
Had we from this carnage *really* learned?
In a place called Flanders poppies grew
Where shells had fallen and bullets flew
Here was a sign for new ways to start
A way to remember from within our heart
The war to end wars was in the past
No more fighting - the die was cast
We'd learned our lesson and learned it well
Conflict and fighting are a form of Hell . . .
Then politicians come to the fore
They talk, have ideas and we go to war
Maybe these talkers should go to the front
And watch poppies die for the ideals they hunt!

Alan R Coughlin, Limavady

Happy Anniversary

Two decades plus three have flown by,
A million plus poets have given voice,
Words that made us laugh, reflect or cry,
Offering the reader a myriad of choice.

But not without problem in earlier days,
When accusers made a vanity press claim,
We're Christian poets, nobody pays,
To spread God's word our primary aim.

For the business-minded opportunities call,
Purchasing anthologies at a reduced rate,
To be resold on the poet's very own stall,
For the entrepreneur successes wait.

For the God-inspired poet you give us a place,
To present God's word and expound on a theme,
A platform for sharing His love and His grace,
A useful tool in God's Holy scheme.

For the dreamer who wants to proclaim his love,
Or the activist with an axe to grind,
The enthusiast who wants to give the idle a shove,
In Forward Poetry your fill you will find.

We thank you all at the people's press,
For giving us a chance to shine,
To one and to all we say God bless,
Continue to do His work divine.

So hip hip hooray, we poets raise a glass,
To celebrate your anniversary this year,
Your books are outstanding, exceptional, first class,
Come one and all, give them a cheer.

Bill Hayles, Prestatyn

Flamenco

Downstage, a woman
steps into a pool of light
in a long, red dress.

She stands very still,
her body a liquid curve,
a gladiolus.

The music begins,
a soft chorus of clapping.
A strumming guitar

strikes percussive chords.
An old gypsy steps forward,
a ravaged beauty,

unleashing a line
of quavering, high-pitched notes
that resurrect love,

lost love lamented,
now recalled in bitterness.
Even the lemons

know the pain of love.
Milk-white palomas have felt
the heartbreak of loss.

The young dancer stirs,
head held proudly high, back straight
as a foxglove stem.

Growing impatient,
her feet tap a slow rhythm.
Hips sway, arms uncurl

svelte hands glide like birds.
Blood pulses feverishly.
The thrumming quickens.

The dancer's red skirts
swirl like the wings of a bird,
as she turns and turns

her scented body
to the frenzied rhythm of
the old gypsy's song.

A flower, ablaze,
her scarlet skirts spread like wings.
Her passion reaches

its flurried climax.
Harsh paroxysmic music
shudders to a halt.

Arms upcurled, lyre-like,
she stands, sweat beading her brow,
back taut as a bow,

her proud breast heaving.
Abruptly the performers
both turn on their heels

and depart the stage,
in opposite directions,
to roars of 'Ole!'

Norman Bissett, Edinburgh

No 22: Craigowl

Everybody on the bus is silent - they've all turned out
'cause these days solitude is what it's all about
apart from the muted growl of early-morning traffic noise
the only sound comes from a baby, laughing at his plastic toys

All the passengers are dead quiet - not a soul dares speak
perhaps they're all depressed at the thought of another week
they're more motionless than mannequins in a shop
responding only to the bell that signals the next stop

Each rider remains hushed - engrossed in their paper or iPod
in my head I laugh, thinking of a cattle prod
they all look so unhappy - their faces are so grim
maybe the CCTV camera is what inhibits them

But I'm desperate to fit in - not a single word do I say
I gaze out the dirty window, my face carefully turned away
until at last my stop is signalled by a cheery chime
as I alight the baby waves at me, laughing one last time.

Kathy McLemore, Dundee

The Mist

The mist hung on the mountain
The hunter in his hide
His trusty dog beside him
Both hidden, out of sight.

At dawn the mist was shifting
Swirling and moving about
The partridge was feeding
Unaware of man or hound.

The dog went out a-hunting
Slowly quartering the ground
The hunter he was watching
For anything moving around.

The dog stood still and pointed
The hunter's gun went up
The partridge rose and cartwheeled
The hunter fired a shot.

The partridge's flight was over
The hound went to retrieve
The sun had revealed its cover
The mist, the mist, had eased.

James Roland Sterritt, Markethill

For Rebecca

Some strive forever for their life's gold, their treasure
Are they satisfied with the venture?
I tell now, I have found my rock
My only and ever anchor.

A delicate flower, a beauty beyond compare
Can, deep within the soul, make stir
The birds of a thousand families flock
Through my heart the open air.

Padraig Donnelly, Keady

The Room

Discarded wrappers, the only remnant
Of a room once filled with
Characteristic brilliance.

Voices distinguished not
As they all collapsed into
One, long murmuring,
But one.

That voice that once held in place
And founded the structure, now gone.
In its wake,
In subtle disguise
Discarded wrappers.

Empty and unstructured now,
The room without its brilliance.
The unknown,
The discarded
And closed.

Anne Taggart, Armagh

My Chosen Path

What do I seek in this world of ours
A chance to redeem myself in the midst of the almighty power
Whom presides over the universe of Heaven and Earth
Which time alone cannot prove my worth.
I seek neither fortune nor fame
Only to serve in His holy name!
The spiritual aspect of my soul is strong
Strong enough to conquer my fears for yesterday's gone.
No man shall hinder my God-given task
With hope and courage I shall seek my chosen path
No longer blinded by false beliefs
For my faith in He has never ceased
Such glorious years now lie ahead
As all life's uncertainties have fled
Guided and protected by His eternal love
He forgiveth all beneath the sun.

Gwyneth E Scott, Colwyn Bay

Autumn Glory

The beautiful colours of autumn
Can make our hearts pound with delight
The colours all blend in their splendour
The yellows and orange so bright
The yellow portrays her true beauty
We value the seasonal glow -
And watch as the leaves tumble downwards
When strong autumn winds start to blow
They make such a wonderful carpet -
A marvellous pattern quite rare
That rustles and glows in its beauty
And leaves the grey trees in despair.
A season so full of enjoyment
Can stir up the artist within -
And bring it to life on a canvas
In style that much pleasure can bring.
All seasons can give us great pleasure,
They vary in colours untold,
But autumn stands out as the grandest
And thrills us with colours so bold.
The colours of autumn enchant us,
They're there for the whole world to share
When days of dark sadness surround us
The memories lift our despair.

Glenys B Moses, Sennybridge

Left To Bloom

The house is long gone, no family left alive,
The old forgotten garden struggles to survive.
Raspberries up against the shed
Help to keep the wild birds fed.
Big pink roses swaying to and fro
Drop soft petals along the floor,
Laying in the sun they scent the breeze
That whispers gently through the trees.
A thrush cracks snails on a big grey stone.
A forgotten spade stands alone
Stuck in the earth, at a crazy angle,
And covered in a Bindweed tangle.
Weeds grow where vegetables stood,
The glasshouse, just a pile of glass and wood.
Long grass covers the old stone path,
And brambles hide an ancient bath
Used to store water years ago
Now on its side by the old shed door.
As the garden becomes more overgrown,
Nature starts to reclaim its own
Hiding man's handiwork all too soon.
Only the roses will be left to bloom
Dropping soft petals along the floor
As the breeze blows them to and fro.

Haidee Williams, Gorseinon

The 17th Flotilla

Down in Portsmouth Harbour,
Around November time,
You'll see old sailors meeting,
Their eyes with friendship shine.

Some are wobbly on their pins,
Some faces lined with care.
But deep within these ageing hearts,
The spirit still is there.

Fifty years and more ago
They sailed the stormy sea,
Through ice and gale and tumult,
To make it safe for you and me.

Young at heart and innocent,
They were called to fight the foe.
Filled with trepidation,
But still so proud to go.

Time has taken quite a toll,
Some have crossed the bar.
But those that live remember,
And raise their glasses to Jack Tar.

They are the 17th Flotilla
And still they're young at heart.
As I listen to their stories,
I am proud to be a part.

Peggy Howe, St Asaph

Ganarew Summer

So, now it's summer -
the brilliant daffodils reduced to dying leaves
the May trees' snowy petals dropped and gone,
the bluebells nearly over,
the delicate lace of early weeping willow
now a full-grown flood of tears,
the tree outside my window
once more blocks the building opposite from view
with its glorious copper colour;
so many shades of green on the wooded hills.
Some parts are already suffering from drought
but we had rain - enough to wet the ground
revive the thirsty plants, still convalescing
after the blistering winter frosts.
Across the way bright buttercups
patch the grass with yellow
amidst the intermittent white of daisies,
Yesterday a neighbour heard a cuckoo
and everywhere the birdsong's a delight.

I've been here now through autumn,
wild, freezing winter and high-coloured spring,
but this is my first May in Ganarew.

Jacqui Fogwill, Ganarew

My Mum

My mum done everything
cooking, cleaning etc.
she looked after us when we were ill
even though we drived her crazy
she still loved us
now that she is gone
to a better place
our lives seem empty and bare
but we must be strong
and plonder on
even though it's hard
our mum knew she was super mum
who could do anything
in our hearts we know that
this is the only way to say goodbye
we will always love you Mum
and you will be well missed
goodbye Mum hope you are
now happy where you are.

Rose Innes, South Carbrain

Dumfries Summer Holidays

Summertime is here at last
School is out
Six weeks fun and play
Everything is okay
I liked to fish
In the river with
Salmon, trout and eels about
So down to the river I go
And see the water flow
And off to the sea it will go
Now along the bank I will walk
And cast my line out
To catch a fish no doubt
Now I'll try again
And yes it's not in vain
I reel it in on the bank
My lovely river it's you I thank
I'll have this trout for tea tonight
It will be a sheer delight.

Gordon Forbes, Dumfries

Pebble Shoreline

I've worn the rhythms of the sea,
amid the anvil clash of waves.
I've watched white fists,
buff the shore,
heard pebbles wail
for squatter's rights;
watched as they decamp
in stridulated backwash,
to the euphony of clinks and
jangled clunks of hobnailed
soldiers on parade.

I've smelt kale and bladder wrack,
inhaled charged ozone ions,
sampled the lingered taste of sand
and thermos coffee on my tongue.
Felt the wind smart my eyes,
tear at clothes and dishevel hair,
before billowing empty deckchairs
with D-shaped spinnakers,
just for fun, and forcing yellow
poppies to touch their toes.

I've seen speckled pebbles as brown as pecan nuts,
onion soup, tobacco spit, exchange
cautious glances, before this brine-powered petulance
tosses them, head and tail, into a long shore drift . . .

It has set hapless tongues clicking and clinking
in agitated motion about yesterday's
discarded broken toys: of tumbled razor shells,
dead limpet crabs, desiccated starfish,
causing fresh alarm, as the wilful sea child seeks
new play fellows on the shingled shore.

John Greeves, Magor

Forsaken

In the hinterland
where the crisp packets
rustle in the night wind
in the underpasses
the rundown parts of town

There is a kind of beauty here
strange off-kilter
where the outsider people roam
among the nettles and weeds
and broken bottles

Desolation land
rotting decaying
and boarded up
the crumbling factories
the sad canal
an empty shopping mall
rusting long abandoned railway lines

At the edge
on the periphery
car parks full of sea gulls
impersonal motels
and dingy cafés
at times
a feral menace in the air

Passing through
on the motorways
belonging nowhere
lonely outside it all
but strangely free

Julian Ronay, Aviemore

Earth In June

Carving beauty from nothing
the saints sway the wind
blooming birds of angelic creed
stand by in tranquil speed

Fresh feet under the sun
croaking doves praise
I'm under wings of love
Heaven's in my gaze

Misty morning rain
as the soil drains
for fresh fields
the hay bails

As evening turns
and summer stays
new days mourn
play me Earth's song.

Patricia Donaghy, Dungannon

Summer Delights

Brightly coloured boats, floating gently in the sea's breeze
Children's laughter fills the air
Ice cream cones everywhere
The smell of hot dogs, doughnuts and candyfloss
Filters softly through the air.

Bikinis, swimsuits, trunks galore!
Donkeys trotting up the shore
The funfair, winning teddies, goldfish, haunted house rides
Helter-skelters, merry-go-rounds . . .

Rock, sugar dummies, kiss me quick hats,
Suntan lotion, brightly coloured buckets and spades . . .

Grannies, grandads with their cauliflowers heads,
Mums dishing out sandwiches, lemonade, cake . . .
Dads snapping photographs
Everyone enjoying summer's delights!

Suzanne Swift, Betws-y-Rhos

Suicide Bombers

Most murderous, destructive these
Mad folk are victims too,
Their ignorance exploited, they
Quite simply have no clue
That they are pawns in other's plots
Against what's good and true.

For violence stirs up violence and
Rejects the better way
That fosters understanding love
By bringing into play
A reconciling of all aims -
Escape from hatred's sway.

Offence is often mutual yet
It needs to be addressed
And then it must be listened to
And ways and means assessed
For finding new solutions to
Change foe to honoured guest.

Peter Spurgin, Edinburgh

Scooby

My little angel sleep tight,
Never will I see your face again in the morning light.
You are now at Heaven's door,
Never have I missed someone like you before,
Can't believe you are lying in that cold grave,
When really you should be basking in your heat wave,
Your little home is empty now,
My room feels cold somehow,
Scooby was your name,
You have lit in me an eternal flame,
May this flame lead you now to the locust laden plain,
Even though my heart is bleeding with pain,
But you don't have to suffer anymore,
As God opens His Heavenly door,
My little angel sleep tight,
Don't let the Bugbeds ever bite . . .

Isla Demuth, Raglan

My Prayer

Place on my head your holy hand
Oh dear Jesus Son of Man,
Give Thy blessing to all alike
As only You dear Lord, can.
The way You renounced all sin,
I'd like to be good, as You were
To love all my fellow kin.
Make me as gentle as Yourself
Lead those that have gone astray,
And comfort all those that do mourn
And strengthen their will today.
Give me a better heart each day
And the grace and means to live,
So all others through me will find
God's love He does freely give.

Jesus Christ the saviour of men
I thank you dear Lord, Amen.

Clifford Jones, Bontnewydd

Reboot Surprise

You'd never think that this will all be gone
That Lisdoonvarna stories will be rare.
This festival of booze and sex and song
Will disappear like rain in your red hair.

She pins me with that enigmatic smile
And squats beside me, where she cups her chin
In alabaster hand and all the while
Her sparkling eyes glow rivalry to skin.

'Don't do it to me,' is her strange riposte.
And I'm as flummoxed as I was back then,
But now I know to ask what? Not so lost.
''Bout time,' she grins and grabs my hand, laughs, 'Men!
Now if you will just come where you are led,
I guarantee you too will flame bright red.'

Perry McDaid, Derry

Forgotten Friends

When I was young my dearest friend
Did everything with me
She only lived across the road
And often came for tea
We went to school together
And did everything the same
She was almost like my twin
Except, she had a different name
My family grew to love her
And we stayed like that for years
Till the time we started boyfriends
It all ended up in tears
We both fell for the same fellow
For he hadn't got a twin
We were eaten up with jealousy
And only one could win
So all those years of friendship
Just emptied like a drain
Then the stupid fellow left us
But we were never friends again.

June Mary Davies, Cardiff

Remembrance

So many years on . . . And the memories fade . . .
Of the horrors of war and the sacrifice made
The price that was paid . . . with the blood and the tears
Those lives now forgotten . . . with the passing of years
When victory came with its flag waving joys
When we cheered and applauded . . . our brave men and boys
What triumph and glory did victory bring . . .
To the thousands who died for their country and king?
And . . . for those who still grieve for a special loved one
What comfort for them . . . more than 90 years on
So pause for a moment . . . remember them well . . .
The poppies still flutter . . . and rest where they fell.

Ann Thomas, Maesteg

Memories

With wistful longing of delight,
Was once a daydream through the night
Where languid ripples seemed to stir
Infectious loving as of her.

The time no longer hurries on,
All is still, the moment gone,
Where reeds move softly at a stroke,
Electric blue in buttoned cloak.

Into the stillness there did come,
Along its banks the bees do hum,
How can they melt into the light,
Or fall asleep when it is night.

I ponder onward at a glance,
I see the spritely moonbeams dance,
On pointed toes they dart about,
And shafts of light send sparks way out.

Sweet music doth it be for me,
To calm my breast so carefully,
Alone in hope it is revived,
The point it is when I'm alive.

To drought there comes with so much thirst,
Can it be, that I am cursed,
About me sings the wooded glade,
Sweet music as has 'ere been made.
With notes so perfect to my ear,
Like harpists' strings the heart do tear.

When I am old and cannot see,
Around about me pleasantly,
Will memories be so fresh and bright,
So perfectly I shall see at night.

So therefore let it all be said,
That all is love when we are dead,
To harbour longingly aside,

Never cast upon the tide,
Of life's clear moments when alive,
That sad in dying we forget,
Together do our hearts confess.

Hannah R Hall

Optimism

I look at my garden at this time of year,
The thought springs to mind
I'm so glad to be here,
It's not just the beauty I stand and survey,
The feelings flowers conjure
Mean much more to me.
They battle the elements, surprise and survive,
Come back every year,
Saying, 'Look I'm alive,'
They give hope for the future
And seemingly call
'Please smile and be happy
We're here for you all.'
Bad weather, bad health, hard up or alone,
The sight of these stalwarts
Urge you to go on.
No matter the setbacks
Carry on, persevere
Just look at the flowers
Be glad that you're here.

Anne Aitchison, Larbert

Untitled

Summer is here and the sky is so blue
Down at the shore what a wonderful view
The beach is busy with lots of people around
Children playing in the sand, what a lovely sound
Gulls swoop down looking for food
Everyone seems in such a good mood
Swimming in the sea,
Having lots of fun and
The beach is ideal for going for a run
Everything changes when the sun comes out
People are smiling, more contented without a doubt
So please winter don't be in a hurry to appear as
We live in hope it will not be like the one last year.

Oira Newman, Erskine

Our City Of Culture
Derry/Londonderry 2013

A City of Culture! Now what does that mean?
A beautiful place crying out to be seen.
A city of bridges, three in all,
A millennium theatre, and a famous guildhall.

An ancient cathedral, with a spire held high,
Lights up like a beacon, in the evening sky.
A city of music, with talent so great,
Hotels and restaurants, famous walls, bishop gate.

We have Free Derry Corner and a diamond so grand,
Pubs, clubs and cafes the length of the strand.
An airport, a hospital, on the east of the Foyle,
Seamus Heaney, Joe Lock, Nadine and Liam Coyle.

To our City of Culture I wish health and wealth,
But don't just take my word!
Come see for yourself.

Frances Meenan, Brigade

Boundry Drawn

So sit in gloom an empty room
Opposed so thought heart hurt wrought
Sweeps life until the cows come back
Again that fire buds moving scene
Into your leaving station keen
Or was it not your era star then
Deliver ideals change for what
Weak strong taste reality haste
Comfort no enter gamble woe
Adults of world plunge gold
Glad on cards compete the heat
Not fixed or listed hard to beat
Sprung from nowhere hit and run
Mature like wine oh summer rain
Lightly dry room collar high
Those years and wrinkles blend
A flight of fancy promised oh
Belated in your confines pile
And piper tune gifted pool
Why love left early over soon
Railing gates frees avenues.

Malachy Trainor, Armagh

A Pleasant Day Out

'Good morning Megan. Where are we going on this beautiful day?'
'We are going to the farm,' Megan answered, 'to see the lambs at play.
I love to watch them as they jump up high,
It's such a pity that, one day, they may be in someone's pie.'

'Oh, why did you have to say that?' said Mair, with a sharp retort.
'Mam's only just come back from the shops, where lamb chops she bought,'
'That's nothing,' replied Megan, with a mischievous smile,
'Did you know that a chicken, with its head chopped off, can run about for a while?'

'Oh shut up,' said Mair, with a greenish look to her face,
'Let us to the farm house have a race.'
It was Gwen, who asked if there were any jobs that day
So they fed the chickens and collected the eggs before they went on their way.

They said goodbye to the farmer, who was covering some tools with grease,
Passed by the pond with its ducks and its geese;
They saw the new piglets, seven in all,
Watched the sheep scrambling through the gap in the wall.

The lambs jumped high with apparent glee
While seagulls flew above well away from the sea
The cows grazed lazily, some chewing the cud
While some horses nearby, were galloping through mud.

The trees were in blossom, the grass was growing strong,
Time for an early cut, before it grew too long,
Flowers were in the hedgerow, the first hatchlings were in the nest,
The new season's insects were becoming a pest.

'Where are we going next?' asked Megan of her sisters both,
'I would go to the old quarry,' said Megan, 'but to do so, nowadays I am loath,
The rubbish that has been dumped is a real disgrace,
Destroying most of the wild flowers and shrubs which once made it an attractive place.'

Missing the quarry, they went through the woods, paddled in the stream for a while,
Before crossing the bridge, then climbing the stile,
They followed the path to the church and the pub,
When Mair asked, 'Isn't it time for a Coke and some grub?'

'Yuk,' said Gwen, 'Why do you use the word 'grub' instead of food?
It's a word which is so crude.'
'OK we'll have some food as well,' replied Mair with a grin,
As, laughing, to the church graveyard, they went in.

Soon, however, they silent became,
As they looked at some gravestones with many a name.
Of coalminers of the same families who had died from a pit explosion on the same day
And of family members who had died of deathly diseases sometimes within a few days.
'I'm glad we have vaccinations and immunisations nowadays,' said Gwen,
'It must have been terrible to have such diseases then.'

'Come on,' said Megan, 'Cheer up. Let's get some strawberries and cream at the fair,'
'But no meat pies,' said Mair with a glare.
'Not today,' said the others.

The fair was in the town park and the strawberries were a delight
After which, the sisters went on the swings to reach a great height.
Then to the town putting green and watching bowls and tennis, money all spent,
Finally, after a good day, they homeward went.

Malcolm Coles, Rumney

Spring In The Park

Gladdening sun and a songful heaven,
Mirroring - shallows as bright as glass,
Daffodils flaunting their crown - gold petals,
Regally bowing as soft winds pass,
You in the park by the shining river,
Running to me over daisied grass.

Here I'll return in the songless winter,
Facing the gloom of a year grown old,
Mourningly gazing on leafless branches,
Grasses withered and paths frost - cold,
Picturing you and the hope - bright springtime,
Child with the hair of sun - glint gold.

Hair gold - silver and soft as April,
Breezes glowing with willow - sighs,
Beautiful girl with the silken lashes,
Ivory girl with the jewel - bright eyes,
You I'll recall when I dream of leaf-buds,
Daffodil meadows and singing skies.

Eileen-Margaret Kidd, Peebles

Budge's Day Out

There's a Pembrokeshire coast town called Tenby
That's famous for seagulls and fudge
And Mister and Missus Finsb'ry
Went there with their sheepdog, named Budge

A lolloping great hound was Budge
All gleaming fangs, slav'ring jaws
With a huge shiny brass studded collar
And thick, hairy, mammoth-sized paws!

Ma moaned that t'beach was too crowded
'Rotten sunbathers ruin t'view!'
'All lyin' an' fryin', row 'pon row
A flamin' human barbeque!'

Pa read notices on t'lamp post
'See these 'ere signs, our Peg?'
'One's summat 'bout fine for dog foulin''
Budge looked up an' raised 'is 'ind leg!

'T' other one says,' Pa continued
'No dogs on beach, May t' September!'
'That's discrimination!' Ma fumed
'Calm down,' Pa said, 'don't lose your temper!'

So they strolled along packed Esplanade
And it was plain 'ow Budge got 'is name
One looked at t'beast an' crowd parted
Just like Red Sea o' Moses fame!

Pa was practic'ly dragged down t'street
For Budge, a small morsel he'd spied
There was young boy with ice cream in 'and
An' Budge slobbered, 'is jaws gaping wide

Little lad's mum was quite overcome
From 'er throat rose a piercin' scream
Budge slipped 'is leash, bounded up t'young lad
An' with mighty gulp . . . swallered ice cream!

With a glare like Medusa o'legend
Lad's mum stood 'er 'ands on 'er 'ips
And watched son bawl 'is eyes out
As Budge sat lickin' 'is lips

Pa Finsb'ry caught up with t'hound
An' slipped lead back on 'is collar
Mum pulled 'er boy away quickly
An' wrapped arms round t'little fellar

I'm t . . . terribly sorry!' Pa panted
''Ave no f . . . fear for thee son
Budge wouldn't 'arm' air on 'is 'ead
He's a veggy-tary-un!'

'A likely story!' she scoffed
'He's almost as big as an 'orse!
I reckon ice cream's just for starters
An' my boy's to be main course!'

'Stuff an' nonsense!' Ma Findb'ry shouted
'Just you listen 'ere, young woman!
It's true, all my 'usband 'as told thee
Aye, we know our Budge is a rum un!'

'He grew up with pigs on Dad's farm
An' I tell thee no word of a lie
Budge 'asn't touched meat since the day
'is best friend was put in a pie!'

Young mum seemed to ponder a while
'That's as maybe,' she answered
'Though a dog that gobbles boy's treat
Is quite impolite an' bad mannered!'

'Oh woe is me!' came a loud cry
Which caught 'ole street's attention
Ice cream man in 'is white van was pacin'
An' tearing at 'air in frustration.

Ma Frinsb'ry asked in concern
'What on Earth's t'matter with thee?'
'I've lost m'gold ring!' man wailed
'T'wife's sure to crucify me!'

Budge nudged Pa's leg with 'is snout
Displayin' wide dazzling grin
An' there, gleamin' bright round one fang
Sat ice cream man's precious gold ring!

'Oh my goodness!' lad's mum gasped
'Ain't that just simply amazin'?
Why, if dog 'adn't scoffed ice cream
Boy could 'ave choked on t'ring!'

She knelt down and patted t'hound
'Oh, what a hero!' she said
Then gave Budge big kiss on 'is snout
An' is face turned bright shade o' red!

'T'ring must've slipped off finger!'
Ice cream man exclaimed with a grin
'That'll be diet's to blame
It's not tight fit, now I'm thin'

'I wonder if Budge knew?' Pa pondered
'An' d'lib'rately made interception?
Some say dogs 'ave sixth sense
Sort o' extra sens'ry perception!'

And so handshakes and goodbyes were exchanged
An' free replacement ice cream for t'lad
'There's summat I'm wond'ring,' 'is mum said
'Why's Budge not on t'farm with your dad?'

'Poor Daddy just disappeared'
Ma Finsb'ry replied with a sigh
'Though it's odd 'ow, cleaning pig sty
We found Dad's false teeth an' glass eye!'

Lad's mum's jaw hit t'floor
There were thoughts she 'ardly dared think
She looked down at Budge with suspicion
An' Budge looked up at 'er with a wink!

Anthony G L Kent, Haverfordwest

There's Life After Depression

I put on a brave face,
Inwardly I'm shaking,
A mask for the human race,
Can't they see I'm faking?

I'm in a black hole,
There's no light,
I have no role,
No strength to fight.

I am *feeling* again!
A ray of hope,
A helping hand then,
I have clasped the rope.

Patricia Bannister, Denbigh

Highland Summer

Summer has come to the Highlands
And has cast its magic spell -
Memories fade of cold, dark days
And of winter rains that fell.

There is a softness in the air -
The views breathtaking, vast.
The grandeur of each mountain range
Can they ever be surpassed?

The tranquil lochs that sooth and calm,
And, mirror-like, reflect the scene,
With tiny ripples on each edge
And islands strewn out in between.

A knot of deer on distant hills -
A watchful eagle sweeping low -
And black-faced sheep that wander free
Oft with a lamb or two in tow.

Highland cattle, sturdy, strong,
Quietly watch as you go by -
The eerie, distant clacking noise
That is the capercaillie's cry.

The many, merry tumbling streams
Winding their way towards the sea -
A movement on some distant hill,
A hare? A fox? Too far to see.

The purple carpet of the heather
Is mixed with shades of brown and green
And everything is calm and still
In this so lovely Highland scene.

The quietness found in wooded glens
Blocks out all thought of urban stress -
You feel your spirits start to rise
And painful worries seem far less.

Joyce Hockley, Stirling

Nonagenarian

Slumped in her seat
She lies oblivious,
Body purple-patched
And ice-floe cold
Slipping forward
No longer at one
With the contours of the chair,
Mouth pouting
Hands drooping
In muscle-sagging sleep.

Eyes remain closed
Impervious to touch of hand
Or whisper of voice -
Just a slight restlessness
Of the foot
In an unconscious effort
To remain balanced,
In control
No sound
No reaction
Just a gentle breathing
Perpetuating a private world
With a clear *no entry* sign.

Audrey Poole, Penarth

Reality

Where is reality
Amid such fantasies,
The existing present
A frustrating fatality,
The fleeting shades of recall
Amongst the unreal presiding state
With no voice to call for help,
Lost, not understanding
This unkind fate.
Deep in the past these memories
Reduced to demented rambles
Of lives that no longer exist,
Who listens? You? You? Few.
Like ghosts reclining
In a wheelchair queue
They sit and stare
Vacant, food stained unaware,
Attended by one? Perhaps!
They are the heroes
Who struggle on unsupported
By those who have
Shut out this world,
Leaving the living dead
To fade away from this cruel stage.
They take so many years,
Years of no future
Deprived of a deserved old age.

Colin Burnell, Cardiff

The Queen's Sausage

Read all about it
today it's front page news
let's ask the Prince of Wales
just what now are his views
saying mam she was just having
a spot of Sunday lunch
the staff were in a panic
she didn't get a munch

Like old Victoria
the Queen was not amused
saying have you seen my sausage
Prince Philip was confused
Camilla was dumbfounded
saying Charles love did you see
what happened to the sausage
it surely wasn't me

Scotland Yard came calling
and searched the banquet hall
the people were alarmed
the mayor he did recall
saying I don't know who did it
it's been almost an hour
I hope they catch the blighter
and lock them in the tower

Someone stole a sausage
from Her Majesty the Queen
outrageous and alarming
no one could have ever seen
a corgi under the table
enjoying a free lunch
it's a shame about the Queen
she didn't get a munch

The Queen had dropped her sausage
on the royal floor
it was snaffled by a corgi
begging her for more
the staff they were assembled
but not one of them could tell
where it went that night
while the butler gave them hell

It's a sad sad story
but if you've just got one
look out for a corgi
going on the run
the staff they were astounded
do you really think it's fun
chasing a hungry mutt
who the deed has done

Never drop your sausage
while sitting at the table
keep it on your plate
if you're surely able
fate will surely guide you
when you're having lunch
don't let the dog distract you
then maybe you'll get a munch.

James Peace, Glenrothes

The Day Of The Funeral

The eyes of the street are closed,
Hidden behind drawn curtains
That shroud each lifeless window.
Grieving friends and relatives gather,
Mouthing useless platitudes.
The buzz of conversation ebbs and flows
Over and around the bereaved,
Who sit in awful isolation,
Red-eyed, unseeing, numb with shock.
'Didn't she look lovely in the coffin,'
Someone says to nobody in particular.
Nodding heads greeted this observation.
'Her hair looked nice,' a voice replied,
'Had a perm last week she did.'
Nimble fingers make more sandwiches -
Just in case,
And the laden sideboard creaks in protest.
The house is awash with cups of tea.

Patricia McKenna, Pontypridd

Memories Of Provence

Pleasures of purple bloomed for miles and miles
Where fields of lavandula's fragrant flowers
Perfumed the air with their distinctive scent
That is intensified by sudden showers.

A heat mist hovered over glassy pools
As pink flamingos, flushed with morning sun,
Outshone the spindly herons, snowy-plumed,
And mingled their reflections one for one.

Beneath a canopy of tangled reeds
The polished lily leaves like floating plaques
Made stepping-stones on ponds of dappled green
For those amphibious, bug-eyed jumping jacks.

There is a place called Fontaine-de-Vaucluse;
Untouched by time, it tempted us to stay
To watch the turning of the water wheel
And feel the rushing river's icy spray.

I crossed the old stone bridge and wished that I
Could stay forever in this state of bliss,
Alighting from life's hectic carousel
To find a peaceful haven such as this.

Celia G Thomas, Aberdare

Life History

You're born as a baby infant then child going to school
The place to get education though some act the fool
When leaving you grow up and find work to do
And trying earn for a living by doing something useful too
Some go to different jobs and get around to live in their day
Others stick to one in their home and rather not move away
You can get married and have a family of your own
Or stay single if you want to be left alone

Forty you're the slip of a lad or lass when life has begun
Mature but still young enough to have a bit of fun
Could be proud grandparents as a proud mam and dad
To see your child's baby must make your heart glad
Fifty you'll feel half a century has gone
That will creep in and let later years roll on
Sixty plus you'll be retired for good
Can do things as you please to suit your mood.

There could be a four generation when joy is tripled for you
And like to get a photo that would be so lovely too
Seventy you're at a three score and ten
With many happy memories to think of now and then
Eighty you've lived forty years over again
Coming to the end of a long memory lane
Ninety to over a hundred could maybe lose your mind
Almost ready to leave a wonderful world behind.

Susan Kelly, Nairn

Been Too Long Going Short

Been standing rigid
Deeply cold
Sociably frigid
Nothing has a hold
Leaving the surface
Sinking low
Ain't no place
You wanna know
Been too long
Going short again
The darkness strong
Vision does strain
All uphill
A high nowhere
Standing still
With nothing to spare
There's so many places
All unsure
With many faces
Born to endure
An endless echo
Of what used to be
A friend turned foe
You couldn't see
Time is reckless
Until it's spent
Your budgeting feckless
Life's last breath the rent
A taken for granted future
In a youthful whirlwind of thought
Succumbs to fate the butcher
Where all that's left is to rot
Don't think too hard
On things that matter
But don't disregard
What can shatter
Don't turn away
From the fear
Learn to stay
See out every year
Written thousands of lines
None of which matter
That life and its designs
Have helped to shatter
There's no special cases
In common one thing the same

Within all the many races
Our last breath's the end game
There's many a misfortune
That can befall you
An' many a full moon
That'll leave you feeling blue
There's no right an' wrong
But judged you'll be
Many strains that are strong
Await for you an' me
The lines ain't uplifting
As the years fade
Thoughts continue drifting
To last forever nothing's made
Don't deliberate
Over nowt
It will create
Even more doubt
For what you see
Is a crash in progress
An' you an' me
Everyone's a victim, I guess.

Mark Tough, Castle Douglas

The Cat And The Cream

I'm a cat. I'm a cat.
A big fat cat.
Money is my game.
I'm an awfully nice guy
But very, very shy
So I won't reveal my name.
Life is rather sunny
Now I've got a lot of money
I'm not giving any of it back
It has left this isle of beauty
So attracts no tax or duty
And you can osculate my posterior.

John McKibbin, Baillieston

The Muse

If I were a painter,
My muse you would be,
Your image to capture,
For all the world to see.

Your image, your being,
Your sense of true self,
There to remain forever,
Framed upon my highest shelf.

All eyes gazing up at you,
There to admire,
Up close, at a distance,
But never straying far.

I'd whisper to you,
As you look out at me,
To look upon your image,
For all eternity.

Rebecca Isted, Cardiff

Every Picture Tells A Story

Art is a form of language pictures from one's mind
Telling people stories they otherwise couldn't find

Putting brush to canvas relaying to what is seen
It's another way of writing I think you will agree

Pictures telling stories of present and of past
Art's evidence of patience can't be completed fast

Some artists are ingenious others seem insane
When paint is brushed on canvas a message is conveyed

Using every detail possible their story it is told
Some believe in art's message and frame their art in gold.

Stephen Maslen, Newport

The Fairy Thorn

Old and gnarled, it clawed its way
Out through the wall beside the church
With roots sunk deep in rich, dark clay
Besides those souls who'd seen its birth.
It started up towards the sun
But soon its trunk began to bow
Then locals, believing in its powers,
Built up a plinth to help it grow.
Young lads lay along the trunk
And fantasised about its powers
The shiny patches worn there
Bore witness to those innocent hours.
I was one who lay and dreamed,
Each dream the previous one surpassed.
Youth's callow hopes could not conceive
How quickly sixty years would pass!
The tree still stands and casts its spell
Conjuring up those dreams and vows
Familiar faces drift through my mind
Forever framed in those magic boughs.

Fred McIlmoyle, Bangor

Angel

I am a tiny angel who follows you about,
I sit on your shoulder when you are out,
I sit on the bus with you, I sit in your car,
I know where you're going, and that's not so far,
And when you talk to me,
I hear what you say,
If there's a bad word spoken, then, I fly away.

Isobel Buchanan, Ayr

Seasons

It was winter when I saw his feet -
white at centre; black at their edge -
made bitter by that relentless frost.
On Henry Street, he rocked, defiant,
but hope, if ever there, was surely lost.

The red of Cruises Street is too enclosed,
even in early spring when the air is fresh;
just as fresh, wafts the scent of bread.
Beset by that aroma, he held a sign -
'I am hungry. Help me,' it read.

It can be just as cold in the summer
out on The Promenade off the Strand,
where, deaf to the laughter, a mother
gives the only thing she has, in one
silent and brief everlasting rupture.

Only leaves stain the ground in Kildare's
most touted village come autumn,
where none need worry about
unwanted calls for investment from
the nation's most familiar quorum.

Each season brings me down to the
South Mall, where the suits are worn.
Behind protected buildings, where
thieves count taxes, lie those overlooked
by charity, being too close to home.

James O'Sullivan, Cork

A Beautiful Season

Summer cheers everyone, smiles and joy abound
People lovingly tending gardens
Bustling activities prevail all around.

Daylight never seems to end
It's rarely dark at all
Two hours after midnight
Birds are beginning their calls

Broken shells litter the ground
Nests of varying sizes are to be found
A pigeon returns with food for her young
The skill of our feathered friends
Never fails to astound.

Late lambs skip and leap
Exercise over, they return to Mum
To rest or sleep
One stands precariously on Mother's back
His balance appears stable
He's obviously perfected the art!

Calves are more timid
Considering their size
Their varying colours
Never fail to surprise.

Foals run after mothers
Sometimes pausing for a drink
Their thirst satisfied
It's time for more high jinks!

We wish the season would last forever
Unfortunately however
That is not our British weather!

Joan Catherine Igesund, Auchnagatt

Hollie

Happy birthday Hollie, can't believe it's here
The day you turn twenty-one seemed so far away
It was only yesterday that I held you in my arms
This small tiny bundle that brought joy to my heart
Cradled in my arms so tight afraid to let you go
I knew that you'd grow up fast but my how time has flown

I remember well the sleepless nights, changing nappies,
Bottle feeds, that first tooth that kept us awake,
But it was all worth it to see the smiles you gave
As I held out my arms waiting for you to take your first step
Toddling towards me with an 'I've done it' look on your face

First day at school, you took it in your stride
New things to learn, new friends to make
It wasn't long before we knew, exams you'd passed
It got you through, university was calling
Our house became an open door
With new friends and old just passing through

I remember the day you were a bridesmaid
Looking as good as the bride
Ivory was your colour as you walked down the aisle
That tom boy image and climbing trees, left far behind
How proud was Grampie on that day of his 'luscious lips'
He was proud of you then, now and always

Family holidays to Turkey, how they made us smile
Seeing all those waiters, although one stood out
'Ice cream boy' was your favourite
There was no stopping you now,
Following on, after your prom
Holidays to Cornwall, one girl among the boys

Hobbies and interests, meant everything to you
So important Disney to Tutankhamen
Next amateur dramatics, acting became your thing
You dance your way forward, acting out your part
When I saw you as Dorothy, it melted my heart
The first day of many roles for you

You learnt to drive and passed your test
The open road is yours, time to leave the nest
Places are calling for you to explore
First stop America off you go
What an impression you managed to make
Winning the heart of those you met

Well you managed to cram so much in these years
How proud are we of what you've achieved
But we know this is just the start of a wonderful life
Go now my daughter full steam ahead,
But remember, I'll always be there at your side
Love in my heart and pride, so much pride

Happy birthday my darling with all I can give
God will guide and bless you
For you will always be the babe in my arms
My daughter, my child.

Jane Bessant, Wainfelin

You're Doing Wonderfully

You're doing wonderfully when you're near to me
You're doing wonderfully when you're talking to me
You're doing wonderfully when you whisper to me
You're doing wonderfully when you creep up on me
You're doing wonderfully
It's like the start of the day when I think of you
Your eyes are so blue, like I thought of you
It's like the heartache of a broken heart
You're doing wonderfully when I think of you
I don't know if it's good or bad
When the rain is falling so hard
When I'm always thinking of you
You're doing wonderfully when I think of you
You're doing wonderfully when I count on you
You're doing wonderfully when your eyes are sparkling so blue
You're doing wonderfully when I only think of you
You're doing wonderfully
The end of the day is very close to me
When the days are so blue, you're doing wonderfully
It's like a song of a broken heart
You're doing wonderfully
Yes, you're doing wonderfully.

David Rosser, Ammanford

Little Grey Men From Mars (Oct 1995)

The grey children are with us,
They are everywhere, in this season
Of darkness and decay;
They envelop and eat the air.

That's why they killed Kennedy;
He knew too much.

Nightmare globose encephalitic heads
Just slits, no noses to speak of,
Their mouths, swallowing words like fish;
Mimer's hands, with only four digits to pray,
Palm forth into space,
Repelled, as though by some invisible barrier,
Push against an infinite barbed wire fence,
The wagon doors which wheeled them away,
Through Europe's midnight marshalling yards,
Onwards to destiny.
In their amniotic sleep and vegetable memory,
Bits of them recall,
The Wailing Wall,
The walled Garden of Gethsemane,
The death camp gardens of Buchenwald, Auschwitz, Dachau,
The gardens where they were laid asleep,
And the smiling disinfected doctors,
Attentive of their every need.
They were human, Jim,
Gypsy kids and Jewish embryos,
Nurtured from Mengele's genetic factory, deep in Peenemunde's darkest woods;
Here the war continues, like some constant rain,
It never really ceased.

While sneering politicians smile unconvincingly
And murmur, 'All is good, all is well,'
Taking bribes, expatiating platitudes as certainty,
The bloom of Europe bleeds.

That is why they killed Kennedy,
He was going to speak,
Tell the poor man on the street, tell us all,
All that we need,
That there is indeed, a conspiracy.

The grey children are everywhere,
Multiplying in the ozone depleted air,
In the polluted breath that we breathe,
Invading our most private dreams and fears,
Cleaving and clawing at invisible wombs for release,
Being made to manipulate cosmic Nazi machinery -
Von Braun's fusion fliegende scheibe, deadly to us.

They are life Jim, but not as we know it,
Their souls are fungal souls,
If they have souls at all,
Borne of the dark Scandinavian woods,
Radium soiled and leukaemia spored,
Nightmares of ill and black half remembered deeds,
They are the wasted wind-blown seed of humanity,
Of spoiled nationhood,
Parasitic upon air, containing no haemoglobin,
As fungi contain no chlorophyll.
They are the undead Jim, who demand rebirth,
Who distil apprehension and guilt into dread,
The bidding Jinni of the fire,
Who are themselves mesmerically led.

Daylight dissolves them,
These phantoms of the Aryan will,
They swim forever in purgatorial limbo,
In the perpetuity of Hell,
Coughing up soundless sores, unspeakable grief,
Not knowing anything, but experiencing all,
Unable to scream, unable to yell,
They silently implore,
But what is even worse Jim,
Kennedy discovered this and was just about to tell.

Prologue:
The following poem posits that during the latter stages of World War II, the Nazis created a highly radioactive flying disg. Homunculi from medical experiments conducted on concentration camp inmates were made to fly it. These experiments continue in America. The narrator is Mr Spock.

James McIntosh Martin, Cowdenbeath

You're Not In Control

(The Chernobyl disaster occurred in Russia in April 1986, with the wind at the particular time, heading westerly. European countries in its path were badly affected with the fallout from the nuclear reactor that went out of control in Chernobyl. Britain and especially Scotland caught high doses carried by the wind)

Mark the day; yes! Mark it well,
Chernobyl's spillage has cast the spell.
The malignant cloud borne by nature's force,
Proved that Man could not steer its course.
Freely spread over many lands,
Radiation conceived by human hands.

Speculation, reassurances, assumptions shown,
Expert advice, facts unknown.
History as always; will relate the cost
No consolation to those who lost.

Learn if not too late,
Mankind who gambled with the world's fate,
Dealing with power in the nuclear role;
It's out of your hands,
You're not in control.

Peter Paterson, Bellshill

Life's Beauty

Crocus, daffs, violets, flowers such hue
Beauty beyond either for you
Sky, stars, sun and moon, a sea so vast
Desert sand, volcanoes, rain, sleet, snow
Beyond control of woman or man
When day is done, and Earth's at rest
The sun setting in the west
We are such tiny specks of life
On this wondrous world of toil and strife
There has to be a stronger force
Stronger than all else it has to be
The God on high, has to be
Has to be, creator of this universe.

Claudette Evans, Hollybush

View From An Open Door

Gazing beyond the open door I see
A hummocked floor with spaces here and there
And seek some argument to minimise
The mad miscellany meeting my eyes -
A sad, half-eaten vestige which may be
The relic of a journey from somewhere.
A crumpled theatre-programme from the past
And fallen stacks of books, amid a vast
Assortment of soiled dresses; underwear
And shoes and costume jewellery; a comb
Resplendent still with tufts of frizzy hair,
Beside a towel stained with henna dye . . .
I close the door and heave a gentle sigh
Of happiness; - my daughter has come home!

Elizabeth Blacklaw, Dundee

Me And My Dog

Let's go for walkies
wagging my tail as we go.
Put on your jacket
let's go running through puddles.
'Throw the ball please'
Off I run to fetch it.
Straight through the wet and muddy fields we go.
Fun we shall have,
then we both fall asleep
on the sofa after our showers.
You stretched out
nose twitchin' and . . .
then the loud
sound
of your snoring
with me cuddling you.

Jessica Stephanie Powell, Pontlottyn

Family History

Family history research,
Can be fun or frustration.
One step on or two steps back,
Progress in moderation.

Excitement, then doubts will come,
Encouragement then despair;
But just keep looking forward
And your triumphs then declare.

Computing, websites, insights,
All aids in this endeavour;
Time and patience will reward
And you will reap the pleasure.

So go forward with head down,
Respect for your devotion.
Details in time and era
Ploughing through generations.

Boasting of your fam'ly tree,
Growing steadily longer;
Who knows what may be revealed,
But your pride will grow stronger.

Janet Bowen, Milford Haven

Toyed Story

While a jack-in-the-box
was flogging a rocking horse
a porcelain doll paraded back and forth
in front of a mirror inside the darkened loft;
then the horse coughed - cough! - the doll stopped
picked up a chessboard (neatly set with family photos)
and turned it edgeways, creating a chequered flag,
which she waved at the jack to make him stop
(quickly jumping back inside his box!)

Robert Black, Annan

View From An Open Door

Gazing beyond the open door I see
A hummocked floor with spaces here and there
And seek some argument to minimise
The mad miscellany meeting my eyes -
A sad, half-eaten vestige which may be
The relic of a journey from somewhere.
A crumpled theatre-programme from the past
And fallen stacks of books, amid a vast
Assortment of soiled dresses; underwear
And shoes and costume jewellery; a comb
Resplendent still with tufts of frizzy hair,
Beside a towel stained with henna dye . . .
I close the door and heave a gentle sigh
Of happiness; - my daughter has come home!

Elizabeth Blacklaw, Dundee

Me And My Dog

Let's go for walkies
wagging my tail as we go.
Put on your jacket
let's go running through puddles.
'Throw the ball please'
Off I run to fetch it.
Straight through the wet and muddy fields we go.
Fun we shall have,
then we both fall asleep
on the sofa after our showers.
You stretched out
nose twitchin' and . . .
then the loud
sound
of your snoring
with me cuddling you.

Jessica Stephanie Powell, Pontlottyn

Family History

Family history research,
Can be fun or frustration.
One step on or two steps back,
Progress in moderation.

Excitement, then doubts will come,
Encouragement then despair;
But just keep looking forward
And your triumphs then declare.

Computing, websites, insights,
All aids in this endeavour;
Time and patience will reward
And you will reap the pleasure.

So go forward with head down,
Respect for your devotion.
Details in time and era
Ploughing through generations.

Boasting of your fam'ly tree,
Growing steadily longer;
Who knows what may be revealed,
But your pride will grow stronger.

Janet Bowen, Milford Haven

Toyed Story

While a jack-in-the-box
was flogging a rocking horse
a porcelain doll paraded back and forth
in front of a mirror inside the darkened loft;
then the horse coughed - cough! - the doll stopped
picked up a chessboard (neatly set with family photos)
and turned it edgeways, creating a chequered flag,
which she waved at the jack to make him stop
(quickly jumping back inside his box!)

Robert Black, Annan

The Tears You Cried

We have heard about the tender tears you cried
About your special loved one that now has died.
You prayed and asked for God's wonderful healing
At this sad time God's healing was not revealing.

Are you feeling sad dejected and alone, deserted?
Perhaps you are taking revenge on God's service
Instead of thinking badly of our heavenly Father
Think about the comfort and love God gives to take after.

Yes you want your special loved one back here again
But to what cost and perhaps terrible pain
Take a back seat and really stop and think
Of God's wonderful compassion, He gives you to take.

Yes your special loved one you will really miss
Oh, the happy reunion when you next meet what bliss
Because over there on that yonder golden shore
You will be with Jesus and your special loved one once more.

Joan McCradie, Cardiff

Thoughts Of Thornhill

Ah! My heart sighs in relief
At the sight of the green rolling hills
It is as well my sincere belief
That no burns can surpass these rills.

I see somnolent sheep and bonny birds
And bunnies hopping hither and thither
With the sound of riders clip-clopping by
And the horizon so stunning against the sky.

All in all it's totally awesome
Here in the heart of Dumfriesshire -
My perfectly peaceful daily diversion
From the noisy life of a townie.

Caroline Anne Carson, Thornhill

Friendship

Elizabeth really is her name, to me it's Betty, just the same
She's a blonde and full of life, but she's had her share of strife.
She's a daughter, and a mother, and her kids just simply love her
Cooking, cleaning, washing, shopping, for our Bet there is no stopping.

She loves her fag, and likes a joke; I sit by her and cough and choke
She said to me, 'I'll give up smoking' I said to her, 'You must be joking!'
Now as for booze, she loves her drink, and downs it like a kitchen sink
And her food, she sure does like it, but at this time is trying to diet.

Bet loves to dance and shake her bum, and always has a lot of fun
Seeing her jive is a real treat, she and Marge are hard to beat.
Jigging, jumping, turning around, stamping their feet into the ground
Chatting, laughing, stepping on toes, dancing while the music flows.

Good old Bet! She's lost some weight, and she's also found a mate
Now she has much more to do, she doesn't mind. I don't! Would you?
I said to her, 'Get one for me,' because it's friends we'll always be
She gives a smile, and nods her head, 'Get your own,' was all she said.

So come on Bet! Let's see that smile, because your life is now worthwhile
The past is over, start to live, for of your best you'll have to give
Enjoy your life; and your new love, he may be sent from Heaven above
And friends we will always stay, whatever happens, come what may.

We've had our lives, gone different ways, both older now, hair of grey
Years have passed, and life is good, our friendship lasts just as it should.
We've both had love, and we've both seen sorrow, but always look for a bright tomorrow
The world will change, for all to see, but Bet and me, will always be.

Enid Thomas Rees, Mountain Ash

Where's Jenkins?

From Dante's Inferno Jenkins saved them
The flying fired flaming fields of Vietnam,
Jenkins grabbed them to safety.
On hearing of Jenkins several
Dashed helicopter flights of rescue,
of many little girls and boys.
I foolishly said, 'I'd have
Shot them to ease their misery.'
Jenkins was shocked as
I was higher ranking, Jenkins said
'If one was only saved it was worth it I'll change your mind.'
Jenkins brought the letters
And the photos of three lovely girls adopted in America
'Sister what do you feel now?' 'Very ashamed.'
Jenkins was a Welsh lady,
Jenkins was a nun,
Jenkins was a student nurse
You'd want in your scrum.
World disasters called her away in the helicopter,
training never completed
Now Jenkins never needs it
A little dainty lady sister dressed in her flowing robes,
Is the one you'd like in your team.
We never knew her given name or her religious name.
I wonder where Jenkins is that gutsy little nun.

Margarte Gleeson Spanos, Llandysul

The Scottish Summer

Power lines down.
Debris on the line.
High winds.
Trains cancelled.
Travelling through a typical Scottish summer.

Barbeque on Saturday.
Forecast says sun.
Barbeque has moved into the house.
Cause the weather has turned lousy.
Socialising during a typical Scottish summer.

Let's go to the beach.
Pack the sunscreen.
We eat ice cream
Huddled together for warmth
Making the most of a typical Scottish summer.

We could all meet in the park.
Let the kids play ball.
As the hail falls. We run home
Cursing our broken umbrellas.
Having fun during a typical Scottish summer.

Mist in the morning.
Sun at noon,
Rain and wind in the afternoon.
Don't you just love -
The Scottish summer.

Dorcas Wilson, Linlithgow

Lost Lines

Seated at a three-cornered table
In St John's churchyard garden.
With an almond cake for company,
And a saucer full of tea
Just watching the world go by.
The sun shy peeping through
The folds of angel wing clouds.
With thoughts of summer
Wrapped up in silken dream.
By the old church door
Under peaceful eaves,
A silver birch tree shivered
And shook off its wet hung leaves,
Just long enough
For an opening moment of grace
And a pair of magpie thieves.

Listening to the nearby market's bustle
With the sounds of flower sellers in their stalls,
The expectant air was filled
With the scent of velvet-tipped tulips,
Along with fresh fruit calls.
A lilac shaded flowering tree
Just by the stone cling walls,
Moves for a short while it stands taller
For gathering sparrows' perching tails
Meanwhile besides the moss stirred stones
Of gentle keeping, a hedgehog,
Unperturbed to any light or visitor
Is still in silent sleeping.

Norman Royal, Grangetown

Damascus Road

And will we learn the error of our ways
And maybe cast a furtive look behind
And simple truths taught at our mother's knee
Are cast aside in Man's new odyssey
Bring forth the magic of the laser beam
Computers flash in all the world to see
And planets wait for mankind yet to leave
As God's creatures gasp in seas of oil to breathe
The headlong rush essential though it be.
For mankind's grasp of new technology,
As nations seek to trespass to the stars
Abandoning all those who've yet to be.
But if we learn to care for God's creativity;
If we save them -
'Then they'll save you and me.'

Windsor Hopkins, Tondu

Untitled

Were you a volcano slumbering
Whilst dinosaurs came lumbering
You've seen all Scottish history without numbering,
Reivers came and reivers went
And you saw their blood well spent
Now a mountain over Hawick you're content to be
Climbing to the top you can see Berwick and the North Sea
So let us put on some leather
And go together
And hang on tight to the heather
Sun's broke through
And I love climbing with you
For I know our love is true
We'll never stop
Till we reach the top
Look at the surrounding view
Border counties all align
The border bonnie counties that are all mine.

Alan Pow, Hawick

Sunshine And Snow

Walking in the snow,
At first with care not to fall,
So more confident in trying
To fulfil the longing
To be out in the sunshine
Glitter on the snow
The soft stillness all around
The snow-laden trees
And the majestic hills
Drenched in white.

Barbro Pattie, Rothesay

The Perfect Waif

Was she the perfect waif?
Stick body, milk-white skin,
The look of a ghost,
Never seeing the sun.

Hair hanging like entangled string,
Black stockings and a Mexican ring;
A sparrow
With no place to sing.

Fingers long and quite artistic,
Brittle bones with look fibristic;
Tired eyes so worldly worn,
The way she's been
Since she was born.

Tragedy's somehow etched in her face;
She is indeed the perfect waif;
A rag doll blown across life's stage,
Always looking older than her age.

Mike Monaghan, Bishopbriggs

Slochd

Please come with me, I beg you,
To a place where I have been.
Prepare to have your horizon spread out,
By the beauty, I have seen.

Immediately my eyes were drawn,
To this place that I had found.
I realised I had discovered,
A vision, so profound.

I had never seen such a place before,
The delight to the senses abounds.
The air is filled with the scent of firs,
With purple heather carpeting the ground.

This place where Bonnie Prince Charlie,
And the Jacobites once stalked.
Where General Wade once wanted,
New roads for us to walk.

In this wild and rugged landscape,
I saw dragonfly, grouse and deer.
Never have I seen painted canvas,
By Mother Nature, so beautifully clear.

I came here as a mere stranger,
But before my stay came to end,
I knew in my heart and soul,
I had made these people my friends.

If you ever come to visit this place,
When you leave, your memories will stay.
Then you will return to your homeland,
And proudly you will say

'I have been to Slochd.'

Ian Archibald, Edinburgh

A Wonderful Shetland Collie

You came to help us back on track
When burglars did our home ransack.
A watchdog extraordinaire
No foot outside but you were there.
Comforted us when we were sad
Jumped for joy when we were glad.
You were so trusting and so true
We really fell in love with you.

Fun and games and walks we had
At first not sure of your 'human' dad
Who walked with sticks - you were wary
They really make you feel quite scary.
But soon you knew no need to fear
As all around held you dear
To save you getting any thinner
Your favourite music played at dinner

You too are gone and I'm alone
Friends and family talk on phone
I thank you folks with all my heart
But somehow I must make new start.
My dog became my true best friend
And I must accept this is the end
But memories great are with me still
They can lonely moments fill.

I never had a dog before
Once bitten scared me to the core
But you're not only *man's* best friend
I'll not forget you to the end . . .
Of my own life be it short or long
You never ever did me wrong.
People do some cruel things
Not knowing the joy a dog friend brings.

Aileen A Kelly, Aberdeen

Return Of Isaac Rosenberg

You were smiling in the sunshine of Africa,
lauded, served in luxury with wine and spice,
Table Mountain beckoned, work engrossed,
friends abundant. But worlds away from home,
art and atmosphere did not satisfy
the pain of creation which was your sustenance.
The avenues of Cape Town could not replicate
back-streets in Whitechapel, no one replaced
the friends who inspired.

Fate sent you a serpent instead of an angel.
He brought you back to London, took you
to the trenches, rats and lice for company,
wet and bleeding guts from torn bellies.
You spurned chances to survive,
always following the difficult path.
A fumbling soldier became
a stiffened corpse beneath sucking mud
and the screaming stare of the serpent.

Bill Torrie Douglas, Fairlie

Hebrides

Where the blue of the sky meets the blue of the sea
where seagulls cry and wind's always high
white sands and marram dunes
flag irises that gild loch shores
the June machair a painter's palette
of multi-hued wild flowers
evocative scent of peat reek
that hangs in the clearest of air
harsh cries of the grey garbed heron
seal song from the midnight rocks
clinking of rigging on fishing boats
and from the sombre Sabbath kirk
the haunting sound of Gaelic psalms.

Pam Russell, Yarrow

Water

Turn on the tap
Gushes out silver!
Sparkling and clean
The essential remover

From hidden caverns
Beneath the Earth
The pliant pipes bring it
Gurgling with mirth.

The crystal lakes
Up in the hill
Fascinate humans
From the dark mills.

Of all the pleasures
To be had in this land
Water answers to
Every demand.

Mavis Downey, Talgarth

Sex

Our bodies are transmitters they tell us what they need
Give us warning of our urgencies allowing us to feed
In circles we spin the words in our minds
Dictating the passion we all need to find.

Each hair a receiver connected to our soul
An orifice we need to fill to make us whole
To expand our understanding of what is right or wrong
Find meaning in the rhythm provide substance to the song.

Small pours evaluate the fragrance of desire
Choosing the most able to reach where we aspire
Their energy accelerates combines, explodes in lust
Feeding power to our muscles, giving us the thrust.

Muscle taught by tension collected in our breath
Coursing fluids overcoming ourselves.

George Campbell, Perth

The Gambler

There's red upholstery upon the wall
The ladies glitter one and all
It's hot and stuffy in this room
And some of the inhabitants
Will meet their doom

For this is where the gamblers come
Where fortunes have been lost and won
Where next week's rent is riding high
And maybe the mortgage says 'bye bye'.

The adrenaline flows when you have a win
Is it worth it though to commit this sin
With loved ones worried until you return
Waiting quietly with the midnight oil to burn.

For the gambler there's always another day
He leaves the other person to pray
That this will end and he will be
Content in his home with his family.

Marion McKenzie, Irvine

Written Words

You'll never know how much I hurt from all your written words,
Quoting countless grievances that in your memory stirred.
Like a poison letter it defined my many faults
And all the many incidents since you became adult . . .

The shock, the hurt, the sadness that you could even think
I was so reprehensible has brought me to the brink
My life has changed forever, it can never be the same,
I ask myself continuously exactly who's to blame . . .

It seems to stem from partnership as another took your name,
When grandchildren came along they were treated all the same . . .
Never favoured one from one, always there to care
Over the years all seemed to change, but speak I did not dare . . .

I had to always bite my tongue so many many times,
Spoke no evil all my life, now heard it in my prime . . .
Now there is nothing left at all but broken relationships
No happy, loving times to care and share all of life's dips . . .

Think on dear child, there are two sides
But on your partner's you decide,
I loved you, love you, always will
Until the day I die . . .

M L Damsell, Plwmp

Life

Fly like an eagle
Soar on the wing
A new life beginning
A wonderful thing
Your trials and emotions
Your hopes and your fears
They're all part of life
A test through the years.

Through joy or through sorrow
Through hope or through pain
Life's a test to us all in every way
We seek peace and loving
A world without hate
But Man's path is not easy
No Heaven he makes.

Yet hope is still with us
Defiance at best
Not to surrender our spirit at last
Perhaps there's a Heaven
Or perhaps there's a Hell
Or somewhere between them
A world without pain.

Gwyn Thomas, Merthyr Tydfil

God Has Called

As you sit by my side near my coffin
With a pain that's in your heart
The tears in your eyes as you mourn me
As this world I am soon to depart

As I go through the door to my maker
At peace you know I will be
God called and he said that he needs me
From this Earth I will soon be set free

He said I would meet friends and relations
The ones who have gone up before
By the gates they will be waiting
With stories and memories galore

They say that in Heaven it's peaceful
The stresses and pain they are gone
And when you scatter my ashes
Your good memories will linger on

As time goes by as you know it will
And when you're feeling blue
Just remember I am not gone
I'll still be watching over you.

Jeanette Davis, Alva

What A Fume

What a fume
Down the road
Left in its wake
A cloud of smoke
Made people choke.

Going places
Up and downhill
At your will
Not to kill
Over bumps
Round bends
Give them thrills and chills.

The engine roars
Doing its chores
Coughing and spluttering
As winter came
Isn't it a shame
If that car had a brain
It would go insane
As if to complain.

Wipers don't work
Running out of luck
Windows dirty
Paintwork rusty
'Couldn't sell this car,'
Mr Claxton said in woe
'The only thing that works
Is the radio.'

The door creaked
The petrol tank leaked
The boot springs open
The car is no hoping.

The brake, accelerator and clutch don't work
We'll have to get a car towing truck.

The truck appeared off to the dump
Clitter, clatter sighs of woe
The dump is the place to go.

At the dump the driver stops
He relaxes and sighs
'That car has had its chances.'
Tyres worn
Metal torn
Ages old, can't be sold.

The car lies there
Like a lump
In all that pile
Or forgotten junk.

John Bain, Oban

William The Right Royal Joker

I drove past the area where he has slept underneath the stars,
A quiet place, where nature ruled true without many taxi cars.
The orange was given as a reminder of the fruit we reap.
One swan's feather, and a match to bridge the timely leap.

The Welsh rain jacket; a child's protective shield nutcracker.
Golden waves for William the right royal joker cracker.
Elizabeth shone from her kitchen that whistled with love.
Blessed loved ones moved, twisted and shook from above.

The little banana ran balancing the golden egg so strong.
Unaware of all around what had been so boldly wrong.
He reached forward with a hand that touched spirits akin.
The window was left open for Art to experience some win.

'Keep ya eye on da ball my son,' yelled young Harry.
The uncle kicked on the ball that his son did carry.
The golden lefty footed skeleton headed the ball onwards,
The skull that stages trust with knowledge teaches upwards.

Caroline Champion, Mathern

Bottom Heavy

All the leaves lie still.
Muted by heat
And the sky is a sheer blue with no edges,
Running on into forever.
Flowers raise stems and trumpets,
Tongues and bonnets.
Turning to follow the sun.
Into this stumbles a bee.
Bottom heavy in its improbable flight.
It plunges into a bright Nasturtium.
Wiggles momentarily then weaves away.
Buzzing drowsily in its intoxication.
Shadows begin to fall across the garden
And a cat stretches,
Too drowsy to catch a passing fly.
The day shimmers and passes slowly
Into the delicate shades of twilight.

Miki Byrne, Walton Cardiff

Yesterday's Blessings

Each morning she rises and looks in the mirror
And feels sad at the sight that she sees.
She once was a beauty with the world at her feet
Drifting through life on a breeze.
From the day she was born she created a storm
With her endearing cherubic looks.
A face that would grace the magazine covers,
Her lifestyle you'd read of in books.
But time marches on changing all in its path,
Yesterday's blessings are not meant to last.
So she puts on her make-up to face the new day,
And dreams of what she had in the past.

Karl Jakobsen, Dumfries

Summer Seaside

Golden sand
Water looks so calm
Children at play
'Oh!' What a glorious summer day
Throwing of a beach ball
Sandcastles built ever so tall
Adults soaking up the sun
Children having lots of fun
Small boat on its own
Sailing across the ocean zone
Laying on the sand
Trying to get a golden tan
If it gets warm
To the water people swarm
Jump in with a splash
Waves coming around with a flash
Playing in the sea
It's everything it seems to be
Water lovely cool!
Children acting the fool.

Marie Coyles, Dervock

Sensing

To hear the breeze's laughter:
See the twinkling eye of the star:
Note the gurgling joy of the spring:
Know the glory of the moonlight:
Hear the steady 'chump' of the worm:
Listen to the music of dancing shadows:
Feel the rain splash at your feet:
See the world of beauty in calm.

Margaret Davis, Chepstow

Vitality

Mercury streams of polythene
Glide between squat ditches.
Last year's remnants bob about
Like aggravated witches.

Solitary fairy thorns
Gnarled branches tied in knots.
Islands in a sea of glass,
Scabby acne spots.

Amber dot stealthily sneaking
Up the dry stone ditching.
Oblivious prey munching grass,
White tails and pink nose twitching.

Vivacious whins in spring attire
Hide baldy, bug-eyed chicks.
Cud-chewing cows wage war
With vicious biting ticks.

Stoic sheep contemplate,
Seeming in a trance.
A fickle puppeteer drags lambs
Through fields on a merry dance.

Secluded robin serenading,
Cultured cockerel crowing.
Haughty chickens pace around
Russet feathers glowing.

Norah Nelson, Newry

In The Park

The hunchback still sits in the park
Not the same one you once knew
A little older, wiser maybe
He still likes to stay out of view
Preferring shadows and dark
That come with the song of the lark
So no one can see him there
'Cause they never did care
Just turn away from his face
What they say has no grace

He asks for nothing
He begs not a question
To leave one out in the cold
Should they be taught a lesson
But never in that moment
Can you know

Only looking back
You will recollect
How you felt
Bewildered he is left
To ponder and consider
But most of all to wither
And await his time
For the door to knock
At the end of his clock.

David McDonald, Kirkcaldy

Nightfall In Paris

Stroll along the Champs Elysees
On warm and balmy nights,
Coffee aromas pervade the air
Cafés swathed in twinkling lights.
Arc de Triomphe towers ahead
With the ever burning flame,
Honouring soldiers fallen in battle
Unknown and without a name.

From the Eiffel Tower a fabulous view
Sacre Coeur and old Monmartre,
Where Parisienne history remains alive
As bohemians study their art.
With easel set and charcoal sticks
Artists sketch each and every day.
And near the Louvre in Tuilerie Gardens
Children laugh and shout at play.

Lovers embrace strolling arm in arm
Along the banks of the River Seine,
The city of love will cast its spell
As night falls o'er Paris once again.

Jean MacKenzie

Where Dryland Meets The River

The river strokes its way across the land
drum deep and skimmed by light white ripples
Cutting its teeth on stranded stones
its tongue into the soft wet earth
High on spring and the taste of bending blossom
Punch drunk, reeling through the corners
sifting sand through all the pores
of its brown flowing body
High on the worship of wheeling trees
their leaves trapping the light in small green parcels
Shielding its waters, from the large eye of the sun
from the blue-white muslin of a looping sky

And I, pigmy-like upon her banks
kneeling amid the small white flowers
Pulled by the spate and mud
Drawn by the pulse and thunder
the scent and roar and echo of her voice
Deafened by the falling dusk
Kept safe, only by the piping of small birds
darting through the roots and spirals
chasing the wings of flies
Held fast by the arm of a tree
Yell back at her
'Time yet to swim in your deep dark waters
Time yet to find my own way to the sea!'

Pat MacKenzie, East Kilbride

The Gardener And The Seasons

Autumn sweeps in with its colourful attire
Cosy evenings in front of the fire.
Shedding of leaves - yellow, amber, brown, red,
Care to be taken on paths we must tread.
Stark branches turned towards the sky
Whereupon once green leaves did die.
The onslaught of winter appears within weeks
Bringing ruddy complexions to everyone's cheeks.

Mornings are dark and evenings seem long,
Birds are scarce and have lost their song.
I wait for the weekends to don my old clothes -
Rain, rain, rain - disappointment shows!
A new day dawns, a blanket of frost,
But it's back to the office - a weekend lost!
Each day that passes seems nearer my aim -
The longing to be back in my garden again.

Awake so early in anticipation
To hear the weather on the radio station.
Hoping that the elements will be kind
To carry out what I have in mind.
Alas, the news is not surprising -
The forecast is rain and the wind is rising.
Another day of patiently waiting
For that which Man has no power in creating.

Trees still bare from autumn leaves falling -
Hurry up weather the garden is calling!
Surprisingly, crocus bulbs are sprouting;
I'm so excited I feel like shouting.
Every day brings forth something new,
Several more shoots come into view.
Spring 'round the corner, an hour's more light,
Winter's at last given up its fight!

Bursting with life the garden awakens,
'Tis well worth all the time it has taken.
And though the months have seemed so long
The birds return in full sweet song.
I know it's all been worth the wait
As I gaze in awe by the garden gate
And set off for work - I *loathe* to leave
But am *grateful* for all that's been achieved.

The splendour of summer soon arrives,
The bees lead busy little lives,
Visiting the beautiful array of flowers,
Bringing them to life between the showers.
Every day there's new colour to see,
The garden is where I've longed to be!
How fortunate I feel to witness such magic -
Nature works wonders - I feel ecstatic.

Up at dawn to the birds' 'Dawn Chorus',
The good Lord provides all this for us.
All that we see is such natural beauty:
Tending the soil is certainly no 'duty'.
The flowers, birds, wildlife are part
Of all the things close to my heart.
I thank the Great Spirit for providing such pleasures . . .
For *these* are surely life's *hidden treasures!*

Vivienne Vale, Tonyrefail

New Life

(Dedicated to Jamie Lever)

And the songbirds keep singing their melody . . .
I love you, I love you, I love you with all of my heart.
Walking through the fields of gold, the scent of the rapeseed,
The undertones of honeysuckle and the sharpness of the summer breeze.

I cannot imagine a more beautiful, precious, delicate moment,
The silence, the anticipation, and the nervous energy exacerbated
By pure emotional indulgence that now overwhelms me.
I feel so faint . . .

The heartbeat, thumpety thump, thumpety thump, thumpety thump . . .
It feels like my life is pounding and there is no exit
My world is spiralling, spiralling, spiralling, and I am here,
Living the moment, a moment no one can touch, it is mine forever.
Hands, feet, body, face and soul. My soul. We are at one.
We are both Kings of Lion, and we will be Kings of Men.

Nothing to want for, no fears, and no inhibitions, no prejudices.
And nothing to love other than love and life.
A life so complete and full of enveloping warmth and support.
Little one . . . You are so loved and so pure . . .

Terry Mullan, Cookstown

Modern Day

In this day and age in which we live, everyday life
is fraught with uncertainty, more so than ages that
have gone before, people are losing a sense of place
and reason, no two days are the same war and strife
and chaos reigns.

Ordinary day-to-day life is disrupted by violence
and needless crime, an old adage of keeping your head
when all about you are losing theirs. Is more true today
than yesterday, we rely on the powers that be to make sound
judgement out of the chaos that reigns.

Fuel bills, taxes, household bills, are draining each family's
resources, supermarkets putting up prices to pay for their
deliveries, health service and pensioner care all cut, no one
is left out of the struggle, modern day technologies run our lives
but what is the cost when chaos reigns.

Will chaos always be with us? As we struggle for our rights
to have a decent life, no one should need to go without
the necessities of life in this day and age, governments
are supposed to look after the people. Yet even within their
high offices, it seems we the people are the ones who lose
out when chaos reigns.

Janet Middleton, Westquarter

The Language Of The Leaves

The city faces the country across a field
The gummy windows of houses are inscrutable
The trees in the woods chatter in sylvan tongues
Incomprehensible, the language of the leaves

At night, foxes forage in gardens
Furtively, their triangular faces
Probing the bins for scraps

Rats dredge ditches
For globs of urban waste
Forefront of the takeaway society

Borders blur at the edge
Buses purr at the terminus
Backs to the wall
Rabbits shrink into their skins
At the roar of engines

Street children mistrust the strangeness of woods
The way trees knot and gnarl
Unpruned, unlopped
The bloody mouths of labyrinthine brambles

Sheena Blackhall, Garthdee

As Time Moves On So Must We

Going back is a dubious game,
Because we are static in that frame.
Like turning the pages of a book,
We go back and take another look.
But lingering too long on what's gone
Is unproductive, and is the wrong
Way to go, 'cause it was yesterday!
In the present we can have our say.
And when we move into the future,
That's where we can enrich and nurture
Our lives, with some new people and things,
Being happy in the joy that brings.

Alexander Winter, Aberdeen

Autumn

Purple coloured mountains
Fields of golden corn
Rose-hips in the hedgerows
Misty autumn morn
Leaves all brightly coloured
Nuts a golden brown
Gentle breeze soon will come
Leaves all falling down
Blackberries so sweet!
Blackberry tart, so good to eat!
Elderberries to collect for wine
Good for colds and when you dine!
Misty golden autumn!
How colourful you are
Summer's put to rest
But of all the seasons
I like you the best!

Maureen Margaret Thornton, Aberaman

Precious Memories

Last year I was in Israel,
And saw in hilly Bethlehem -
Steep steps to the silver-starred church floor,
Where Jesus was born in poverty.

We went down a hill on Olive's Mount
To the garden of Gethsemane -
A tree - two thousand years of age
May have 'seen' the Christ in agony.

Via Dolorosa in Old Jerusalem
We one day walked - a holy place -
(Though now it shops and markets sport)
The way of crucifixion then for Him.

We saw the small skull-eyed cliff face
Where many say that Jesus died -
On Calvary - a' top the cliff -
Taking our punishment - stupendous love!

Then walking through a little path
We saw the holy garden where
Jesus' tomb is situate,
Where He rose in resurrection power!

One day on the way to Galilee,
The beautiful blue Dead Sea we saw -
Here you can float, reading the news,
Such salt and minerals are there.

We stayed in Galilee some days -
The lake a few minutes from us there.
What an honour it was, just down the beach
To paddle in the Sea of Galilee!

We also went to Nazareth
And saw the Bible Gardens there.
A weaver, a shepherd, a carpenter
Wore costumes as in Jesus' day.

And so, last year, we flew back home
With precious memories of that land -
Of the holy places that we'd seen,
Because of God's all-embracing love!

Wendy Prance, Cardiff

Bloodlines

It runs in the blood, they say.
So when the day has pocketed its shadows,
and late sun seeps the last bead of plasma
from the marrow of the yard,
I'll go inside, and there you'll be,
bustling and clattering in the kitchen,
capillaries chattering, arteries brisk as bees.

And when you turn to me, and I see tiredness
like an old dog stoop its weight
against your legs and shoulders,
I'll think of how, each day, you juggle
that busy hive of leukocytes.
And when a sudden bruise appears,
crushed blueberries on your skin,
or breath is struggled away on a skirl of breeze,
then I'll remember how it runs in the blood,
faster than we can catch it,
quicker than a skipping rope can turn,
quicker that the flickering of a vein.

Kathy Miles, Ffos-y-ffin

Adieu

Be still my heart,
Whenever my love is near,
Don't tremble!
It makes my feelings clear,
He waits for the smile
That touches his mind
And a kiss that caresses
Gentle and kind,
In hope he continues
To show faith and expect,
When she looks in the mirror
His love will reflect,
Lonely is the man
Set apart;
As the girl of his dreams
Shares naught with his heart,
Goodbye seems so harsh,
In saying to you,
Softly my love
Can I just say 'Adieu'?

William F Park, Clydebank

The Moment Of Truth

Huddled around your bed
Did we appear looming
Like figures in a dream
As you departed?

Was Father
Waiting there
For you?

Was there a loss of colour
Especially of those you loved
Of spring and summer hues
Autumn leaves and
Winter berries?

Or sound like the wind
Down our stack
During winters past
When you talked
About the fairies
And the dark
Shadows of night?

Have you travelled
Far or as quick
As your morning walk
To St Mary's?
Where each stone
Knew your step
And every window
Carried a reflection.

How do you look, now
Or are you as you were?
Or at the moment of truth
Did all end - is there no more?

Liam Ó Comáin, Derry

Leaving

Standing in the garden
she said are you a gardener? Meaning she isn't.
Yes I said and smiled
My mum likes gardening she said.
Relief flooded, heart stopped pounding.

Minutes and hours, days and months and
years of love are in this garden.
I've cut my teeth on it,
sharpened my secateurs, honed my hoe
tested the soil, dug in the compost.
Learned what does
and doesn't love ph neutral
and salty south Westerlies blown from the shores
Of Columbus's discoveries.

Watching the seedlings disappear overnight
I fought the snugs, midnight raids
with buckets of brine.
Fed the birds, watched the fledglings
counted the butterflies.

Loved and nurtured soft hued plantings,
blues and pinks, mauves and lilacs.
Relished the hot and spicy beds,
ate the gooseberries.
Cut and clipped and brushed and tidied
to within an inch of its NGS Open Garden life.

Croquet and cream teas,
barbeques, bridge and babies on blankets
Ladies' lunches and Mah-jong,
it's seen it all.

And now it's someone else's turn and
it will be what it needs to be.
All the joy it gave to me will carry on
with different hands
and little feet to shape its heart.

Susan Clarke, Llantwit Major

Pour Moi

What is right for me?
I look around and see
A changing scene
A time that's been
The future yet to be . . .

To keep a hopeful heart
Is where I'm best to start
A helping hand
A steady stand
An interest in fine art . . .

To keep my calm for sure
My cool the double cure
A bright outlook
A real good book
Good luck that's pearl pure!

Norma Anne MacArthur, Edinburgh

Where?

In a little wood which almost
No one knows, is a little
Stream hidden deep in a gully
Too small to be called a ravine.

Here the stream whispers secretly of
Its beautiful unseen waterfall
Haunt of grey wagtail and solitude.

Such a sweet, seductive sound
I have to confess I shall keep
Forever in my heart, never
To be found.

Robert Wynn-Davies, Whitland

Sky Surfer

The plane soars high and higher still,
Fear fires my pulses
Yet exhilaration damps the fire
And blazes with its own wild flame;
This heady game I play
In the wide playground
Of the sky, where others only fly,
Is the extreme, the ultimate thrill,
The zenith of excitement,
Before which, all other sports
Seem pale imposters - I surf the skies!
High in the wide expanse of blue
And marbled white,
Turning, twisting, sailing
The seas of Heaven on my craft -
The flat and fragile board
Beneath my feet; I see the line
Where Earth and Heaven meet
And all my senses flare and fill me
With a joy that overrides my fear;
Above me, the plane,
A silver spear slicing the clouds,
Circles, then shoots away clear
To the far horizon;
Earth hangs above me briefly
As I spin and loop,
I feel the drag of gravity
Pulling me faster, faster to the ground,
One short sharp tug, I spin around,
Then I am floating, falling
Free and safe, under the folds of silk.

Betty McIlroy, Bangor

I Am Happy In Jesus

I am happy in Jesus
I am trusting in His word
Though shattered by the storms of life
I shall not fear
For He will see me through
He will walk with me
And He will talk with me
So why should I fear?
He tells me I am His own
And that He loved me so much that
He suffered and died in my place,
That I should live a victorious and
Happy life by His grace.
One day He is coming to take me to
His lovely home above
What a day that will be!
The rule is that I must humble myself
To walk with Him.
He is the King of kings.
He reigns on high.
Leaving to go to that beautiful home
I can take nothing with me
But I can send it on ahead.
I hear His voice saying,
'All this I have done for you.
What hast thou done for me?'
Yes! He loves me.
He tells me I must be faithful
And true to His word
To be His own.
He will take me by His hand
And lead me to the Promised Land.

Joy Wilson, Clogher

Day's End

A swift soars over the hedge.
Without slowing it swerves
to avoid another bird.
Undeterred it flips
over the wall to the sea
whose grey vibrates blue
with a liner's passage.
The waves crash on rocks,
foaming water sluices down,
sparkling.

A flight of swans like an arrow,
targets a red-gold cloud
on the sunlit summit.

Martins stop foraging
the air over the wilderness
of grass and wild flowers,
rustling in the warm wind.
The shrill oyster catchers quieten.
Silent eiders, float in cliques -
brown females and brindle young,
black and white males;
all plunges for food over.
The herons position a leg,
ready for the night vigil.

The sun dies in red
as day ends.

Fleming Carswell, Argyll

How Beautiful Are The Mountains

Ben Lomond stood proud,
In total and complete reflection,
Majestic in the mirror of the Loch,
I looked up high unto the hill,
I looked down low deep into its waters
And fell deeply mesmerised, all in one moment.
Where did mountain, sky and water begin?
Where did water, mountain and sky end?
The glorious vortex enchanted and numbed my senses,
Till I was drunk with its watery vision.

The road stretched out ahead, it sank down
As golden hills rose up on either side.
The Trossachs became sandy dunes
In the golden Spring light.
The withered grass, clothed the hills
Dead tufts, glowed like velvet sand.

A pause to look back on the Trossach desert and
Down into a sharp valley 3D in its vista.
Once again a vortex enchanted and numbed
My senses with its vertigo vision.
On that hillside, I felt like an eagle
Ready to take flight into the still, warm air.
To soar to hang in the purple sky, to rise and circle
To be free in flight forever.

Cracks and fissures opened up as
Streams cascaded down the hillsides, in trickles and gushes
A precious refreshment for the parched rocks
A lively, bubbling drink to quench the dry rock's thirst.
Living water, breathing water, cool water, clear water
Let me touch you, dip my feet and hands in you.
Dropping fast - the mountain's life-blood
Its source of life - as it falls,
Melts into the stream, to the river, to the loch
And slides slowly into the sea.

Katriona Goode, Earlston

Come Next Winter

I will wait with my son in my hands
Forget not coming to my land my friends

When the woods bloom with flowers of snow
When the Boreas bring you hell with blow
When your hearts crave for warmth and glow

Forget not coming to my land my friends
I will wait with my son in my hands

You shall nest in pastures new
Clover is green and foes are few
I will show you some ethereal view

Forget not coming to my land my friends
I will wait with my son in my hands

You shall bath in hot water spring
Wrap into sweaters the sunny days bring
Stroll on the plain where the sun rays cling

Forget not coming to my land my friends
I will wait with my son in my hands

Tell them the stories of light and hue
Tell them the stories of green and blue
Bring with you some more friends new

Forget not coming to my land my friends
I will wait with my son in my hands

Pack in thy bags some fairy tales
Wrap in thy lungs some homely smells
My son will jump to see doll belles

Forget not coming to my land my friends
I will wait with my son in my hands

Bye bye o birds if we cannot meet
Forgive me friends if I cannot greet
Forget not the sky you flew with me
Forget not the land you roamed with me

Worry not to come next winter my friends
My son will wait with my name in his hands.

Mukeshkumar Raval, India

Birds On The Wing

Birds on the wing
in they fly, from faraway places to our summer places
of gardens and parks, from overseas faraway places,
into our summer days, to here and there,
they come on into our lives, with summer songs
through summer days, birds on the wing they fly on in
for our lives to be cheerful in cheerful places
gardens parks country places
where the corn is high, and dragonflies fly,
by brooks and slow-running streams
where we free our dreams of summer ways and days,
and trees are of many greens.

Birds on the wing
that spring and summer brings,
with cheerful songs
from faraway places
into parks and gardens of rose beds and flowers.

Arthur May, Newport

The Enlightment Of Love

The man he can be stubborn
the woman can be vain
but they are both victims
'cause they are much the same
suffering is a part of life
that they will both endure
whether they are wicked
whether they are poor
trust is the essence of love
both equal in their own wee way
try to think of someone else every single day.

Yvonne Clark

Friendship (To Bonnie)

I'm here for you, if you should need me,
In good times and in bad
To share your happiness with you,
As well as pain and when you're sad.
Thousands of miles between us -
My arms cannot enfold you;
My love and thoughts, however, will,
For they're sincere and true.

I feel your heartache and your sorrow,
Share your anxiety and fear.
Everything has its tomorrow,
When clouds may pass, and skies will clear,
When life again will be worth living,
When everything feels good again;
When health returns, your heart is singing,
And you'll forget the pain and strain.

Through all of this, we'll fight together,
Friendship we share in thought and word.
Where sorrow's shared, the storms we'll weather.
Compassion is a powerful sword,
Unleashed against the darkest hour,
It combats all, it fights for light.
True friendship has an awesome power.
And in the end, all will come right.

Helga Dharmpaul, Tain

The Winter Rose

Blustering winds, temperatures below zero.
Wet and murky soil all around.
There standing the most beautiful red velvet rose.
Seemed to say let me stay.
To everyone that passes let them feel the glow
Of my red flame of colour
As my petals fall one by one
Let me fade into a summer elsewhere.

Joan Kelly McChrystal, Derry City

The West Highland Way

(95 miles from Milngavie to Fort William)

We set off in August time,
To walk the Highland Way,
From Milngavie, then to Carbeth,
We stopped for lunch today,
Then up and on again we walked,
Till Drymen we did spy,
There we rested for a while,
Then to Balmaha when dry,
Arriving there for B&B,
A caravan for the night,
Breakfast and a big packed lunch,
We set off fresh and bright,
Rowerdennan, heading north,
Along Loch Lomond side,
Inversnaid was our next stop,
A bunkhouse to reside,
The people there were friendly,
In the Inversnaid Hotel,
Showed us to the bunkhouse,
We were welcomed very well,
After breakfast we set out,
For Inverarnan now,
Over rocks, up hills and glens,
Yet we survived somehow,
Tough and dangerous sometimes,
But the scenic view was great,
Then Crainlarich was in sight,
A few miles to the gate,
Of a lovely little cottage, bright,
B&B awaited there,
What a beautiful feeling, though,
We were a tired pair,
Next morning bright and all refreshed,
For Tyndrum we set out,
Many miles stretched ahead,
And then, without a doubt,
We stopped for lunch, then off again,
To Bridge of Orchy next,
Found a farmhouse for the night,
B&B was fixed,
Then up again, with lunch all packed,
Inveroran, here we come,
A break for lunch, then off again,
The Rannoch Moors begun,

What a glorious sight we saw,
Hills and mists and heather,
The rain came on, the first we'd seen,
But we didn't mind the weather,
Miles and miles of open moors,
The Kingshouse Hotel we spied,
The head of Glencoe, we were there,
Its beauty not denied,
Once more we stopped for B&B,
A bath to ease our pains,
Aching from these miles and miles,
From self-pity we refrained,
Up again next morning bright,
Kinlochleven we were bound,
The Devil's staircase winding up,
Was difficult we found,
When we reached the top of it,
The road was nice and easy,
Breathtaking scenery we did see,
And the weather bright and breezy,
Kept us cool and helped us on,
As up and down we walked,
Valleys, glens and waterfalls,
Awesome as we talked,
Of all the beauty, that was there,
By far the greatest sight,
Massive hills surrounding us,
Filled us with delight
Then Kinlochleven we saw there,
Down in the valley deep,
Another hour and we were there,
The coming down was steep,
Then once more stopping for the night,
Grant's garage, had some ground,
And in the back, a caravan,
In bed, we slept so sound,
Next morning, up and off we went,
A long haul had begun,
14 miles we walked or more,
And that was our walk done,
It rained so heavy every step,
Poured from Heaven above,
We walked it humbly, sponsored too,
And the reason was for love,
Our sister in the hospital,
Had had a massive stroke,
We raised the funds for a unit,
To give other people hope,
For when she passed away, we thought,

How nice if we could do,
A sponsored walk, in memory,
Of that lady we all knew,
Then something good, will have come out,
Of the suffering she went through,
So it was worth those weary miles,
We both did it dear, for you.

Janette Campbell, Cumbernauld

Last Night In Blantyre

It was my last night in Blantyre
Time for me to retire
Memories of days gone by
Glimmering in objects that caught my eye

Paintings pictures and photographs
Captured moments of our past
Time and time moved so fast
Blantyre boys were not made to last

Hopes of one last good night
Fell apart from blinding sight
I had become the man who deconstructs
Packing my suits and my tux

I may be gone but I'll dream of this place
No matter where I am in time and space
I will always remember
Blantyre boys forever . . .

Then dreams woke up
And sun down went
My time in Blantyre
Had been spent.

Gavin Knox, Ballinamallard

On This Desert Night

On this desert night,
I have an earnest yearning.
I need a light wind.
Let me rest my mind.
Let me rest beneath palm trees.
Let me find relief.
I feel such a thrill!
It comes unexpectedly!
Oceans excite me!
The Supreme Being,
He knows my aspirations.
He liberates me.
On this desert night,
Orange clouds glow in the dark.
Sunlight is fading.
On this desert night,
The distant water sparkles.
I see the diamonds.
On this desert night,
My palm tree looks like fireworks.
It brings me solace.

Laraine Smith, Indiana

Poetry

Who needs it?
Who reads it?
The sad
The mad
Chancers
Wanting answers
Who don't belong
Who hear a different song
Alone in bars
Gazing at the stars

Also some quite ordinary people.

M G Sherlock, Colwyn Bay

A Winter Solstice Journey

We were freezing cold if the truth be told,
The wrong time of year for a journey we thought.
Over the High Downs; to reach the next town
The sun furthest off making all days short.

But on we must go, ground covered in snow,
Narrow lanes filled deep up to the hedge top;
Travelling together, we battled harsh weather
We prayed in our hearts - 'God let this wind stop.'

Our ears were ringing and faces stinging
With night now on us; feet sore and throbbing
We found dry ledges under wide hedges;
My wife, big with child, quietly sobbing.

With many a yawn we awoke at dawn
Blinking our eyes in the harsh morning light
Our hearts disapprove, but on we must move;
The new-fallen snow squeaks under our weight.

On gaining the hill in awe we stood still,
Seeing the vale outspread in sparkling array.
Cold desolation; no vegetation;
The winding river now frozen and grey.

Down there is an inn with a room within,
I think of another birth long ago.
But we must descend to our journey's end,
Pondering what God wills for us below.

Wendy A Nottingham, Ogmore-by-Sea

I Wonder What Birds Do All Day

Looking up into the tree,
I wonder what they do all day

Do they soar through the heavens
Wings broadened out, faces
Caressing the fluffy clouds.

Or do they fly to the top of
The highest tree, and
Build a home there,
Cuddling their shelled young.

Or perhaps they soar to
The highest mountain top
And capture food, keeping it in
Their unattainable homes
For later use.

Do they fly to a safe
Tree branch, only to ebb
Closer and closer to the
Weakening twig to
Shower the flightless world
Beneath with their soulful song

Perhaps they stand on the
Branch closest to the bark
And sighing down upon the
Pond with squirming specimen
Wishing that they could swiftly
Escape the air and
Jump into the coolness of fish.

Shiksha Dheda

At Peace By The Sea

As I sit staring out at the sea
I forget how you hurt me
That was back in spring
It's the new start that summer brings
So I watch as the sea hugs the shore
I know I deserved more
The blue crystal glare
Banishes every care
The summer sunshine
Clears all thoughts from my mind
I get lost in the melody
Of all that's around me
I just sit here
No longer shedding a tear
Just taking in the atmosphere
It's so much better than there
I hear the birds singing their song
One I hope continues on and on
I see people everywhere
But when I'm here
I feel like it's just me
Me and the sea
They laugh and run
Having so much fun
But still in this place
They are not invading my space
That's the beauty of the beach
You're close but you never quite reach
No matter how many people there are
They always seem so far
I feel warmth off of the sand
Something you don't get from other land
The night seems so far away
During this endless time of day
The clouds rare in the sky
Creating pictures only I see
Leaving footprints as I walk
This place has a way that talks
Capturing my heart as each moment passes
Not just mine but those of the masses

There's a reason why everyone flocks here
Escaping all their tears and fears
Where we all want to be
At peace by the sea.

Sara Burr, Inverurie

Mankind

This world's so full of hatred now,
If God came back he'd wonder how
Since first light when it all began
He let the world be run by Man!

For everywhere there's spite and greed
Where one man hates the other's creed
And some men stained with racist sin,
Detest the colour of their neighbour's skin.

Yet black man, white man, what's the odds?
We're all the same in the eyes of God,
We'll all end up beneath the clay
So what's the difference anyway?

Man grabs his neighbour's land, his oil
Invades his neighbour's sovereign soil
Creates more weapons at a frantic pace
Whilst trying to win the arms race.

If only Man would stop and think
Perhaps we'd move back from the brink
The voice of reason would not be lost,
And the world would avoid the holocaust!

James Quinn, Dumfries

The Farming Brothers

One, tall and thin as a rake, the other stocky
Plump as a butter ball
The same blue childlike eyes stare out of the brothers'
dissimilar faces.
They walk as one, talking loudly, both together
Each wanting to give you the yarn
With the occasional 'Aaaay' as they pull on their braces.

Clean living, hard-working virgins they
Toiling the land as their parents before them
Approaching the year 2000 with no trumpet call of honour
The long years of work, no monied wealth brought there.
Instead the farm with machinery and carts all gleaming clean
And brightly painted, heralding an age long past
Stand in lime-washed sheds like well dressed patrons in a church of prayer.

The modern tractors work the interminable rows
In weather fair and foul
Each long day and into night
The brothers still maintaining rustic health.
One can see them as boys, when Mother put them to their beds
Telling them stories of the land, their precious right.

As children, ankles tied to win the race
Coming abreast together to the line
The two old brothers working at the harvest
With a smooth unchanging pace
Yet using all their age-old skills.
Not heeding science with all its fashioned progress
To kill attackers of the soil and grain
Yet every day they watch the telltale sign
Of pesticides, insecticides on other people's land.

The ruination of the crops for greedy gain
The devastation wrought on plain and hills
Men's arbitrary response to warnings of great gloom
Sweeping on, relentless, seeking to impress
With mammoth bulks of food to hold in store
Thrashing the very goodness from the land,

The brothers see soil drift across the roads like sand
They work away - for all this they abhor
Trying to keep their earth in virgin balance whilst they live
Wondering how much more they can withstand.

Pamela Gibson, Duns

The Day I Became A Christian

40 odd years ago, something good happened to me
I was at the Youth Fellowship and oh what a-glee.
Do you know what they said - I have not forgotten
If I gave my heart to Jesus - salvation begotten.

Wait, I could not, till He'd take me forever
I prayed - forgive my sins and leave me never

He sees me through trouble and even while I laugh
Jesus the best friend, there is, on my behalf,
Everything He is, so precious and lovely,
I sing hallelujah, Almighty, Loving, Holy.

Anne Black McIsaac, Motherwell

Despair

I stand on your shore not knowing why
Unaware of the thunder of sea and sky
The sand slips gently from beneath my feet
At each menacing sound of the sea's heartbeat
It embraces me swiftly with clinging hands
To warn that life has but fragile strands.

In the wind I hear whispers of danger to me
From lost souls in your prisons beneath the sea
They cry out from dead ships in which you chain them
Imprisoned forever in Neptune's vile kingdom.

Yet screaming defiance in each wind that roars
As the sea's green fingers at my body claws
'Go back,' they implore, 'to life's safe beach
Where our captor's cruel arms are powerless to reach.'

I drag my feet from treacherous sand
And fought my way back to now precious land
Thanking those lost souls whom I'd so nearly joined
For the peace they had brought to my troubled mind!

Owain Symonds, Pontllanfraith

The Mirror Of Your Soul

The mirror of your soul, is the part I love the best.
When looking at them, temptation's the test.
The mirror of your soul, is your beautiful eyes.
When looking at mine, they do hypnotise.
I feel under your spell when our eyes meet.
My body's yours, and I surrender defeat.
They're just like a magnet, pulling me, to your side.
And then, how much in love we are, is impossible to hide.
When our eyes meet, the whole world, stands still.
And up my back, I feel this wonderful chill.
Like two china dolls, we stand and stare.
Shall we make contact? If only we dare.
Our bottom lips drop, as we stand so amazed.
Each other's emotions, we have now raised.
Two pairs of eyes, are burning with desire.
So in the grate, there must be a fire.
The eyes are showing the world, the one thing we treasure.
The eyes are showing the world, our feelings of pleasure.
There's no need, to open our mouths, or speak one word.
For, in the silence, not a single thing, is heard.
And out of our eyes, flow the words, the ones, we've not said.
The words in our eyes, that everybody else, seems to have read.
Actions speak louder, than words, they say.
And our feelings transmit, without delay.
The mirror of the soul, is God's gift to us all.
So in the wrong person's arms, it's impossible to fall.
Yours, are the eyes, that I know I can trust.
Yours, are the eyes, for which I lust.
They have, a certain longing, that makes me feel wanted.
They, make me feel, like I've almost been haunted.
We just, forget, all trace of time.
As our eyes freeze, in one straight line.
We forget whether it's day, or it's night.
To break the contact, like two magnets, we fight.
The warm glow between us, cannot be broken.
And yet, still, not a single word has been spoken.
Because the feelings we share, are so strong
That together, in our hearts, we belong.
That our lips, must stay sealed, forever and a day.
Until in eternity, our bodies will lay.
But how in God's name, can we break the spell?
If, no one on Earth, we can tell.
We'll keep, the secret, until we die.
And realising this, I shed a tear and cry.
Stronger than love, are the emotions, we feel.
And I thank God above, as I go down to kneel.

'Thank you, for bringing, this man, into my life.
Although, I shall never, be his wife.
He's given me, back, my dignity and pride.
By saying I'm beautiful,' tears of joy I now cry.
'He's put back the part of my life, that, was broken.
And the best words, he has said, his eyes, have spoken.
So our mouths, needn't say the words, 'I love you'.
Because, when you've got eyes, they will do.'

Linda Jennings, Glais

The Stolen Angel

High above the mountains where the sky meets the seas
Leads me to fields as she plays pale and fair
Gentle soul, clusters of snowdrops running so free
Trees of lilacs, sweet smells fill the air.
Your time was short your beauty beyond compare.
Death was not for you, it should have been me.

My perfect angel your tiny life was ahead
Dead dark clouds make my eyes so blurred.
I hear your laughter your smile is led
Instead the silence, not a sound on mists heard.
Snow flutters, flying angel's wings of a bird.
How lost the moment, the illusion of words said.

My soul lifts to the golden enchanted land
Hand stretched through the winding bluebell wood.
Leads to those tangled iron gates so grand
Stand open wide, a beautiful vision is now stood.
Angels wait, my darling daughter looking so good.
Fair, pale no more, that cherub face I understood.

Most certainly I knew her, I knew she would grow
Show the tears of joy, in God's Heaven I can pray
Ray of sunshine now, the fears have ceased to flow.
So long I have waited, so much having to say.
Towards the light hand in hand we walk our way.
My precious daughter together at last, our love we know.

Anne Williams, Llanelli

Northern Ireland 2011

I feel so lucky
To have lived my life
Through days of heartache
Sadness and strife
Through murder and mayhem
Wondering will it ever cease
Surviving years of conflict
To finally enjoy the taste of peace

Now yesterday's enemies
Today work side by side
I feel so lucky because
For years those thoughts had died
All the bitterness
That made life Hell on Earth
Led to the peace and babies' arrival
And I was at the birth.

Jim Emery, Ballymacoss

The Last Goodbye

The last goodbye
Will span a lifetime
With memories of
Fond feelings shared

Those happy days
And treasured moments
Will live forever
In time and space

For it goes on, and on
And on, and on, into infinity.

Grace Minnis, Holywood

First Crush

At primary school we first met, I was four, you were five.
I took one look and could never forget
Your bright blue eyes and jet-black hair;
At playtime we could never get near
For boys played in one yard and girls in the other
So - we never kissed.

We both passed our eleven plus then went off to grammar school,
To catch my bus I had to pass right by your house!
Hoping for a glimpse of you my steps slowed down.
Sometimes, you appeared at your door, my heart stood still,
But, we never kissed.

I helped you with your homework when you came to my house,
The teachers knew because our answers were the same!
My mam was friends with your mam,
So we used to visit; you played a record 'When I Fall In Love',
But - we never kissed!

We went to parties at our school, we had to catch a bus,
I wore a party dress and wellingtons - it poured with rain!
'Wellingtons!' you exclaimed! I looked up at you -
There was no one about and the moon was out . . .
I wish I had been bolder, but - we never kissed!

Time rolled on, we went our separate ways.
We met years later and I had changed from an ugly duckling
to a swan!
You didn't recognise me at first,
We smiled and chatted about old times,
But we never kissed - I wish I had been bolder,
But - we never kissed!

Ruth Lydia Daly, St Dials

A Trip To The City

At Drogheda on board I got
A bus to Dublin bound,
The fare, it was not large
Ten euro was the charge.
Then into Dublin I did go
The Liffey there I crossed,
On Shank's mare then I did proceed
Of traffic worries I'd no need.
Down Talbot Street I went
Into the Scripture Union,
And young Valmai there I met
She did some poetry get.
In Grafton Street a young lad sat
At an opensided piano,
His living there he sought to make
And income from CDs to take.
A shopping centre I did find
And tastefully it was designed,
Down in St Stephen's Green,
- Sure the clothes were fit for a queen.
Then on to St Anne's Cathedral
And next to Trinity College,
Some history there to view
Past the tourist centre too.
A lady she sat beside its door
Playing the harp with a beautiful tune,
The passers-by they stopped to hear
The lyrics falling on their ear.
Across to St Patrick's Cathedral
And into Dublin Castle,
What a beautiful architecture!
Too late for a tour or a lecture!
With sore feet I returned
From a very enjoyable trip,
The day it fled too fast
The memories they will last!
Some day the journey of life will end
How soon we do not know,
'Tis good to trust the sinner's friend
Our Lord, who to the Cross did wend.
From Heaven to Earth the Saviour came

The journey of life to make,
That we through simple faith in Him
A place in Heaven then should win.

Ruth Edgar, Dromore

The Lifeline

She'd phoned to say goodbye, she said.
She had phoned several times before
But now her life was at an end.
She'd bought the pills; the whisky too.
Tonight would be her last on Earth
The quiet, kindly voice enquired,
'What makes you feel you can't go on?
You must be feeling pretty low.'
And slowly she retold her tale:
The car had crashed, her husband dead
And she herself a crippled wreck.
She'd battled on for ten long months
But things could never be the same.
Her active life would be no more.
No one could help her get through this.
The quiet voice said, 'We are here.
You've got us now to see you through.
We'll talk all night if that will help
And while you need us we'll be there.'
A sigh, a pause and then she said,
'No one has tried to help before.
Perhaps with you I might survive.
Perhaps I'll put the pills away.
Your being there has helped me live.
Thank you, dear Lifeline, it is good
To know that someone cares for me.'
Her mood had changed; she felt relaxed;
Her suicidal thoughts had passed.
The phone went down. A life was saved.
The 'quiet voice' had done her work.

Kathleen Wendy Jones, Rhyl

Empty Overcoat

The silence of winter
spent
embalming flowers
with
Toom Tabard's
regret.

A drowned voice lost in noise
dying from the outside in
as many before
and those
who never begin

So
leave the dead
to their dreams
and moments of magic.

Grant Cameron, Aberdeen

Mother Nature

The nature's changing its energy course
and it's forgetting to comfort the air
and the blue and black clouds are just floating everywhere.
The electric downpours of the rain
are making the riverbanks burst
and the seasons of the weather are getting worse.
The eternal sun stands motionless
when it used to shine with delight
and now underneath the lonely moon
the stars are dim at night.
Mother Nature is making this world sad
and lonely each day
and all that we can do now for things to change
is to get together and pray.

Veronica Davison, Misterton

A Poem In Time

I'd like to be a poet
I thought as I sat down
But words just seemed to elude me
They kept going round and round

But then I began to realise
That life is a poem in time
And the uniqueness of each verse
Leads to many a different rhyme

The poems of life can be short or long
When providence takes control
And the vivacity of the content
Comes from deep within the soul.

Life is short for everyone
No matter how long we live
So why do we complicate it
Just learn to love and forgive.

Forgiveness is a freedom
Whose legacy makes us rich
So why not write a poem
Whose aim is to enrich.

Teresa Bell, Moneymore

Soul Searching

As I search the souls of those I know, seeking what is true . . .
It's disappointing after time finding truth in few.
Why do they tread their paths in life in that impassive way,
Never taking time to stop to wish a friend good day.
With honest thought, from the heart, and meaning every word,
Too much to ask, I'm sad to say, they'd find the thought absurd.
Relationships built on sand are much what most prefer,
And some built upon the rock, still seem to cause despair.
Yet, each of us who search for truth, will find it's not in vain,
We'll only lose what's false in life . . . the truth will be our gain.

Ronnie Simpson, Blairdardie

The Puppeteer

And I will be an author,
And I will play my puppets,
Make them move and dance, or falter,
For the strings are in my hands.

And I will weave my fancies,
As the Turks they weave their carpets,
Give them pattern give them colour
For the strands are in my hands.

And I will take a beggar,
And I will rise and fall him,
Give him life and then discard him,
Let the strings fall from my hands.

And I will make a kingdom,
And people it with princes,
Let them love, or fight, or suffer,
But the strings stay in my hands.

For without me, they are lifeless,
But without them, I am nothing.
Who is puppet? Who is master?
The strings are in whose hands?

Betty Westcott, Newport

Wake

Vision reveals a sun glowing love
and warmth unto body and soul.
When all is sun rays, the horizon of life
is an evaporation of clouds.
Enjoy the rapture of her love, for it holds
keys to doors that express, Heaven.
Blame not harshly your mind or self for hiding away.
Wake and come back unto the realms of your identity and meaning.
To walk a path on a crooked bumpy road is one way to travel,
but you and your reservations are as a weight of unnecessity.
Unravel your feathers my fine graceful friend and fly.

Nick Purchase, Grangetown

Wet, We Live - Dry, We Die

Moving in a desert, moving with the wind
Without the wets, it's just like living in a dream
It's like someone injects
Lots of sand, in my veins
And then just a drop makes me alive
Because
Wet, we live - dry, we die

From the smallest life, to the largest being
A small bird's species ever seen
Everything depends on wets and greens
The crawling creatures, bird that fly
Because
Wet, we live - dry, we die

I learned the importance of wets and thy
Without them no one can and may
To wish for fruits and colours around
Without them there is not even a single sound
On all wetlands, forests our future lie
Because
Wet, we live - dry, we die

Imagine us, without souls
A soul without useful thoughts
Same will happen, if we end the moist
We'll lose everything, even if we survived
If someone has to choose between the two
The unending hunger, and water the blue
The first choice will be water, all of us knew
Without it the fruits will never grew
And will end up, including me and you
Just save your wetlands, at least start to try
Because,
Wet, we live - dry, we die

We should wish, we must say
Our wetlands, forests be saved everyone pray
We cannot, without them take a single lift
We must take care of God's precious gift
We will save them
Never will say goodbye
Because
Wet, we live - dry, we die.

Zoha Khalid, Islamabad

Sprite

There she sits in the secret glade
With her arms wide open
To the sky.
And all around the nightingales fly
Upon the breezes
That form from her senses
As she sends them heavenwards
To capture her dreams.

There she waits in the deepening meadows
As the spring comes calling
And see how
She works the air all around her.
Watch how the willows
Bend and gently rustle now
To the song of the streams
That run through her feet there.

A light rain falls
On the upper reaches
Of the age-rent oaks,
The giant beeches.
Yet far below
No patter is heard or felt
Just a sparkle upon
Her flower-strewn shirt.

A pale owl flies by
And calls to the girl
With sun in her hair
And her eyes meet his.
No words are spoken
No signs are shared
Just thoughts and memories
Across the airs.

And in her songs
There lies a tale
Of lives and loves
Still to come
For one so young.
She spins a dress of wintergreen
To wear when her lover comes
It's one he has never seen.

Then from deep without
The forest glade
Where only magic walks on summer eves
A call is heard upon air
That sends a shimmer to the stars.
And through the ground
A tremble starts
That shakes the leaves of autumn's heart,
See, her lover comes!

From the hills that lie between
A glimmer now takes hold.
In a forest glade
Where footsteps fade
And rustles are no more,
A lady with hair of the sun
Is dancing with her love.
In green they're clad
On Earth they tread.
To the stars they'll fly
On wings that are never heard.

Julian Bishop, Fasnakyle

Awakening

Stark severity, winterish 2010-2011
Activity protracted
Proceeded springtime 2011-thaw
Heaven's magnetism, region succumbed
Radiance dissolve frostiness, snow
Perishing remnants fluctuate
Climatic dormancy emerge
Species, manpower, interaction abound
Kaleidoscopic transpose land
Raising extant magnificence
Avant-garde Cardiff capital city
Renowned.

Pam Ismail, Llanishen

Crazy Sayings

Don't put off till tomorrow
What you can do today
But as tomorrow never comes
How come tomorrow's another day?

Don't put all your eggs in one basket
Don't count your chickens before they are hatched
But if birds of a feather flock together
I'd say they were perfectly matched.

Half a loaf is better than none
Well that's what somebody muttered
But who in their minds would eat only bread
Unless they knew on which side it was buttered.

No more of these crazy old sayings
Good and bad luck comes in threes
So if money is the root of all evil
How come it does not grow on trees?

Barbara Fowler, Merthyr Tydfil

The Cranes

One morning, glancing up at a pink-flecked sky,
I saw two giant cranes, at rest before the day's work,
Facing each other, the frames almost touching,
As though about to engage in an intimate kiss.

Their metal gleaming in the early morning sun,
These mighty features of Man's creation,
Perfectly angled towards each other,
Reflected a bizarre beauty all of their own.

Do they have souls, these lofty structures
Dominating the awakening city's skyline?
Are they whispering sweet nothings to each other
Or murmuring, 'See you after work.'

Alison Drever, Edinburgh

The High Mountains

Majestic mountains regally crowned
Snow capped tiaras, leather bound
'Neath blue skies freedom is found
And living is ever sweet.

Fragrant air free from pollution
There one finds the perfect solution
Reaching God to seek absolution
From all earthly deceit.

Clouds send o'er summits in gay abandon
Swirling down valleys taken at random
Where man has n'er put his brand on
Such beauty reaching on high.

Exhilaration gained in mountain sealing
Leaving behind all misery and wailing
Pulses throbbing and never failing
Absorbing pleasure with a sigh.

The sun creeping o'er a distant peak
Sunbeams cavorting down into a creek
Chasing shadows that persistently streak
Into dark valleys beneath.

Sweet fragrance of the elegant pine
Spreading cones in a mantle so fine
One can stretch and gently recline
Upon the luxurious heath.

Never to return to the rat race below
Noise and bustle that's forever go
Worldly traffic incessant flow
That's not for me.

Give me the clean air of mountains sweet
The great golden eagle circling his beat
God's creation makes life complete
That's where I'd love to be.

Bill Barker, East Wemyss

Hot Ice

A damp mist embraces the crowd
And the wind chimes they rattle aloud
Blades they scream across the ice
With figures so hot like spice
Mesmerised in the heart of sound
Tangled bodies unbound
As the drums begin to burn on fire
To the music axels grow higher
Then costumes change and change
And back and forth from age to ice age
With elegance and grace they steal the show
With energy they set the stage aglow
Off burning lasers and water fountains
Where skaters bang metal against tins
Blades skate to the rhythm
With girls and men with them
Twisting their bodies into perilous shapes
In lycra suits and flinging capes
Flying above the ice, flapping their arms
Hot ice steaming below, as the applause it charms
Taking folks on journeys with wonderful sights
Sexy and toned beautiful delights
With shining hair in different styles from years ago
They parade on ice in solo and pairs and synchro
With spirals and lay-backs and death drops
Replenishing our souls till the music stops.

Cameron McIntyre, Newtownards

The New You

Now take a look at yourself
And then you will know
It's time to lose weight
Why not have a go.

Cut out the junk food
Take plenty of fruit
You will soon find
You'll fit your Sunday suit.

Now cut out those greasy fish and chips
Don't dare let one across your lips
Remember to always drink plenty of water
As this is the key to this healthy matter.

But don't forget take two meals a day
This will help you in your work rest and play
Pears and bananas, apples and grapes
These are the things that help keep us in shape.

Up early in the morning and on your skates
You will soon find the drop in your weight
Start yourself to walking mile after mile
On your face you'll soon have a smile.

So get out and start walking and without a doubt
Soon you will have something worth smiling about
Now you're beginning to feel good and healthy
Remember it's more important than to be wealthy.

Mary Morton, Keady

The Fisherman

One day as I was walking down by the River Bann
I saw a figure standing there an ancient fisherman.
His hair was grey his face was tanned his body old and bent
His eyes were on the water with a look of deep content.

I stopped to watch a moment to see him cast his fly
And said old man be careful for the water's running high.
You should not fish alone I said as he slowly turned around
You're not a young man anymore I'd hate to see you drowned.

He said now these Bann waters are known well by me
I've fished the Bann Backwater the Braid the Roe the Rhee
My family is all scattered my friends beneath the sod
I have nothing left to care for now but this old fishing rod.

Now if there is a Heaven and this I'll never doubt
Then surely there are rivers there that's teeming full of trout.
For where would all the men have gone who fished on Galilee
They must be fishing up there still upon a Heavenly sea.

Soon after this they found him upon his lonely bed
While he was sleeping peacefully his poor old soul had fled.
I stood beside an open grave and said a silent prayer
I hope you find your Heaven friend tight lines when you get there.

Robert Simpson, Ballymoney

Student Life

The old sofa they sat on in the garden
Is now in a skip
Their student days of fun are over
Three years of study now gone
No more sit down Frisbee games outside
Or evenings spent drinking as they watched the sun set
Frightened, lonely Freshers grow to confident students
Fun is mostly what it is all about
Then it is off into the world for a gap year
Or hopefully to find a job
Some never leave this place but go on for higher degrees
At the University of Wales by the sea.

Melanie M Burgess, Aberystwyth

My Reverie

I know a place, where the greenest grass grows,
In a circle surrounded by trees.
Birch, beech, and lofty pine
Spread out their branches and entwine
A parasol of leaves.

I know a place where the air is still,
Peace and tranquillity reign.
Sorrow and joy, and free from pain
Where life and love could begin again
In a circle surrounded by trees.

I know a place where I can go,
To reflect my secret thoughts.
Where I can plan fantastic schemes
Imagine my romantic dreams
In a place where the greenest grass grows.

Joan Littlehales, Rhostyllen

Poetry Within The Soul

Poetry doesn't have to rhyme
At least not every time
Sometimes the message
Is loud and clear
And you know what poems mean.
Other times
The meaning is deeper
Like abstract paintings in a gallery.
The rhyme is
How poems are read
And not in how they end.
Modern poetry can leave you confused,
Which really makes you think.
So if poetry is within your soul
Just let the words unfold.

Catherine Keohane-Johnson, Penydarren

Just Stand And Wait

Not a place in life now
As the poor still stand and stare
At a road of cars and lorries
And new houses everywhere
In the years when work was tough
Man played a role with pride
But now his life is pushed along
By the woman at his side

In a world where crowds stand idle,
Oh! Brains how could you
Deprive us of the golden rule
In the days that we once knew
A computer styled with letters
There on a screen to view
A perfect picture shimmers
And the answer's given to you!

The greatness of a modern life
Brilliance mixed with brawn
If you could see beyond today
And warn us of our wrongs
Capture a joyful picture
Or sadness to beguile
We would love to be with you
And live here in great style.

We know no picture holds
Time enchanted there
For in this world of cruelty
The poor stand back and stare
They always wait for better things
Then surely they will come
When their lives are over
And death claims everyone.

John Monaghan, Ballygawley

Once

I see the sea, the expanse of grey under a cloudy sky
The rise and fall of the swell, the latent power
That is dormant in each wave, yet this force can be so
Gentle as it smoothes its way upon the sand
But you are not at hand.

The billowing clouds that crown a southern sky
And rise so high above the rolling hills
Are flecked with colour from a setting sun
As the rush of day time slowly quiets down
But you are not around?

The gentle trickle of a brook meandering through reeds
Upon the mountain flank, that then cascades a hundred feet
And becomes a rushing stream that into the valley flows
And dodges around the rocks that line its way
But where are you today?

The crags that crown the mountain summit that then
Swoop down into a greener gentle land with fields
Of corn and wooded patches here and there
The farms, the cottage nestling by the hill
Where are you still?

These days I cannot see a view but think of you
The sea, the clouds, the hedgerows and the trees
The scent of flowers on the evening air and carried
by the gentle breeze
Caress your person, or did one time
But now you're gone
No longer mine.

Cyril G Payne, New Inn

The Blossom On The Dee

The blossom falls upon the Dee,
Like brides in white
They sail by night
Into a wider sea.

White petals gleam
Upon the stream
They fall so silently.

Green branches sway
Buds torn away
To a new destiny.

No flower in spring
So fine a thing
The bride's white purity.

How fresh and lovely they begin,
How soon they fade
Night closes in,
The blossom on the Dee.

E Hawkins, Denbigh

Winter

First she moves slowly
Creeping upon you eerily bringing dark evenings,
Temperatures drop below zero.
With her long white hair and ice crystal dress
She scatters the frost in the chill of the night.

As time moves on she becomes more cruel.
High winds cause fear and devastation,
But she has no remorse.
As we sleep nervously in our beds
Her evil mind is deliberating her next punishment.

The sun being her only real enemy,
She calls upon her many friends to help her with her callous tasks.
Thunder, lightning, hail and fog
All jump to her every command
Her pace now hurried, ensuring chaos all around.

Alone in her ice castle
She drums up another plan,
Heavy snowfall and then flooding, destruction once again.
As lives are lost and homes destroyed
She grins an icy smile,
For winter is just evil, cruel and unkind.

Chelsey-Leigh Clatworthy (16), Blaengarw

The Blacksmith

Leather-aproned, stooped with pliers,
Fetlock wedged between his knees,
He prises the worn-down metal crescent
off the beast with a skilful squeeze.

Now the iron - beaten - ringing
between the anvil and the forge
as, bellows snoring, the amber-glowing
slumbering fire begins to surge.

Red-hot ingots shaped and fashioned,
dipped and hissing, belching steam,
tempered, fitted - acrid burning,
metal forged with a skill supreme.

Shoe completed, nails inserted
hammered home with practised ease,
the blacksmith arcs his back surveying
this stamp of his dying expertise.

Fred McIlmoyle, Bangor

Summer

Last summer season's come and gone
But happy memories linger on
I travelled o'er the British Isles
And everywhere was wreathed in smiles

I wandered through your barley rigs
I sang your songs and danced your jigs
I laughed and cried and drank your wine
And pilgrim prayed at holy shrine
I walked your lanes
I fished your streams
I shared your most fantastic dreams
I climbed your hills and breathed your air
And wished again that I were there

The season's days will wax and wane
But summer will roll back again
No mortal man can change the face
Of this green and pleasant place.

Frederick Osborne, Bangor

The Visit

In the still and silent night
Like thieves they come, as vicious might.
They come to disturb sweet peaceful sleep.
They come to disrupt and to keep
You awake.

They bang at the front door
The window the back door.
Rash to confuse you
Remarks to abuse you.
They've come.

A baby starts crying
A mother starts praying
There's no need to plead
Let them take what they need.

Papers, books scattered the place
Agony, torture showed on my face.
God give me courage from within
Let me know that soon we will win.

George Du Plessis, Boksburg

Spring And Summer

The spring is here - joy at last
The winter has gone - in the past!
As leaves unfurl and flowers bloom
It helps us all to forget the gloom
As we watch the wonders grow
A little bird darts to and fro
And builds its nest way off ground
We marvel at nature, it has no bounds
The summer follows in a spectacular blaze
And feeds the eye - as we stop to gaze
Trees and flowers in their Sunday best
That leaves the gardener little time for rest
Hedges to cut, lawns to mow,
Always busy and on the go -
Without God's help - there would not be
A coloured flower, or a leafy tree
A singing bird or a busy bee
Without our help, you must agree!
God as the gardener?
Is jolly untidy!

J Pressly-Allen, Knutsford

When Will It All End?

When will it all end?
Simple answer, it won't
There is no start
There is no end
We all just change form
Then we do it again

Yes it seems dark
When you are alone
But this is your planet
This is your home

Yes your human body
May end in time
Don't worry your head
You'll be just fine

No matter your troubles
We all face the same
Your body will disappear
But you will always remain

You might be a bird
Maybe a lion in the past
You will always be here
Your spirit will last

So lift up your head
And focus on life
Give yourself purpose
Give yourself drive

If not for you
Then for some others
Remember we are all the same
My sisters and brothers.

Anthony Dunne/O'Regan, Kilkenny

Pain

Why did you leave me why did you go?
I am trying hard to find the answers but I really don't know
I tried so hard to make you love me, to want me
Was I so bad that it made you feel you wanted to be free?

You have been gone for so long I am in so much pain
Living, laughing it's all so much of a strain
These feelings I have for you what do I do?
They say time heals, that you'll feel better but it's so untrue

They are always there filling my heart up with pain
Getting through each day what for? What do I have to gain?
Each day I try harder to be stronger
But inside the pain just seems to stay longer

I wish I could talk to you, for you to phone
I wish I could ask you why you left me alone
What I would give to feel your arms holding me tight
Holding me close making everything feel alright

I didn't think you would leave again, not twice
But I felt safe and paid the ultimate price
I made myself feel happy for the first time in years
It felt good to be with you to kiss away the tears

I felt myself feel feelings which I have always had
Even though I knew that things could turn bad
I trusted you even though I shouldn't do
Because you knew how my life was, how bad it was without you.

But I guess it doesn't matter it feels like you didn't care
Because suddenly you were gone and my life feels so bare
What did I do wrong? I guess I'll never know
What do I do now my life has nowhere to go?

I guess you can love someone too much.

Nancy Tamagno, Ladywell

My Country

The land of song my homeland creso glorious Wales
'Calon Lan' 'Myfanwy' are vocalised through hills and vales
Rugged majestic mountains many, stately castle exalted everyone
Testament to years of battle, some lost, but mostly won
The rills, the stream and rivers, babbling, tumbling as they go
From mountain tops to valleys, cascading then meandering as on their way they flow

Past pit heads most now silent, black sentinels of Yore
No miners' feet clatter the roadways home, their lamps are lit no more
Pit ponies now out grazing, green meadows and the sunshine to enjoy at last
The wooden pit prods crumbling, their job done, long in the past
Slag heaps now are landscaped, nature's beauty reclaimed at cost
Miners no more breathe black dust, therefore, not all is lost
Our coastline quite outstanding, awesome cliffs, some sheer outcrops
Miles of sandy beaches, pretty harbours, colourful yachts
Children happy building sandcastles or jumping over some small waves
The bolder ones, exploring rock pools, the grottos and deep caves
The daffodil, leek, red dragon proud emblems most dear each one
Ancient history our heritage many valiant deeds well done.

Marjorie Leyshon, Swansea

In Our Yorkshire Garden

The frost, the cold, the snow, have gone
Spring is here again
The flowers and shrubs and bulbs appear
There's colour and green all around

Now summer is nearly here
The yellows and blues of the alpines
The pinks and yellow roses too
The foxgloves entice the bees
Up each flower they do crawl
Collect the pollen and away they go
Over the fence as they have done before.

We sit in our garden with our cup of tea
We watched everything happening and yes everything is free
The birds are singing a happy song
All of them glad that winter has gone.

Marjorie Langhorn, Darrington

The Monster Within

Gareth tried to bully me
I'm twice his age and half his size
So what a coward he must be.

He will not prosper nor succeed
Unless he listens and takes heed.

He hurts the people who are kind
It doesn't occur to him to mind
Or care about the damage done,
He targets people who are fun,
He thinks he is the only one
To find life rough, so what! And tough!

To achieve success and happiness
He'll have to sort out his own mess.

Rachel E Joyce, Cardiff

The Seasons

Autumn leaves fall, the trees begin to look bare,
Weather changes windy, wet, cold and sometimes fair,
But even in these days there is a beauty to be seen,
In the leaves with their hues of red, gold and green,
Then followed by winter dark early at night,
Maybe some snow so pretty a sight,
More time spent at home cosy and warm,
But poor birds and outside animals cold and forlorn,
Daffodils look glorious and now spring starts to appear,
More plants, leaves come back on trees and you know summer is near,
Lazy days spent enjoying the warmth and glad of a gentle breeze,
Time for holidays, beach trips, outdoor activities and all that you please,
Each season has beauty in its own way,
It is exciting to see the changes in every season day by day,
Let's not even complain when we think we get too much rain,
Some countries have none and it causes sorrow, sickness, death and pain,
So let's enjoy each season and look for the pleasure it can bring,
Summer, autumn, winter and spring.

Patricia Todd, St Helier

Coach Journey To Scotland

We went to the station in a hurry
The coach was waiting for the passengers to come
They said no need to hurry
You've time for a tea and a bun.
We started the journey proper
With the driver in command at the wheel
He said we're heading for the border
If I fall asleep you just squeal.

It rained most of the way in a fashion
But inside we were dry and content.
We left it to his intuition
It seemed as though he'd been sent.
We stopped once or twice for the usual
And left what we stopped for behind,
We felt better for the break in the journey
And everyone seemed very kind.

The hold-ups were not very frequent
But one was stretching for miles.
It's a good thing we're not back this way tomorrow
As traffic is in single file.
From then on we motored to Scotland
Over hills and through picturesque glens.
The colours were really magnificent
An artist's palette had touched every strand.

At six-thirty we arrived at the castle
The courier was on in a flash.
You rooms are all numbered and ready
You'll just have time for a splash.
The welcome we got was tremendous
And it stayed like that all the time.
We've been fed, sheltered and cared for
With affection and love that's sublime.

The entrancing beauty of Scotland
We've seen as never before.
Over hills, on lochs and in glens
Leaves us looking and yearning for more.
Tomorrow we return to the homeland
With an ache in our hearts, that's true
It's not goodbye that's forever
It's adieu our kind friends, it's adieu.

Margaret Kent, Beauly

An Odyssey

Following a narrow stream
travelling on tendrils
wafted by weeds
at one with the flow,
I have come into being.

Tumbling out
into huge spaciousness,
a vast soft cavern,
I find a place to burrow in
to take root and grow
a seed in the earth.

In a bubble of fluid
I am floating,
finding form
curling, stretching, spiralling
a waterborne astronaut,
my cord, a lifeline.

Like a sensitive receiver
my cells pick up messages
transmitted from the outer world
do I open to life or defend myself
am I welcomed nourished, carried with love
or in a toxic place, starved and rejected.
I twist, turn, smile, frown, kick, rest and play,
a dance of movement and growth.

Slowly life changes
where there was space, now confines
the place of floating freedom
becomes a tight caress.

Enclosed and trapped
I push and feel resistance
toning my muscles,
building my power.

These prison walls are crushing me.
I can't survive in here.

I must escape.

I am preparing
for a new journey.

Lesley Downie, Findhorn

Dragons Amidst The Clouds

From a vision of a child who sees the shapes in the clouds as fierce dragons . . .

The sky is just white
But I see
Beyond the morning light
Their long triangle tails
And fire-blowing flames
Dragons I see
Looking down at me

Their mythic beauty fascinates me
I hold their tail and pull them down
Holding their orange moustache
Like a crown

The sky is just white
But I see
Beyond the morning light
The sharp swords at the neck
Seem to me like cards on a playing deck
Dragons I see
In the sky set free

As the lines of pink in the sky go dark
The clouds change shape
But I still make out
Where the dragons would be

The sky is just white
But I see
Beyond the morning light
The teeth are sharp like a shark's
Their howls thunder but still sound like barks
Dragons I see
Calling me

They jump on each other
In a dangerous yet good-humoured fight
They jumble around in their battlefield
Turning their tail into a knot quite tight

The sky is just white
But I see
Beyond the morning light
They've black under their eye
Thumping their feet across the sky
Dragons I see
Combating me
As dusk sets the sky

And stars twinkle
I still see beyond their light
For the last time
At the dragons amidst the clouds
This time;
Waving goodbye . . .

The sky is just white
But I see
Beyond the morning light . . .

Nikita Biswal, Delhi

Nut Farm

Welcome to my new farm -
It's going to be a big success!
The crops have just been planted
And once they've all come up
I'll have the raw materials
To put the plans in gear.
A soon as the pignut crop matures
I'll have a herd of pigs
And once the money nuts come up
I'll be supplying pet shops.
Once the peanuts have grown peas
And the coconuts grown cocoa
I'll sell to supermarkets by the ton!
Yes, I know that there's a problem -
I haven't got a farmhouse -
But there's a cheap solution on the way!
I'll put the house together
When I've got enough components -
When the walnut field
Has grown a crop of walls!

Dilys Jones, Hull

Eventide

The shadows gather as the night enfolds the countryside,
The warm sweet breath of eventide through trees and bracken sighs.
And mountain tops are hidden in a dark and mystic spell,
As moonlight cast a tapestry on hedgerow, field and fell.

The scent of summer blossoms, meadowsweet and rambling rose,
The fluttering of the bird's frail wings, that seeks the night's repose
And out upon the fell side, the sheep in plaintive cry,
As a sharp-eyed owl on soundless wing, swoops through the branches high.

The barking of a sheepdog, and the cattle's gentle low;
The whispering sounds of insects, and the firefly's flitting glow;
And deep in field and ditch, the scurrying sounds of tiny feet,
Of woodmice, voles and rabbits, and the badger's lone retreat.

I sit beside the casement, rest my head against the pane,
And in the darkness see the lamp at the ending of the lane.
Its mellow glow that lights a patch amid the night's lone hours,
And sends to me the comfort, like a rainbow after showers.

Beryl Shepard Leece, Wallasey

Times Gone Bye

Today I sat and talked with you
About anything and everything till we turned blue

We spoke of memories of years gone by
Times that hurt us when we'd ask why?

Speaking only in truth, trying not to cry
Because there was no reason for us to lie

I'll finish this poem by writing now
Accepting each other without raising a brow

Listening intently, hearing every word
Safe in the knowledge every verb was heard.

Deborah Wilson, Norton

Summer Morning Walks

Summer morning walks with you
Well girl, you ease my mind
Keep me steady on my feet
Fill me with your love every day
And I realise just what you are
Girl, you're a credit to this world
That's what you are
Summer morning walks with you
Well girl, you ease my mind
Little talks, no holding back
The way you laugh, the way you walk
Girl you take all my troubles away
See them floating over the bay
Bouncing, now, screaming, let us stay!
Yes, girl, you took all my demons away
And now the sun shines on my face every day.

Terry Ramanouski, Widnes

Jenny

The epitome of youth
Painted this song writer's light
Just as luminous stars
Shone - celestial bright
And
To a time-honoured poet
Such synchronised bond
Was as lyrical music
While strength of mind traversed on
Never by chance - was our meeting
But a power - timely placed
When all is reaching
Connecting
In Divineness and Grace.

Irene Gunnion, Perth

Our Wonderful Mum

It's been a year since you've gone
We're all still trying to figure out, what went wrong
You were taken from us, way before you're time
Sudden death, why is it such a punishable crime?

We never got a chance to say our proper goodbyes
Thoughts left unsaid, through the heartache, pain and cries,
Words cannot be found at such a loss,
We're all still trying to understand the meaning of 'someone lost'.

You've left a void, such a vast emptiness,
We're all left abandoned here so helpless,
Your headstone inscribed on it' 'je pense plus'
For the love we all had for you, you never really knew.

You were a woman, with a heart of gold,
For your life was so precious, never to be sold,
If there is a Heaven, you're surely there
Perhaps I'll maybe see you there sometime in the future.

You were an angel, that was put on Earth,
As if sent here by the Almighty Himself,
As children, you kept us safe from harm,
Your shoulder, a haven to always cry upon.

You taught us to be always good, never to be bad,
Now coming to terms with your loss, is so terribly sad,
So God rest your soul, we all can pray,
That we know in our hearts, you're with us every day,
So, we will leave our flowers and tears now at your grave,
For a woman, mum and gran you were so brave,
Goodnight Mum, sleep well xx.

Robbie Hillhouse, Ayr

Coatbridge Gran

I'm feeling really down today, I could do with a great big hug.
But the one person, who does this best, has been taken up above.
God decided it was time, time for her to go.
Why did He have to take her, I guess I'll never know.

It's never been the same, since you were taken away.
I wish God could have spared you, even for one more day.
Then maybe I could have fitted in one last special hug.
Just before He took you, away up high above.

I'm talking about my 'Coatbridge Gran' she meant the world to me,
And anyone who met her loved her instantly.
She was such a lovely person, so warm and so kind,
And a nicer person in the world you could never find.

I wish you were still here, sitting in your chair,
Or making apple pie for all of us to share.
I wish you could have been here, to meet all your great grandkids
I tell them all about you and everything I miss.

The thing I miss the most are your great big hugs,
They made me feel so happy, they made me feel so loved.
Sometimes when I hug the kids, I say, 'It's from up above,'
And tell them it's from Coatbridge Gran, she's sending down her love.

I think about you every day; sometimes I shed a tear,
It's really hard some days; I wish you were still here.
I'll keep on passing on those hugs, and sending on your love,
Until we meet again, somewhere up above.

All my love Coatbridge Gran
Always thinking of you

Love
Diane x.

Diane Thomson Miller, Uddingston

Nursing Home

You have to be nice to the staff
in this godforsaken funny farm.
If you don't you'll get a frown

or a slap on the arm.
You're not allowed to laugh
so I keep the head down

like a horse in a stable,
a human vegetable.
Where's the young man

who broke every law in the book?
(Gone for his tea, I'm afraid.)
Look at him now: down on his luck,

wishing he could meet
the people from Civvy Street
where everyone is the same.

It's different now. I'm ashamed
to call myself human.
A sociological calamity,

strangers call me by my first name
(the modern disease of familiarity)
and I have to accept it.

As far as health goes I'm not too bad
no visible neuroses
or incipient osteoporosis.

The hours are like days
in here but I don't let anything faze me.
You become a digit

forgetting you're bored rigid
as you attempt the latest jigsaw,
treating it like a cure for leprosy

or the parting of the Red Sea.
For years now I've been sitting here
looking out at the same sunrise,

the same polite young men
who tell me forgivable lies.
They smile sweetly at me

as they raise a spoon to my lips
so I don't dribble.
Fair enough; I don't want to quibble

about house rules.
But I'm looking at ways
of being a disgusting old fool.

I could refuse to watch 'Countdown'
for instance, or do a number two
in my dressing gown.

Thrill-seeking for oldies is dirty.
It's eating your After Eights at 7.30.
Could I have them at seven, or even six?

Maybe I'll hit matron with my crutch
and get locked up with the geriatrics.
Could I go on hunger strike

for some lost cause? Maybe not.
How can you make a point by refusing
something you don't even like?

(You couldn't call the food here hot.)
Maybe I'll put a Harley Davidson engine
in my fifth-hand wheelchair

and do multiple somersaults
up and down the stairs.
Or even become a kamikaze bomber.

I could put a stick of gelignite
around my waist. That would
give some people a right fright.

Maybe, the dossers in the Dail.
(Who's miss Fianna Fail?)
Or those f*****s in the HSE

who put me here.
I'd be doing a favour for all of us.
But who'd stretcher me to the bus?

Aubrey Malone

Breaking My Family Ties

Sitting on the curb of Fourth and Main
I barely escaped the reign of fear and pain,
Still have the scars to prove it:
My past was corrupt, but my future won't be abrupt.
He's probably driving around in his Cadillac,
Searching for someone to hurt and smack,
He's no longer my daddy,
He turned into a needle fiend,
When I needed my father,
He didn't want to bother.
Used to make me feel special,
Now that *special* seems surreal,
And now I'm sitting here asking God, 'Why me?'
But He sends no reply,
I can't decide if my father truly loves me.
With an actor's heart,
He played his part,
No one had suspicions at the start,
My soul morphed into a ghost,
Since he's the parasite, I became the host,
My trust dissipated because I anticipated the truth,
It seems my prayers never went through,
My anxiety grew,
I felt enraged since I knew my mother's cries weren't staged.
The woman I look up to put herself aside,
She had no one to confide in,
Got fed up and my family divided,
But after all the things that he put us through
Can you tell me why I'm crying?
I couldn't separate myself from the pain I grew accustomed to,
My ivory-coloured skin returned to black and blue,
But now that I'm staying with him,
My patience is wearing thin,
Every day I'm like a ticking time bomb,
Detonate, then gone.
Something's keeping me here although it's hard to bear,
Every night I cry myself to sleep,
Struggling to find the 'old me',
But I'm drowning in all his lies,
It's so hard to see,
I can't take anymore, I'm at my last resort,
'God, I think it's time to meet you,'
I ran and I never looked back,

He dialled 'nine-double one',
I was gone faster than a heart attack,
(Heaven) arrived at 4:11.

Kalie Eaton, McDonough

Thoughts

I write these words for you alone
Please do with them what you will
For answers that are wrote in stone
Leave questions we will never ask.

Times and memories we'll never forget
As the future will become the past
And then all the people we have met
Their words still haunt our minds

Life is treated as a game
Love is what we're always denied
Lies and truth are one and the same
And friends refuse honesty

Love is lonely, yet I love you so
And freedom from guilt denied the innocent
Who can tell or care what we want to know
As day by day faith becomes belief.

Lee Connor, Norton

The Sea

The sea, so vast and endless
Always moving with the tides
pulling, this way and that.
The flashing foam of sea horses
The churning of the storm
The endless cries of seagulls
welcoming ships to land.

Christine B Dobbie, Rothesay

Cygnus

The azure blues against each other,
rippling gently across the morning breeze.
The swans gliding across the surface,
lose their grace to pachyderms.
A neck, a trunk; beautiful feathers, great ears.
No arrogance, but lazy, labouring movements,
a great weight to be borne by strength not elegance.
The swan bends.

She preens her feathers, while her counterpart
lazily scratches his ears.
Plunging neck, head into the turquoise depths,
his trunk in the clouds.
Both searching; her for life's sustenance,
him for the philosophy of life.
Meeting, not in embrace, but a consummation.
The elephant blinks.

He catches a glimpse, fleeting and ephemeral,
perhaps the life he may have dreamed of.
He blinks again, all memories removed.
She feels heady, suddenly, a vertigo
not of her own coining, but forced upon her,
head further in the clouds than she's ever known.
The swan rises.

She sees the sun, not a navigational tool,
or the marking of the day, but as a flaming star,
full of aspiration and future.
Her faithful pendant in the depths of cerulean,
is sated where no thirst had before existed.
The swan soars.
The elephant drinks.

Susie Crozier, South Hylton

A Mother's Pride

I remember the day my daughter was born
It was early one Tuesday morn,
When they put her in my arms
She won me over with her charms,
With her blonde hair and smiling eyes
The colour of clear blue skies,
I couldn't wait to take her home
Fill in the baby book as big as a tome,
Put her in clothes all pink and frilly
Making sure she did not look silly,
Taking her for walks in the park
Oh, we were going to have a lark,
But back at home her teething did start
Her cries of pain did wrench at my heart,
Get through that then the terrible twos
Her naughtiness gave me the blues,
At last it's off to school full of pride
As my tears I try to hide,
Too soon a teenager she has become
It seems she no longer needs her mum,
So many friends are at the centre
It's a circle I cannot enter,
But then one day she's a mum herself
And I am brought down from the shelf,
I do all I can to help her
She knows that I will always be there,
Now she has two teenage daughters of her own
Oh, how my little girl has grown,
And my tears of joy I try to hide
As I look at my daughter, I am full of pride.

Valerie Smallwood, St Helens

The Consciousness Of A Crumbling Society

At the centre of the consciousness of the human mind
Lays all the hope to dreams we cannot find
After eight days nights of work and no play
That's when we think of what we want to say

Why is the day longer than the light?
Why do we seem blind to what's in sight?
Do we dare achieve when we're told not to?
Is it always so hard to say I love you?

Choices we make cause problems later in life
With consequences coming after all the strife
And then society crumbles before our own eyes
For we believe the truth behind all lies

Friends come and go, so easy, so fast
Like a faded memory, now living in the past
Emotions come and leave just the same
Leaving us desperate to pass the blame.

Graham Connor, Norton

Cruel Sea

A silence falls as it starts to get dark
In the distance I hear the sound of a dog bark.

Stars start to twinkle in the night sky
I stare out to sea with a tear in my eye.

The fishermen have a hard job to do
The skipper looks after all of his crew.

It started off like an ordinary week
The sea was a bit rough, sky was bleak.

Then I got the call that we wives all dread
An accident at sea, crew all dead.

Doesn't matter who you are in life or what your stature
There's nothing that can beat the cruelty of nature.

Ali Gina Shotton, Ovingham

Genuine Hope

What does it mean for someone to have genuine hope?
the kind that summons faith, belief, the ability to cope
to move them from hopelessness, their ditches of despair
towards pastures of purposefulness, the land of fresh air?

Sometimes we wonder why answers to our prayers never come
waiting in angst and anticipation, our pleadings just ramble on
materialising into non entity, and our prayers coming to nowt
we become reclusive, or rebellious with exasperation and shout.

Hindsight points to beyond the wait that answers mystically appear
post frustration and rejection, just as the biting hurt begins to sear . . .
thence in that moment, as we apologise and ask for forgiveness
the ineffable invades our mist, suffusing us with its brightness.

And it's as if in this handing over, our pain is taken away
numbness preceded calmness, the mind seems to go astray
we focus on something else, a divertissement or design
and in reflecting we are puzzled as from pain we resign.

But within this melancholic softness, there is a transforming
As nerve endings enter their nirvana, they prepare for evolving
mindfully different schemes . . . mysteriously change has arrived
the impossible put to one side, and now the possible will be tried.

We ponder over this irrational behaviour, how we adapt to life
why it is we worry wearing ourselves out, and bring on strife
for we must find solutions, but fail because we are far too near
to see the bigger picture, the meaning of the learning from fear.

It's not until we grasp this, that learning itself becomes emotional
knowledge and experience help, but sometimes it's the irrational
which confuses our understanding, assumptions about our reasons
we become uncomfortable, so entertain short-sighted extrapolations.

We could also see this process as the handing over of power
drained and exhausted through mental labouring hour by hour
our quixotic concerns transmute into a surrendered servility
as we let go of the must to have and know we accept reality.

The mechanics behind manifesting is the melding of energy
congruency occurs as minds work toward a common synergy
based on awareness, respect and tolerance for self and others
genuine hope arrives when we liberate the fear from ourselves.

Bob Gleeson, Glasgow

Tiny, The Stray Cat

Those big sad eyes
They break my heart
Where in life
Did she start?
With those so cruel
With hearts of stone
That's why poor Tiny's
Skin and bone

A little nutrition
And a little love
Then you'll see her play
Like a little dove
Those big sad eyes
They tell no lies
And this is where
Her story lies.

Patricia Angus, Glasgow

Granda Grey

Granda, Granda Grey
Would you let me out to play
I won't go near the water
To chase the ducks away

Oh how I miss them, but who cares?
An old man's feelings count for nought
A stranger in my own town, lost
A stranger to my grandchildren
They walk past, never to know me
Such a shame, evil has won.

Michael A Johnston, Ballycarry

The Free Spirit

You lived amongst the stars
Capturing the planets with your
photographic lens
And danced in the great spaces,
The whole universe your playground
You felt the sun
To be your flaming fingered friend,
Slept in the arms of the dark moon
And at the end of your short life
You rode the comet
As it streaked across the sky.
But you never looked back
As you held the hand of the day
As it sank out of sight
You wandered away
And the dawn could not find you.
But your spirit was stellar
Are you playing hide-and-seek
In the giant glittering Christmas tree
Of the Orion Nebula?

Jean Mitchell, Aberdour

Running Streams

Running stream
From mountain high
Please take my dream
When you pass by
Towards the sea
That ebbs and flows
And set it free
So no one knows
Its final destiny.

John Mangan, Liverpool

Lost

Can't say I've seen
Every corner of this world
Can't say I've met
A thousand people
Can't say I've found
A love that will last
Can't say I've danced
Beneath a fountain
Can't say I've heard
Every song that's been sung
Can't really say
That I've done that much
But I have chased
A dream or two
Even gotten lost along the way
But that's been half
The fun
Finding the way back
Was the adventure I
Didn't expect to have
Could have given up
But then
I wouldn't have
Travelled the roads I have
Nor the adventure
I have had
As I searched for
A way back
Getting lost
Wasn't such a bad thing.

Oliver Waterer, Accrington

Family Crest

We decided to have a family crest,
Tattooed on every member's chest.
The picture showed a farmyard hen,
Which laid an egg just now and then.
One day it laid a hot cross bun,
And then confessed, "T'was just for fun.'
It followed with an Easter egg,
Produced when standing on one leg.
One aunt who didn't like the crest,
Said it was improperly dressed!
'The hen at least should wear a crown,
And robe herself in bridal gown.'
The hen itself could not care less,
And thumbed her nose at good Queen Bess.
She pecked the tattooed chests for corn,
And when she found some, blew her horn.
As she clucked around with head held proud,
The rest of the farmyard rose and bowed.
'And so you should,' the posh chicken said,
'There's only me has a tattooed bed.'
The family crest is widely revered,
By those clean-shaven and those with a beard.
Soldiers salute it, others raise hats,
Dogs stand to attention and so do cats.
We have a march past about once a week,
With limericks painted on the hen's beak.
They're rude and they're funny - written by Dad -
To help kids grow up both twisted and bad.
A family crest is a must in life,
Especially for men without a wife.
It helps them grow upright, proud of their kin,
And encourages girls who like their gin.
So get yourself a rousing motto,
Like, 'Let's play bingo or maybe lotto.'
Then your name will ring round the halls of fame,
If you manage to win a single game.

Kenneth Cox, Brigg

Mirrored Through The Mists Of Time

Folk awaiting at the lock head
For trawlers anchored in the bay
Terraced houses . . . smoky chimneys
Dockers queuing for their pay

Children laughing, playing hopscotch
Babies' nappies on the line
Soldiers waiting at the station
Spellbound - once upon a time

Harvest supper at the mission
A snowman with his carrot nose
Bluebell Wood and Primrose Valley
A Valentine - a Christmas rose

Coloured pebbles on the seashore
Sunrise at the break of day
Furrows on the fresh-ploughed landscape
Reapers stoking new morn hay

Starlings whirling round the rooftops
Clematis climbing garden walls
Horses in the brewery courtyard
Tat men voicing out their calls

Handshakes at the last farewells
Hugs and trusted smiles
Picnics by the old mill stream
Rambling over country stiles

Frosted patterns on the panes
Sunsets on the sea
Beauty in the summer skies
Kingfishers and bumblebees

Embers flaming far horizons
Apple blossom, full-blown corn
Rutted tracks scaring the meadows
Sparrows mustered on the lawn

The joys when guns fell silent
Tears for those who fell
Poppy wreathes at cenotaphs
Coins thrown in a wishing well

Mirrored through the mists of time
Forever there will be
Beauty, happiness and tears
Life's unsolved mystery.

Malcolm Wilson Bucknall, Hornsea

Morningstar

The pain I feel from the wounds hurts not,
When compared to the pain in my soul . . .
To be cast from my father, my creator, my reason to be . . .
To be cast down amongst the savages who doubt his very existence . . .
With only despair to keep me company I gaze up into the sky
And the rain upon my face falls like tears . . .

I am fallen, wings burnt and charred, never to see again the glories of the divine . . .

I walk amongst you silently and unseen . . .
Listening to you call my name . . .
Seeking justification for all your sins . . .
Making me the one you seek to blame . . .
To escape the justice of my father . . .
And to enter his kingdom blessed and guilt free . . .

I scream unto the heavens that I am innocent . . .
I pound my fist upon the doors of my father's house . . .
I cry into the night begging for my sire to hear my plea . . .

My pain in my heart cleaves my soul, my wounds do not heal . . .
I pray for forgiveness knowing it can never be . . .

I am fallen . . .

Peter Madden, Mytholmroyd

Gardenia

I read in the paper, I heard it on the news
Another failed adventure, another one to lose
I'm going to a forest with flowers all around
I'll wear a pair of moonboots and stomp them in the ground
Cos who needs all these flowers
And all these stupid trees
And who'd've thought a flower
Could have brought me to my knees.

And you were my Gardenia, a name that's nice and new
If only all the others had been a bit like you
But love affairs like ours happen once upon a time
And undiscovered poets sometimes find it hard to rhyme
But who needs all these flowers
They only make you sneeze
And who'd've thought a flower
Could have brought me to my knees?

They're smiling when they see me, friends with tales to tell
And love that's made in Heaven must sometimes live in Hell
A pretty little flower has left me all alone
And our particular garden is where no sun has shone
And who needs all these flowers
They just attract the bees
And who'd've thought a flower
Could have brought me to my knees?

Phillip M Rowland, Padgate

No Feeling

Laying in my bed in shadows of doubt,
every little thing just causes me to freak out,
Cold and bitter you made my heart,
you pushed and shoved me making me break apart.
Knock me down to my knees as I beg and plead,
but you refuse to listen making my mind freeze.
I don't want to feel no more
as you never felt for me at all . . .

Shona-Lee Gallagher, Birkenhead

Miner

His work was hard
His work was honest work
At a time when coal reigned supreme
In, out and throughout our lives
There was a job waiting for us
There was a job to be done
Generations of the family
Became miners
I was no different
Except
When my turn came
The mines closed
Jobs went, livelihood lost
And I began to carve my life
Away from the place
That I once called home.

Kauser Parveen, Halifax

Untitled

I sit here watching the TV
And eagerly await kick-off at three,
The Midlands, versus the North
One in blue, one in red,
A corporal back from Afghanistan
A true blue City fan
Meets the teams and shakes their hands
The band strikes up and the anthem sung
Whistle goes and match begun.
Both sets of supporters in the crowd
In good voice and singing loud
The new Wembley is packed full
Now kicked off and it won't be dull
Second half, Man City now one-nil up
Five minutes to go, before they lift the cup.

Janice Jackson, Oldham

Sheds

At the end of each new garden
Stands a small neat shed for tools,
Is it used that very often
Or there to match the neighbours' moods?

Where are the sheds of yesteryear?
Pieces of patched up fencing
Leaving us to ponder what's inside.

- Are they housing parts of engines,
Storing lost machines, bits of bikes,
Or lots of junk to scrape your shins,
Cast-off toys and children's trikes?

A workshop? There's a smell of woody
shavings, just the place to mend
Old household things which find their end
Here, in this disintegrating hut.
Just a glimpse with door half shut,
Will tell if there's a railway layout.
There're old armchairs! A place to brew!
To meet the mates you know.

Doris Thomson, Middleton

British History Born Anew

During the year two thousand
On a ceremonial August birthday
Reverence was paid to our dear Queen Mother
With love and devotion we smiled her way.

Elizabeth's life spanned a century
When dark days of war, made 'peace' shine like gold!
And with a few more months of true dedication
Her death touched the hearts of young and old.

She sadly departed to pastures new
But memories shall not fade or sever
Our minds will recall that sweet shade of blue
Royal moments lingering forever.

Joyce Hemsley, Sunderland

A Magical Moment On A Summer Day

Sensations aroused in the heat of the day,
As the hot summer sun sprinkles its rays.
A partner exclusive to me in my world,
A passionate moment, my mind in a whirl.
A hot satin kiss blows by on the breeze,
As silky soft skin burns with ease.
Goosebumps appear like an army's salute,
A soft smile, a knowing look, from a lover so cute.
A diamond-studded sky at the end of the day,
A satisfied embrace then we walk on our way.
A magical moment in a troubled world,
To treasure and caress for many a year . . .

Gwen McNamara, Bagby

A Star Spreading Supersatisfaction

If you want to reach high spirits anew,
Come to a Daniel O'Donnell concert for you.
The songs with heart and soul entwined
Cover romance of a special kind.

Irish ways and Irish days
Remind you of the best displays
Of music past and songs before
Sung with sincerity, soul and more.

Danny Boy is a keen song for mothers
Sung by Daniel O'Donnell like no others
A highly enticing quality that's devout
Makes life a Heaven on Earth about.

When love is in the air you find
The joy that Jesus Christ had in mind
Time to stop for Daniel's CDs when found
Makes each day allow high spirits abound.

Dorothy Kenny, Burnley

Searching For You

A little Irish girl in a strange new land,
Doesn't fit in so clings to Mum's hand.
She changes her accent, her clothes and her hair,
Hoping that nobody notices her there.
She changes so often she forgets who you are,
And soon you are nothing; a distant star.
Then one day she sees that you've gone far away
And starts on a quest to make you come back and stay.
She searches so hard she can no longer see.
She's lost in the darkness, fighting to breathe.
No longer sure who you were at the start,
No longer sure if she can trust her heart.
The blackness was scary and terribly cold,
She thought she'd stay lost and never be told,
The truth about you and where you were hid,
The feeling of emptiness, she'd never be rid.
She stopped trying to look and then heard a sound,
All of a sudden you were there to be found.
The real inner girl she'd been trying to find
Was right there inside her all of this time.

Caroline Corley, Huddersfield

A Little Ditty

If life were a poem
There'd be no way of knowing
How long it would keep going
How long the words would keep flowing
Before slowing
To a stop.

Rachel Sutcliffe, Golcar

The Future

My home falls out of view
As I travel to my future
A future of unknown, unseen
A cursed future, I knew.
I watch my new friends approaching
And gaze at a life once mine
An innocent life, a quiet life
All over in a matter of time.
I dreaded to hit the ground
When reality struck painfully
I take a breath and prepare for the fall
And relish my last moments of glory.
As I finally arrive
I see a member of family
Another and another
They're all slightly different
Different from each other.
I cross a black desert
Broken up by a white river
A river which breaks indecisively.
I gaze at two lights
As they expand to fit my eyes.
I heard about these, a car, I think
And it came as no surprise
That the lights did not stop for me
But carried on going, as I pray desperately
I pray to awake, but this is reality
And away slips my future.
I saw my veins turning red
My body crinkly and dry
I felt throbbing in my head,
As I realised all future is,
Is but to die.
I begin to weaken and collapse
As the tarmac hit my underneath
But nobody will be bothered,
Because I'm only a leaf.

Connie Walsh, Bramhall

One, Two, Three

I remember
The very first day that we met.
We went for a walk.
It rained, and we both got soaking wet.

I remember
Saying I love you
And acting the goat
The words as usual
Sticking in my throat.

I remember
How we used to
Kiss and cuddle
And do all those silly things
Like splashing around in
Some great big puddle.

I remember
How you took my
Breath away
I remember
Finding myself speechless
Not knowing what to say.

I wake to thy beauteous face,
I wake to thy warm embrace.
I wake to the morning dew,
I wake to 'Eyes of Glossy Blue'.

I wake to take thee in my arms,
I wake to the magic of thy charms.
I wake to steep my lips in bliss,
I wake to dwell an age on every kiss.

I wake to take thee by the hand,
I wake to trace thy name in sand.
I wake to a tranquil sea,
I wake to no one, more lovelier than thee.

To me
Our love is beyond compare,
And I know it's something rare,
It's not often that you see this kind,

I find you're always on my mind.
I always listen for the sound
Of you coming through the door,
Each day I seem to love you more.

Ted Brookes, Dunscroft

The Earwig

I asked my mum one morning
To go out for a run
She smiled and said it's a lovely day
Let's go and have some fun
The garden centre was our first choice
And we wandered among the trees
When suddenly my mum fell down
And landed on her knees
She screamed and yelled and pointed to
A movement at her neck
Where a little earwig wriggled about
I was terrified by heck
A man arrived and tried to take
The insect from her bosom
Then my father turned up much to my confusion
He yelled and shouted at the man
For daring to touch his wife
And attacked him with his crutches
So that the man ran for his life
I think it will be a long, long time
Before I go out again
With my mum to the garden centre
I haven't recovered since then.

Zena Bain, Kincorth

Man's Greatest Enemy

Man has conquered Everest
And journeyed into space.
Invented many wondrous things
To aid the human race.

He's tamed the mighty ocean wild
And made the sky his own
Discovered things and places
That were hitherto unknown.

He's found a cure for many ills
And learnt to subdue pain
Has triumphed on the battlefield
Sweet victory to gain.

It seems there's very little left
On Man's 'to conquer' shelf,
Except, of course, his last
And greatest enemy - himself!

Jean Percival Ford, Almondbury

Poppy

Fur black and shiny
Like polished ebony
Eyes so round and
Innocent, belying a
Hidden mischief.
Prowling and stalking,
Hiding and playing,
Leaping in joyful ecstasy
Bottlebrush tail
Waving like a flag at
Full mast.
Sleeping and purring
Cat and human
In perfect harmony.

Elizabeth Doroszkiewicz, Northenden

Index

Adrian McRobb, Cramlington 97
Aileen A Kelly, Aberdeen 283
Alan Ernest, Sheffield 58
Alan Pow, Hawick 280
Alan R Coughlin, Limavady 228
Alexander Winter, Aberdeen 302
Alex Branthwaite, Sunderland 112
Ali Gina Shotton, Ovingham 370
Alison Drever, Edinburgh 338
Alison Scott, Heaton 182
Allen Beit, Birkenhead 129
Alma Taylor, Manchester 115
Andrew Gill, Chester 113
Andrew Gruberski, Dewsbury 157
Angela Butler, Allithwaite 59
Angela Cole, Llangunnor 215
Angela McLaughlin-Bolton, York 77
Anita Cooling, Boston Spa 186
Ann Ashworth, Swinton 20
Anne Aitchison, Larbert 247
Anne Black McIsaac, Motherwell 325
Ann Eddleston, Worsthorne 160
Anne-Marie Pratt, Howden-le-Wear 6
Anne Taggart, Armagh 233
Anne Williams, Llanelli 327
Annie McKimmie, Portsoy 206
Ann Thomas, Maesteg 245
Ann Voaden, Nantymoel 204
Ann Warner, Prestwick 122
Ann Warren, Grange-Over-Sands 48
Anthony Dunne/O'Regan, Kilkenny 352
Anthony Gibson, Hartlepool 120
Anthony G L Kent, Haverfordwest 252
Arthur Aston, Townville 36
Arthur May, Newport 314
Arthur Pickles, Waterfoot 164
Arya Mati, Manchester 81

Asraa Hafeez, Cheadle 28
Aubrey Malone 364
Audrey Poole, Penarth 256
Audrey Watson, Wakefield 71
Austin Baines-Brook, Gomersal 181
Barbara Bentley, Appletree Village 12
Barbara Fowler, Merthyr Tydfil 338
Barbara Rodgers, Belfast 207
Barbara Sherlow, Preston 191
Barbara Turner, Sale 56
Barbara Ward, Pickering 81
Barbro Pattie, Rothesay 281
Barry Bradshaigh, Blackpool 21
Bernard Shaw, Barwick-in-Elmet 110
Beryl Eastwood, Hull 108
Beryl Mapperley, Bridlington 24
Beryl Shepard Leece, Wallasey 360
Betty Allison, Gilesgate Moor 25
Betty Graham, Whitefield 142
Betty Lightfoot, Swinton 195
Betty McIlroy, Bangor 309
Betty Westcott, Newport 334
Bianka Hannam, Ellesmere Port 109
Bill Barker, East Wemyss 339
Bill Hayles, Prestatyn 229
Bill Torrie Douglas, Fairlie 284
Bob Gleeson, Glasgow 371
Brenda Hughes, Holland Moor 60
Brenda Liddy, Belfast 211
Bryan J Holmes, Wheatley 175
Cameron McIntyre, Newtownards 340
Carole Bloor, Cadishead 9
Carole Revell, Hull 135
Carolie Cole Pemberton, Manchester 67
Caroline Anne Carson, Thornhill 275
Caroline Champion, Mathern 291
Caroline Connelly, Faifley 57

Caroline Corley, Huddersfield	382
Carol Taylor, Wakefield	127
Catherine Keohane-Johnson, Penydarren	343
Celia G Thomas, Aberdare	260
Chelsey-Leigh Clatworthy (16), Blaengarw	347
Chris Mary Creedon, Fulwood	1
Christina Batley, Rochdale	125
Christine B Dobbie, Rothesay	367
Christine Naylor, Airmyn	90
Christine Pudsey, Cleethorpes	63
Christopher Hayes, Bolton	170
Christopher Robin Slater, Newcastle Upon Tyne	160
Claire Gordon, Mottram	198
Clare Marie Zeidrah Keirrissia Marshall, Langley	94
Claudette Evans, Hollybush	272
Clifford Jones, Bontnewydd	244
Colin Burnell, Cardiff	257
Colin McCombe, Moreton	79
Connie Walsh, Bramhall	383
Cynthia Gibson, Ripon	91
Cyril G Payne, New Inn	345
David Charles, Lytham	96
David John Hewett, Dyfed	213
David McDonald, Kirkcaldy	295
David Rosser, Ammanford	269
David Sim, Normanby	34
Dawn Williams-Sanderson, Newbiggin by the Sea	179
Dean Beardsley, Old Denaby	55
Deborah Wilson, Norton	360
Denise Clitheroe, Preston	49
Denise Evans, Thornaby	173
Denise Jarrett, Leeds	82
Diane Thomson Miller, Uddingston	363
Dilys Jones, Hull	359
Donald John Tye, Wallsend	158
Dorcas Wilson, Linlithgow	278
Doreen E Todd, Portglenone	217
Doreen Goodway, Airedale	84
Doreen Tattersall, Cowpen Blyth	196
Dorinda MacDowell	91
Doris Thomson, Middleton	380
Dorothy Jessup, Keighley	126
Dorothy Kenny, Burnley	381
Dot Young, Durham	132
D Ritchie, Roseworth	121
Ed Collins, Southport	108
Ed Gardner, Boston Spa	149
Edna Mills, Riding Mill	146
Edna Sarsfield, Southport	57
E Hawkins, Denbigh	346
Eileen-Margaret Kidd, Peebles	251
E Joan Knight, Great Houghton	119
Elaine Briscoe-Taylor, Shipley	189
Elaine J Seagrave, Woodseats	105
Elaine Sands, Standish	177
Elizabeth A Wilkinson, Runcorn	52
Elizabeth Blacklaw, Dundee	273
Elizabeth Doroszkiewicz, Northenden	386
Elizabeth Mary Dowler, Bulwark	188
Elizabeth Mason, Knutsford	73
Elizabeth Phillips Scott, High Valleyfield	221
Emma Simister, Morecambe	47
Enid Thomas Rees, Mountain Ash	276
Eric Hyland, Aspull	19
Eric Prescott, Southport	161
Eric R Sephton, Stretford	72
Erin Fitzgerald, Liverpool	123
Ernie Graham, Millom	145
E S Arries, Houghton-le-Spring	61
Fleming Carswell, Argyll	311
Florence Broomfield, Ashton-in-Makerfield	176
Frances Gibson, Beragh	197
Frances Meenan, Brigade	248
Frania Vickers, Leeds	10
Frank Oldfield, Hackenthorpe	124
Frederick Osborne, Bangor	349
Fred McIlmoyle, Bangor	265
Fred McIlmoyle, Bangor	348
G Aldsmoor, Broughty Ferry	213
Gary Austin, Southport	78
Gary Thompson, Whitefield	43
Gavin Knox, Ballinamallard	318
Gay Horton, Bollington	40

Gaynor Evans, Bridgend	216
Geatana Trippetti, Heaton Mersey	182
Geoff Kendall, Chorley	39
George Campbell, Perth	285
George Du Plessis, Boksburg	350
George Gutherless, Withernsea	172
Gladys Brunt, Beighton	5
Glenys Allen, Pendine	227
Glenys B Moses, Sennybridge	234
Gordon Forbes, Dumfries	239
Grace Minnis, Holywood	328
Graham Connor, Norton	370
Graham Thomas, Llanelli	218
Grant Cameron, Aberdeen	332
Gwendoline Douglas, Hull	193
Gwen McNamara, Bagby	381
Gwyneth E Scott, Colwyn Bay	233
Gwyn Thomas, Merthyr Tydfil	288
Haidee Williams, Gorseinon	235
Hannah R Hall	246
Harry Patrick, Carlisle	65
Heather Aspinall, Heaton	180
Heather Pickering, Horsforth	30
Helen Smith, Darlington	53
Helga Dharmpaul, Tain	315
Henry C Culpan, Halifax	44
Hilary Jean Clark	155
Hilda Marjorie Wheeler, Llanon	226
Howard Peach, Cottingham	109
Hugh Campbell, Lurgan	222
Ian Archibald, Edinburgh	282
Ian Bosker, Leigh	154
Ian Lennox-Martin, Carlisle	187
Ian L Fyfe, East Kilbride	225
Ian Lowery, Upper Denby	138
Ian McNamara, Belfast	199
Irene Gunnion, Perth	361
Irene Patricia Kelly, Bolton-on-Dearne	166
Isla Demuth, Raglan	243
Isobel Buchanan, Ayr	265
Ivy Bates, Lymm	64
Jackie Richardson, Underbarrow	169
Jacqueline Bartlett, St Martins	201
Jacqueline Bulman, Great Harwood	174
Jacqueline Burns, Salford	38
Jacqueline Zacharias, Naburn	116
Jacqui Fogwill, Ganarew	237
James Hazell, Rochdale	66
James McIntosh Martin, Cowdenbeath	270
James O'Sullivan, Cork	266
James Peace, Glenrothes	258
James Quinn, Dumfries	323
James Roland Sterritt, Markethill	232
Jane Bessant, Wainfelin	268
Janet Bowen, Milford Haven	274
Janet Middleton, Westquarter	300
Janet Rocher, Wirral	118
Janette Campbell, Cumbernauld	316
Janice Jackson, Oldham	379
Jeanette Davis, Alva	289
Jean MacKenzie	296
Jean Mitchell, Aberdour	373
Jeannette Facchini, Hartlepool	8
Jean Paisley, Hebburn	76
Jean Percival Ford, Almondbury	386
Jenifer Ellen Austin, Sproxton	103
Jennifer D Wootton, Bradway	116
Jenny Bosworth, Louth	147
Jessica Stephanie Powell, Pontlottyn	273
Jessie Horsley, Bolton	39
Jillian Minion, Millom	178
Jim Emery, Ballymacoss	328
Jim Spence, Dufton	144
J Malcolm Robinson, Bentley	17
Joan Catherine Igesund, Auchnagatt	267
Joan Evans, Upholland	130
Joan Kelly McChrystal, Derry City	315
Joan Lister, High Pittington	165
Joan Littlehales, Rhostyllen	343
Joan May Wills, Kendal	89
Joan McCradie, Cardiff	275
Joan O'Toole, Blackrod	53
John Bain, Oban	290
John Dillon, Pendlebury	2
John Flanagan, Leeds	92
John Fudge Jnr, Sunnyside	93

John Greeves, Magor	240
John Harrold, Bettws	207
John Mangan, Liverpool	373
John Masters, Marske-by-the-Sea	152
John McKibbin, Baillieston	263
John Monaghan, Ballygawley	344
John O'Connor, Little Hulton	88
John Sears, Congleton	128
Jonathan Curry, Killingworth	68
Joseph Knott, Whitworth	90
Joshua Peters (12), Redbrook	220
Joyce Adams, Lakeside	14
Joyce Hemsley, Sunderland	380
Joyce Hockley, Stirling	255
Joyce Hudspith, South Stanley	140
Joyce M Chaffer, Yeadon	84
Joy M Humphreys, Preston	56
Joy Wilson, Clogher	310
J Pressly-Allen, Knutsford	351
Julian Bishop, Fasnakyle	336
Julian Ronay, Aviemore	241
Julie Merdassi, Castlefields	24
Julie Spackman, Leeds	3
June Knight-Boulton, Newton-le-Willows	122
June Mary Davies, Cardiff	245
J Williams, Swansea	203
Kalie Eaton, McDonough	366
Karen Collins, Wrightington	98
Karl Jakobsen, Dumfries	292
Kathleen June Jinks, Eston	180
Kathleen McGowan, Newcastle Upon Tyne	150
Kathleen Wendy Jones, Rhyl	331
Kathy Denton, Horwich	133
Kathy McLemore, Dundee	231
Kathy Miles, Ffos-y-ffin	304
Katriona Goode, Earlston	312
Kauser Parveen, Halifax	379
K Chesney-Woods, Sacriston	163
Kenneth Cox, Brigg	375
Kenneth H Wood, Ormskirk	93
Kiran Ali	161
Laraine Smith, Indiana	319
Lee Connor, Norton	367
Lee Smith, Woodhouse	83
Leila McLeish, Carnforth	143
L E Marchment, Hathershaw	85
Lesley Downie, Findhorn	357
Lesley Elaine Greenwood, Bradford	51
Leslie Hogarth, Carlisle	100
Letty Linton, Sunniside	33
L Growney, Crosby	46
Liam Ó Comáin, Derry	306
Lilian Kujawiak, Widnes	5
Lillian Fitzgerald, Moston	9
Linda Gray, Ashington	136
Linda Hardy, Southport	168
Linda Jennings, Glais	326
Lorena Valerie Owens, Durham	25
Lorna Hawthorne, Armagh	202
Luke Greggain, Whitehaven	92
Lyn Crossley, Burnley	151
Lynette Coote, Harrogate	167
Malachy Trainor, Armagh	249
Malcolm Coles, Rumney	250
Malcolm Wilson Bucknall, Hornsea	376
Manal Ahmed, Leeds	18
Margaret Bate, West View	153
Margaret Davis, Chepstow	293
Margaret Kent, Beauly	356
Margaret Mathers, Barrow-in-Furness	16
Margaret Non Williams, Saundersfoot	209
Margaret Robertson, Gt Lumley	50
Margaret Whitaker, Brighouse	141
Margarte Gleeson Spanos, Llandysul	277
Margery Rayson, Daltongate	151
Margie Fox, Cheadle	45
Maria Jenkinson, Blackpool	152
Marian Williams, Davyhulme	189
Marie Coyles, Dervock	293
Marie Greenhalgh, Burnley	75
Marion McKenzie, Irvine	286
Marjorie Langhorn, Darrington	354
Marjorie Leyshon, Swansea	354
Marjorie M Armstrong, Carlisle	102
Mark Tough, Castle Douglas	262
Marlene Jackson, Wath-upon-Dearne	166

Mary Braithwaite, Southport	74
Mary Hoy, Bootle	86
Mary Leadbeter, Beaufort	212
Mary Morton, Keady	341
Mary Parker, Maltby	13
Maureen C Bell, Gateshead	104
Maureen Cole, Felin Foel	208
Maureen Dearden, Keighley	148
Maureen Margaret Thornton, Aberaman	302
Mavis Downey, Talgarth	285
Melanie M Burgess, Aberystwyth	342
M G Sherlock, Colwyn Bay	319
Michael A Johnston, Ballycarry	372
Michael Harrison, Aintree	131
Michael McGuigan, Carrive	212
Michael McNulty, Runcorn	29
Michael Riley, Farringdon	121
Michael Spencer, Hessle	7
Mike Monaghan, Bishopbriggs	281
Miki Byrne, Walton Cardiff	292
M L Damsell, Plwmp	287
M Noad, Thornaby	150
Molly Timpson, Leeds	8
Mukeshkumar Raval, India	313
Nancy Tamagno, Ladywell	353
N G Charnley, Blackpool	141
Nick Pearson, Gipton	134
Nick Purchase, Grangetown	334
Nicola Karunaratne, St Helens	185
Nigel Miller, Sandbach	183
Nikita Biswal, Delhi	358
Norah C Darbyshire, Daisy Hill	87
Norah Nelson, Newry	294
Norma Anne MacArthur, Edinburgh	308
Norman Bissett, Edinburgh	230
Norman Mark, Carlisle	140
Norman Royal, Grangetown	279
Oira Newman, Erskine	247
Oliver Waterer, Accrington	374
Olivia Barton, Balderstone	85
Owain Symonds, Pontllanfraith	325
Padraig Donnelly, Keady	232
Pamela Gibson, Duns	324
Pam Ismail, Llanishen	337
Pam Russell, Yarrow	284
Pat MacKenzie, East Kilbride	297
Patricia Angus, Glasgow	372
Patricia Bannister, Denbigh	254
Patricia Donaghy, Dungannon	242
Patricia McKenna, Pontypridd	259
Patricia Todd, St Helier	355
Paul Hough, Barnsley	165
Pauline Uprichard, Lurgan	223
Pauline Walsh, Blackburn	162
Paul Judges, Leavening	159
Paul Kelly, Walton-le-Dale	111
Paul Kurt Lockwood, Welshpool	214
P Brewer, Cleveleys	37
Peggy Howe, St Asaph	236
Perry McDaid, Derry	244
Peter Branson, Rode Heath	124
Peter Cardwell, Keighley	137
Peter Corbett, Liverpool	70
Peter Madden, Mytholmroyd	377
Peter Paterson, Bellshill	272
Peter Roebuck, Prestwich	184
Peter Spurgin, Edinburgh	243
Philip Corbishly, Rossendale	169
Philip J Mee, Kinmel Bay	219
Philip Moore, Walton Village	101
Phillip M Rowland, Padgate	378
P Mitchell, Morecambe	134
Qesma Mohammed, Manchester	54
Rachel E Joyce, Cardiff	355
Rachel Sutcliffe, Golcar	16
Rachel Sutcliffe, Golcar	382
Rachel Van Den Bergen, Levenshulme	126
Rachel Wilson, Silksworth	125
Rae Alderson, Flixton	21
Ramandeep Kaur, Bradford	64
Ray Lennard, Macclesfield	2
Rebecca Isted, Cardiff	264
Robbie Hillhouse, Ayr	362
Robert Bannan, Townhead	202
Robert Black, Annan	274
Robert Hogg, Guisborough	158

Robert H Quin, Knutsford 117
Robert Lockett, Bootle 100
Robert Simpson, Ballymoney 342
Robert Wynn-Davies, Whitland 308
Rodger Moir, Allerton 162
Roger Paul Fuge, Llwynhendy 215
Ronnie Simpson, Blairdardie 333
Rose Innes, South Carbrain 238
Ruth Edgar, Dromore 330
Ruth Lydia Daly, St Dials 329
Ruth Margaret Rhodes, Knaresborough 33
Samantha Forde, Magherafelt 223
Samantha Taylor, Oldham 11
Samuel McAlister, Carrickfergus 210
Sandra Meadows, Lymm 159
Sara Burr, Inverurie 322
Sarah Harrop, Priest Hutton 10
S D Sharp, Stockport 123
Sheena Blackhall, Garthdee 301
Sheila Donetta, Swansea 190
Sheila Storr, Gargrave 200
Shiksha Dheda 321
Shirley Gray, Sheffield 183
Shirley Johnson, Falkirk 221
Shirley Temple Beckett, Widnes 69
Shona-Lee Gallagher, Birkenhead 378
Snowman, Lymm 80
Stephen Maslen, Newport 264
Stephen Wooley, Croxteth 22
Stuart Elsom Wright, Halifax 80
Sue Gerrard, St Helens 194
Sue Hardy-Dawson, Harrogate 99
Susan Clarke, Llantwit Major 307
Susan Kelly, Nairn 261
Susie Crozier, South Hylton 368
Suzanne Beevers, Earlsheaton 41
Suzanne Swift, Betws-y-Rhos 242
Sylvia Joan Higginson, Timperley 190
Sylvie Alexandre-Nelson, Swansea 205
Taranom Movahedi, Leeds 23
Ted Brookes, Dunscroft 384
Terence Leslie Iceton, Leeds 107
Terence Powell, Dresden 15
Terence Smith, Sheffield 63
Teresa Bell, Moneymore 333
Terry Mullan, Cookstown 299
Terry Ramanouski, Widnes 361
Thomas Speight, Halifax 7
T McFarlane, Wavertree 188
Trevor Huntington, Emley 26
Valerie Lancaster, Southport 35
Valerie Smallwood, St Helens 369
Vera Seddon, Gatley 42
Veronica Davison, Misterton 332
Violet Burggy, Kilmuir 214
Vivienne Fitzpatrick, Bradford 164
Vivienne Vale, Tonyrefail 298
Wayne Barrow 171
Wayne Pugh, Brasside 106
Wendy Anne Flanagan, Rishton 156
Wendy A Nottingham, Ogmore-by-Sea 320
Wendy Prance, Cardiff 303
William F Park, Clydebank 305
William Jebb, Endon 192
William Nicklin, Widnes 153
William Reilly, Liverpool 6
William Waring, Belfast 206
Windsor Hopkins, Tondu 280
Yvonne Clark 314
Yvonne Valerie Stewart, South Shields 114
Zena Bain, Kincorth 385
Zoha Khalid, Islamabad 335

Forward Poetry Information

We hope you have enjoyed reading this book - and that you will continue to enjoy it in the coming years.

If you like reading and writing poetry drop us a line, or give us a call, and we'll send you a free information pack.

Alternatively if you would like to order further copies of this book or any of our other titles, then please give us a call or log onto our website at www.forwardpoetry.co.uk

Forward Poetry Information
Remus House
Coltsfoot Drive
Peterborough
PE2 9BF
(01733) 890099